Gotcha
CAPITALISM

Gotcha
CAPITALISM

How Hidden Fees Rip You Off Every Day— and What You Can Do About It

BOB SULLIVAN

Ballantine Books • New York

Gotcha Capitalism is a commonsense guide to personal finance. In practical advice books, as in life, there are no guarantees, and readers are cautioned to rely on their own judgment about their individual circumstances and to act accordingly. Readers are also reminded that this book is intended for informational purposes only and is not meant to take the place of professional advice.

As of press time, the URLs displayed in this book link or refer to existing websites on the Internet. Random House, Inc., is not responsible for the content available on any such site (including, without limitation, outdated, inaccurate, or incomplete information).

A Ballantine Books Trade Paperback Original

Copyright © 2007 by Bob Sullivan

Published in the United States by Ballantine Books,
an imprint of The Random House Publishing Group,
a division of Random House, Inc., New York.

BALLANTINE and colophon are registered
trademarks of Random House, Inc.

LIBRARY OF CONGRESS CATALOGING-IN-PUBLICATION DATA
Sullivan, Bob.
Gotcha capitalism : how hidden fees rip you off every day—
and what you can do about it / Bob Sullivan.
p. cm.
ISBN 978-0-345-49613-3 (pbk.)
1. Fraud—United States.   2. Consumer protection—
United States.   I. Title.
HV6695.S74 2007
351.3'4—dc22   2007029738

Printed in the United States of America

www.ballantinebooks.com

4 6 8 9 7 5 3

Book design by Mary A. Wirth

To Iñigo López de Loyola

Patron saint of reformation from within

Competing by cheating has become a way of life for . . . many of these corporations, many of the most reputable of them. Because it's done by AT&T, MCI or Sprint, people are reluctant to use that word, but when all is said and done . . . these are scams.

Connecticut attorney general Richard Blumenthal

Contents

Preface

While it's always better to be on vacation than at work, any economist will tell you it's usually terrible to be a tourist.

Last Christmas season, a New York City hot-dog vendor demonstrated this for me. I was walking across the street from Radio City Music Hall, on my way to Rockefeller Center, dragging a piece of luggage on wheels behind me, taking in the sounds and smells of Christmas in the city. I stopped for a snack at the corner, something I've done far too often, so I know my way around pushcarts.

While my salesman pulled out the bun, I handed him a $5 bill. He handed me back $2. Street dogs cost more like $1.25, and never more than $2, in Manhattan, so I knew something was wrong. I grabbed the bills, made a funny face, and then said, "That's $3?"

"Yeah, man," he answered, without hesitation.

"Well, that's the most expensive hot dog I've ever had in New York," I said, responding with culturally sensitive hyperbole.

"Well, you know, it's Christmas," the vendor offered back, this time a bit more sheepishly. Then he whipped out the mustard.

After beating back the moment of self-doubt that always arises at a time like this (maybe they do raise prices at Christmas?), I began to mentally gather my options: Start talking very loudly about the price, scaring away other customers? Find a bored-looking cop to involve? Whip out my press badge or a camera?

Perhaps my consumer-affairs-reporter nostrils started to flare, because the vendor began to make idle conversation.

"So, what are you doing?" he asked me.

"Going to work around the corner, right there," I shot back, point-
ing toward Rockefeller Center.

I don't know if the proximity of my office gave the vendor a
change of heart, or it was my accent (I was sure to say caw-nah). But
that did it.

"I'm sorry, man," he said. He reached behind his till, grabbed a
dollar, and handed it to me. "I thought you were a tourist."

I grabbed the bill, mustered my best "I'm so disappointed in you"
glare, and walked off as he cried after me "I'm sorry" two more times.

Tourists and locals are always treated differently. Tourists always pay
more and get less. Think of any trip you've ever taken—particularly
overseas—and those moments when you don't know where to go,
what to do, or what the local rules are. You always pay more than
you should. If you're lucky, and smart, you quickly attach yourself
to a local and start finding the better restaurants, the higher-quality
lamb's-wool sweaters, and a fair exchange rate.

America's massive corporations long ago noticed this and set
about to make us all tourists. When you sign up for cell phone service, get a new credit card, or subscribe to satellite TV, you are entering a foreign land full of arbitrary rules no normal consumer could
anticipate. At every turn, whenever you make a mistake, you violate
one of these unimaginable and unpredictable rules and it costs you.
Corporate America is making a killing by charging this tourist premium on everything—one $2 penalty fee at a time.

This is what I call "Gotcha Capitalism."

The butcher on the corner of days gone by would never think of
adding such sneaky fees; if he did, he would have been run out of
town. But satellite-TV firms and cable companies don't have offices
around the corner. To virtually all Americans, these firms are disem-

bodied entities that exist in some virtual reality a world away; we know them only by the slips of irritating paper they mail us once a month indicating that, once again, we owe them more than we think we should. Got a problem? Send off a letter to this disembodied entity in Never Never Land, or worse still, call on the telephone, sit on hold for an hour, and talk to someone who quite literally works a world away, at a phone bank somewhere in India. This detached virtual world is every consumer's reality now.

But you don't have to be a tourist in it.

This world does have rules. It does have social conventions. Simply by knowing the language of Gotcha Capitalism, by letting a company know you are a local and not a tourist, you will save hundreds or thousands of dollars every year. The electronic equivalent of a New York accent, a letter or call that deploys the right magic words, or simply a well-timed question, will produce immediate results. By showing you know what you're doing, that you know your way around the world of Gotchas, you will literally have everyone from hot-dog vendors to cable-television companies handing you dollars to get you to walk away quietly. That's when you've become a local in the world of Gotcha Capitalism.

It's not fair that you have to waste your time learning these rules, and I wish you didn't have to. But failing to learn the language will cost you—research we did for this book suggests at least $946 annually—perhaps more than you save for retirement every year. My goal is to help you get back most of that money. Let me be your local guide.

In this book I will show you how companies size you up. I'll take you inside the dark rooms where committees dream up insidious ways to cheat you. I'll introduce you to terms like reverse competition and shrouding—tactics you've probably never heard of that cost you hundreds of dollars each year. Then, after showing you the madness in these methods, I will break apart thirteen industries that hit you with more than a hundred sneaky fees each year, and show you how to stop losing all that money. In the back of the book, you'll find a tool kit packed with sample letters, telephone scripts, and other handy tools you can use today to get refunds and satisfaction, and to get around in the world of Gotchas.

I know you are busy. In fact, I know you are already too busy to read all that fine print companies throw at you every time you buy something. The last thing you need is more homework. So I've designed this book to be interactive. Each industry has its own chapter, and most fees have their own subhead. The book is designed so you can pick it up and refer to it as needed. To really understand the sea change that's happening to the U.S. economy, you'd be best off reading the introductory chapter that follows, which will open your eyes to the hidden world of sneaky fees. But if you are really hell-bent on saving money and invoking your rights right away, by all means, skip ahead to the company or industry you intend to challenge. Start saving money now.

Gotcha Capitalism is a strange land with strange rules, but it doesn't have to be. This book is meant to be your travel guide to this foreign land. Here are the secret rules for surviving as a consumer in twenty-first-century America.

The World of
Gotcha Capitalism

Shrouding, Reverse Competition, and Other Corporate Tricks That Attack the American Way of Life

Some will rob you with a six-gun. Some with a fountain pen.
Woodie Guthrie

I. Paranoia?

Let me make a confession. I hate getting cheated. I mean, really, really, really hate getting cheated. I mean veins-pop-out-of-my-forehead, glad-I'm-not-getting-my-blood-pressure-checked-today hate getting cheated.

And yet, I feel like I'm getting cheated all the time.

I often open the mail with dread. It makes the hairs on the back of my neck stand up, as if I were some primal creature readying for a fight. I walk into a cell-phone store, check my online statements, or just turn on my television, and I feel like everyone is out to get me. I suffer from what a therapist might call low-level, background anxiety. I think someone is always trying to steal something from me.

Am I crazy?

When I was a child growing up just outside New York City during the 1970s, I learned to be afraid of getting mugged. But this is not that. The criminals I'm talking about don't bop anyone over the head and steal hundreds of dollars. These criminals slowly take $5, $10, and $20 from me, often with a smile. They pop a surcharge onto my monthly phone bill. They pad my TV bill with services I didn't ask for. They drain my bank account—drip, drip, drip—when I'm not watching. These hidden fees keep me up at night like the sound of a leaky faucet. I feel like I have to watch everything all the time because it's so easy to miss some statement on some form with some asterisk that means the company can take even more money from me. And when that happens, I suffer from what I call small-print rage.

Am I crazy? Or am I just paying attention? One thing I know for sure: I'm not alone.

I'm not a therapist, or a sociologist, but I feel on firm ground saying that small-print rage is a close second only to road rage as a source of stress in America today. As author of *The Red Tape Chronicles* on MSNBC.com, a twice-weekly column that exposes small print, corporate sneakiness, and other twenty-first-century headaches, I invite readers to share their woes with me. Tens of thousands have e-mailed and left comments on my blog as a desperate last attempt to get justice. I can see the exasperation in the amount of CAPITAL LETTERS that show up in their notes.

So I know: You suffer from small-print rage, too.

Sneaky fees peck away at us like a swarm of mosquitoes that ruin an otherwise beautiful summer evening. And like mosquitoes, an individual bite might seem trivial, barely more than a nuisance, but repeated bites can actually change the way you live. They chase you inside, make you build a screened porch, and in extreme cases make you sick.

As a too-sticky summer night breeds mosquitoes, today's business environment breeds sneakiness. Companies under pressure to keep advertised prices low have seized on trickery to pump profits up. The most successful firms are now the ones that hide their prices best: under asterisks, deep inside terms and conditions, in fees they call taxes, bills that come months after the fact, even around dark corners in auto dealerships where the manager's office is. Then, right when you think you just got a good deal, an unexpected bill comes, or a car salesman jumps out from behind the corner and yells:

Gotcha!

One Gotcha might be irritating. A few might make you angry. But

Gotchas are everywhere you turn now. They are a way of life for consumers. They are our new economic system, replacing our former system, the free-market economy. In Gotcha Capitalism, your personal finances are under siege. Mosquitoes might threaten your life with death by a thousand bites; Gotcha Capitalism threatens your finances with death by a thousand fees.

"C'mon, Bob," you might be thinking. "We're talking about nickel and diming. It's not *that* bad."

Yes, it is. I've got research to prove it.

During November 2006, I asked independent researcher Larry Ponemon of the Ponemon Institute to conduct a nationwide survey of fees and surcharges. Together, we asked consumers around the country how much they believed they'd lost to sneaky fees in the past twelve months. To be fair, we didn't allow much speculation; instead we asked consumers to identify the amount of hidden fees they'd later discovered in ten important product lines one at a time, such as cell phones, groceries, and travel.

The result? Those $5 and $10 charges really add up. Even with these limitations, Americans told us they lose $946 to sneaky fees every year, enough to stock a sizable retirement fund. And when you add up all sneaky-fee revenue, the total is simply massive. According to the survey, corporate America's take in the ten industries surveyed was $45 billion. To put that number in context, $45 billion is about equal to the amount of money stolen through the fastest-growing crime in the country, identity theft. ID theft is such an epidemic that presidential task forces have been formed to fight it. There are entire divisions of law-enforcement officials being trained to stop it. There is an entire industry of companies that has grown up to prevent it. However, I know of no single agency or company devoted to stopping the explosion of hidden fees, which cost our society just as much as identity theft.

Of course, the crime of hidden fees is not so dramatic. There are no spectacular million-dollar diamond heists accomplished in the name of deceased CEOs. Instead, hidden fees are a slow drip-drip-dripping out of Americans' hard-earned salaries. Cell-phone users, for example, reported to us that they pay about $5 to $10 more a month—on average—than they expect to, thanks to sneaky fees. That doesn't sound like much, until you consider there are more than two hundred million cell-phones users in the United States alone.

Now perhaps you'll think like I do, that the proliferation of hidden fees—and not identity theft—is the fastest-growing white-collar crime in America.

For consumers making $45,000 or less a year, that $946 in hidden fees can mean one less vacation per year, or no evening classes for additional job training. It can take a huge bite out of a family's retirement savings.

And that number is conservative. For starters, to make the study manageable, we limited the survey to ten likely culprits: cellular phones, credit cards, banks, airline travel, hotels, cable TV/satellite, home Internet access, retirement services, insurance, and groceries. Detailed industry-by-industry discussion of these fees can be found in the Toolkit Section, Chapter 4.

Remember, this $946 total is an average. So for every consumer who manages to exert Herculean effort and minimizes hidden-fee expenses to a tidy $200 or $300, there's another who pays nearly $2,000 a year. It also only represents the sneaky-fee take among those ten industries—obviously, other kinds of companies stick their customers with fees, too.

Finally, this $45 billion total—that's just the sneaky fees consumers know about. Others are surely lurking out there underneath mountainous monthly bills that busy consumers miss, and couldn't reveal to us when asked.

It's easy to calculate sneaky-fee estimates that are much higher. Simply adding up analysts' estimates of total fee income from credit-card late fees, homeowners' title insurance, wacky hotel-resort fees and the like, consumers lose well more than $100 billion a year to hidden surcharges.

But the real total is probably even more than that—in 2004,

Consumer Reports guessed it was around $216 billion annually. Your family's portion of that would average closer to $4,000 each year.

Gotcha! Perhaps those mosquito bites are starting to itch. But I have yet to describe the biggest bite of all.

That $4,000 annual drain is nothing compared to what Gotcha Capitalism is doing to your retirement. In the biggest fee swindle ever invented, hidden fees—siphoned off in total silence by Wall Street—will force you to work four, five, even six years longer than you should. They're stealing roughly one-third of the money the average American has set aside for old age. And get this: the better the investor, the greater the penalty. Later in this book, I'll show you how Wall Street fees can suck up fully 80 percent of the money a twenty-year-old invests for retirement. Eighty percent!

Hidden fees are so drastic now that they may even be screwing with the national inflation rate. Companies often don't supply surcharges and fee data to the Bureau of Labor Statistics, so when it computes inflation rates, fees aren't reflected. As a result, our national inflation rate is held artificially low.

Yes, hidden fees are a big deal.

These numbers might surprise you, but I'll bet you've had a sixth sense that something was amiss for a while. You wondered why the government keeps saying inflation is the lowest it's ever been, yet you feel squeezed tighter and tighter by monthly bills. And I'll bet you feel small-print rage once or twice a month. You know the feeling well. There you are, lying in bed at night, trying to convince yourself to forget how irritated you are at that $39 "courtesy overdraft fee" you just paid to your bank for buying a $3 hamburger with your cash card one day before your paycheck cleared.

But you don't have to take all this lying down. In my paranoia to avoid getting cheated, I've discovered something, and I want to let you in on the secret. We don't have to pay sneaky fees. And if you've already paid, don't worry: There are ways to get your money back. *Gotcha Capitalism* will tell you how.

Companies have spent years and billions of dollars conducting extensive research, learning just how to confuse you and take away your rights to a fair deal. This book will show you how they do it, and then show you how to reclaim both your money and your rights. With any luck, we can all start a movement to reclaim our economy from hucksters with huge market capitalizations, and create a marketplace where fair companies actually stand a fighting chance.

II. Tales from the Mouse Hole

The journey into the world of Gotcha Capitalism may temporarily increase your sense of rage when you find out what *they* think of *us*. You'll discover, for example, that corporations have armies of fee consultants who study more and more sneaky ways to separate you from your money. You'll see that they snicker behind your back while they trick you into one-sided contracts using typography that's so tiny, industry insiders call it "mouseprint." You'll learn that while you weren't paying attention, the idea of customer loyalty was thrown overboard by many American firms, and they now believe that *pissing off* customers is good business. You'll find out the U.S. Supreme Court has ruled that mailing you a single notice, even one you may or may not read, can constitute a binding contract.

Now to really learn how to hunt down hidden fees and kill them, you've got to know your enemy. You've got to learn to think like the enemy. To really understand mouseprint, you've got to meet the mice. So let's crawl into the mouse hole for a bit and have a look around.

AT&T: "NOT EVEN LIKELY TO OPEN" THE ENVELOPE

What if, as a company, you want to be really, really sure consumers won't read the contract you give them? You ask your marketing people to study the problem. Marketers are experts at getting people's attention. So couldn't marketing tactics be thrown into reverse, and used to make sure some fine print slips by unnoticed?

In 2001, AT&T wanted its sixty million customers to quietly agree to waive their right to sue the company. It wanted no fuss, and no mess. So it carefully crafted a mailer that was specifically designed to be *discarded*.

This tale of deception dates all the way back to the breakup of AT&T's monopoly. After reading it, you might never toss junk mail into the recycling bin again.

The telephone behemoth was dissolved back in 1982, but the firm's complete deconstruction took decades. Almost twenty years later, regulators were still dealing with the fallout.

Before the breakup, AT&T had to obtain approval from federal regulators to increase prices. The process was called "submitting a tariff." But after the breakup, AT&T's monopoly was dissolved, and the tariff process was eliminated. AT&T was told by regulators to form normal contractual relationships with its customers by sending a contract home to every one. The company took the opportunity to stuff the contract with goodies, and took the concept of small print to new lows.

As AT&T prepared to send notices to sixty million people, a special "detariffing" team was formed. It carefully prepared a mailing that no one would notice.

Getting consumers to ignore the mailing was critical, because that meant they would silently submit to the new contract terms, however one-sided they were. No uproar, no bad publicity. The detariffing team decided the document would utilize what was called the "negative option"; consumers who didn't respond to the mailing were assumed to be in agreement. No "yes" required, no signature. Silence meant consent. Recycling meant surrender.

In July and August 2001, millions of the notices were mailed across the country. AT&T was not worried they would cause a stir. Its research had concluded that many of its customers were "not even likely to open" the letter. The company expected every one of them would be fooled into consenting to this absurd contract.

But not Berkeley resident and AT&T consumer Darcy Ting. She actually read the document. A Taiwanese immigrant and professional consumer advocate, Ting spent her days helping educate Asian Americans about consumer rights for San Francisco–based nonprofit group Consumer Action. Ting knew enough to scour AT&T's fine print. She noticed that the detariffing notice included a "legal remedies" section that forced consumers to surrender their rights to sue the company under virtually all circumstances. Disputes were to be taken to mandatory binding arbitration instead. The contract also barred consumers from participating in class-action lawsuits. Disturbed by the prospect of waiving so many basic rights so quietly, Ting enlisted the help of Consumer Action, and sued. Court documents from the case reveal just how far AT&T was willing to go to sneak its customer-service agreement past consumers.

The detariffing team at AT&T extensively researched the letter's language before sending it out. As a member of AT&T's detariffing team put it: "I don't want [the letters] to tell customers . . . pay attention to the details."

So the firm made sure to put in bold type near the top of the cover letter, "There's nothing you need to do." And in a research document called the "Qualitative Study," AT&T team members wrote that "after reading the bolded text . . . [at] this point most would stop reading and discard the letter."

Note: When a company says there's nothing you need to do, watch out.

Even the most enterprising consumers who scanned the document and went to the trouble of calling AT&T with questions faced still more hurdles. In a document titled "Detariffing—Customer Handling Experience," which was circulated to customer-service managers, the strategy for distracting consumers from the real point of the mailing was made plain.

"Canned responses will be provided to service reps which will reinforce that the customer needs to do nothing," it said. Everything was carefully designed to keep consumers from finding the heart of the matter.

Call it reverse usability testing, if you like. I call it systematic deception. A federal judge called it misleading and declared the contract invalid.

The victory was short-lived, however. Corporations around the country were undeterred by the results. The mice and the fee consultants just honed their craft a bit, making sure not to leave incriminating paperwork like AT&T's Qualitative Study lying around. Today, they are not one bit shy about the contracts they continue to mail home, and the Gotchas they continue to pack into the fine print included in our monthly bills. And the type just keeps getting smaller. Consumers are today bombarded with meaningless disclosure notices, voluminous privacy policies, and incomprehensible forms—many designed so they will go straight to the recycling bin. Getting consumers to ignore the details, to skip the small print, is the name of the game.

To that end, tricking you to throw contracts into the trash is one tool, but it's hardly the best tool. For the mice, the real action is in the asterisks.

THE TWENTY-SEVENTH LETTER

We live in a world of ast*erisks*. Ignoring them is indeed a risk, and will cost you dearly.

I have become obsessed by these asterisks. Not the "Roger Maris hit his 61 home runs in 162 games," kind of asterisks. I mean the "Free checking unless you access your money from a cash machine or talk to a teller or write a check or let your balance slip fifty cents below $5,000 for a nanosecond" kind of asterisks. These are the ones that can really hurt you.

Asterisks surround your financial life now; they are part of perhaps every single transaction you make. They are so common, I believe they have become the 27th letter in the American alphabet. And behind each one is a bunch of words that always add up to just one: "Gotcha!"

You didn't fill up the rental car with gas?
    Gotcha! Gas costs $7 a gallon here.
Your bank balance fell to $999.87 for one day?
    Gotcha! That'll be $12.

You miss one payment on that eighteen months same-as-cash loan?

Gotcha! That'll be $512 extra.

You're one day late on that electric bill?

Gotcha! All your credit cards now have a 29.99 percent interest rate.

Knowing what often lurks behind these asterisks, I am driven by a need to link them with their parent paragraphs. My obsession with asterisks is the reason I found myself one day crawling on top of my pickup truck in a vain attempt to read some very, very small mouseprint.

I was doing some reporting in a Seattle suburb along Highway 522 when I spotted a billboard with the words "Free Internet Bill Pay" in enormous, twenty-foot letters.

Actually, I left something out. It really read:

"Free Internet Bill Pay*"

I don't know how fast you read, but perhaps you missed that asterisk as your eyes flew by that paragraph we just passed. I can tell you that at fifty miles per hour, a lot of people missed the asterisk when they flew by on Highway 522. But being sensitized to asterisks, I spotted it. And I decided to investigate. I hit the brakes hard, made a legal U-turn, and circled back to have a look at the billboard again.

I passed the board, did another U-turn, and pulled over to the shoulder for a closer look. From the highway, I could see there was a blurb of text at the bottom of the sign that seemed to correspond with the asterisk. But even at a standstill, it was far too small to read from my vantage point. Fortunately, I have a pickup truck, so I was able to ramble across an unpaved lot and get near the foot of the sign stanchion for a closer look.

But even that didn't work. Now, because of my close-in angle, the platform under the billboard that supports the lights blocked the bottom third of the sign. I could still read "Free Internet Bill Pay*" well enough. But I couldn't possibly see the small print at the bottom of the sign.

Again, I felt glad to have a pickup truck, and I refused to be deterred. I opened my door, climbed up the side of the truck, then pulled myself up onto the roof of my cab. With that improved angle, I was able to see the important terms and conditions of this bank's offer.

"*See banker for details."

Now I am a big believer in personal responsibility. The answer is, yes, we are all responsible for what we sign. In fact, as you can see, I do think people should be responsible for going to some lengths to find the devil in the details when they are making purchases or signing contracts. But cheating is cheating. Misleading is misleading. Obfuscating is obfuscating. None of that philosophical personal responsibility talk should be used as a rationalization to allow companies to do things they know will mislead many people. Consumers should never have to climb on the roof of a truck to read the fine print. It's time to draw the line somewhere.

Cable TV seems like a good place to start drawing.

A SEA OF WORDS, BUT WHERE'S THE PRICE?

Not long ago I saw an offer from Comcast for cable, Internet, and phone service sold as a bundle. Get all three for less than $85 a month, the mailed postcard read on the front. On the back, the deal was split out with more detail—$30 for cable, $30 for telephone, $25 for Internet. In a font that was about one-eighth the size, the company included the phrase "(per) month for 3 months" next to each price. OK, that would tip off most people that the price was just a tease, and it would go up after an initial period.

The key question remained unanswered, however: What was the real price? What happened after three months? Finding that out was much harder than climbing onto the roof of my truck.

The Comcast postcard was five inches tall and eight inches wide. Below the price listing, running all the way across the bottom half-inch of the card, was an asterisked parent paragraph with type so small that calling it mouseprint would be an exaggeration. Let's call it flea print. It could easily have been mistaken for dirt smudges.

Only with the aid of modern technology could a typeface this small be generated. I have better than average eyesight, and I physically could not read it. I don't believe a literate mouse could have read it, either. The words were so tiny it hurt to focus on them. But that's not the only reason the block of text was unreadable. The words ran across the entire eight-inch width of the card. At that font size, that meant there were more than sixty words on every single line of text, an impossible amount to follow. For comparison purposes, I picked up the nearest book and counted a line of text. It ran twelve words across. The ability to follow words across a line of text, and to jump to the next line, is something designers call "tracking." Poor designs make tracking very hard, and readers tend to give up when they have to track too far. I can tell you that I still have not read this paragraph of Comcast marketing text because I physically could not track that long. It was hard enough just counting the words on a single line.

So, to find out the true price of the service, I tried randomly hunting around this sea of text. I did find some important information using this method, like this: "Additional monthly charge of $10 will apply for customers who do not qualify for multi-product discount." And this: "Equipment (including cable modem) is required and unless specifically included in offer, must be rented at Comcast's standard rates or purchased at retail."

Then, after a bit more looking, I spotted the information I needed. Sort of. "AFTER PROMOTIONAL PERIOD REGULAR MONTHLY RATES APPLY." And that was it. What those monthly rates were—I had no idea. They were not on the card.

I will give Comcast this; that monthly rate notice was capitalized. One can only imagine that someone inside the firm's promotion department had a pang of conscience about the two-point font thing. Naturally, the pang was not strong enough to actually say on the postcard the *only information that actually mattered to consumers.* That being, how much did Comcast's services really cost?

To intentionally echo a popular marketing campaign, Comcast's advertisement was, quite intentionally, priceless.

III. The Big Problem: Pricelessness and Stealth Inflation

Almost everything today is priceless. Not the "isn't that sweet, he took his kids to a ball game" kind of priceless. I mean quite literally "without price." Price tags are dead. You won't find them on jars of mayonnaise at the grocery store. You disregard the ones you see on automobiles. And the price tags you find on cable-TV ads and cell-phone ads are flat-out misleading.

How much does your cable TV cost every month? How much did you *think* it would cost when you signed up? How about your cell phone? What will the bill be next month? Go through your list of monthly bills and consider the surprises you find on every one. Time after time, you open the mail not knowing what to expect. But didn't that nice man at the store say it would only cost $29.99? Didn't the cable ad say the price was $85 for everything?

These days, nearly every service we buy is priceless. There is one price on the advertisement or the store window, and then a second price, which includes the surcharges and fees—something I call aftercharges. Price No. 2 is always more, and nearly always elusive. It usually doesn't reveal itself until the first bill comes, weeks later, when it's too late to get out of the deal. Often, the price continues to change, continues to grow, as more and more small print kicks in. The price of cable TV is never what the cable company says on the postcard, not even in the first month. And after six months? It's often 50 percent more.

What the large print offers, the small print takes away.

As a result, comparative shopping is dead, murdered by corporations that profit from consumer confusion. How can consumers compare prices when they don't know what they really are? Also dead: capitalism's built-in reward mechanism for the most efficient, well-managed companies. Now, the rewards go to the best cheaters, instead. And consumers, instead of shopping, must now feel their way in the dark, guessing at what things will really cost, always nagged by this feeling of being cheated.

This new "priceless" economy is more than just unfair. It's a fundamental shift in our economic system. Consumers aren't the only target. Honest companies are getting thrown under this bus, too. In a true market economy, transparency allows the best products and the most productive companies to succeed. In a priceless economy, cheaters succeed and efficient, honorable companies struggle to survive. Later in this book we'll meet a hotel chain that adopted upfront, no-fee pricing as an experiment—it later had to abandon the practice after consumers repeatedly abandoned their hotel beds. Lured by lower come-on prices from competitors, consumers dropped the honorable hotel chain. It's a sad statement on our business environment, but in America today, companies can't afford to be fair.

LIKE MOTHS TO A FLAME

Here's the secret companies long ago learned about you: There's no penalty for playing with prices, and consumers can't seem to resist a good price come-on. Like moths to a flame, you are drawn to low, low advertised prices and you're terrible at making choices based on the eventual price you pay. You pay close attention to the big price at the top of the bill, but almost no attention to the little price at the bottom of the bill. You'll do almost anything to save a few pennies today, even if it costs you a few pounds tomorrow.

Take gas purchases. As prices rise, people become much more price sensitive. In fact, a survey conducted in 2007 by petroleum retailers found that half of consumers would go to some trouble to save 3 cents per gallon on a fill-up—they'd make a left-hand turn across a busy street, for example. But one in four said they'd go even further: They'd drive ten minutes out of their way to save three cents per gallon.

That makes no sense. Taking that extra trip saves a driver 36 cents on an average twelve-gallon fill up. But saving that 36 cents costs the driver nearly $2! If the driver averages 45 mph, getting to that magical discount gas station will end up taking the driver on a fifteen-mile detour, round trip. Assuming the car gets twenty miles to the gallon, and the price of gas is $2.40, the extra trip costs $1.80, nearly five times the amount saved.

You might be too busy to accurately assess the pros and cons of a penny-wise, pound-foolish drive (using the example above, the gas price would have to be fifteen cents a gallon less for the driver to break even!). But don't worry; someone else is hard at work doing the mathematics for you. Companies know how effectively discounts entice you; they know the pull is generally a bit stronger than the negative reaction you have to aftercharges. So they know precisely how much of a fee they can tack on to your monthly bill before you'll complain (about $10). And they know you can't resist a good-sounding, low-ball deal. By the time the actual price is revealed to you, after all the fees, surcharges, and penalties are laid on thick, it's usually too late for you to back out. You've already signed the cell-phone contract or you're sitting at the closing table with your banker and your attorney.

Setting optimal floating prices in a fast-moving economy requires sophisticated technology; companies have it, and you don't. Make no mistake: Every day, you are engaged in an information war with corporate America. And you are losing badly. Sophisticated computers are constantly observing our behavior, selecting optimal price points, and designing traps that cost you. Credit-card companies know exactly how to lure you with a low "fixed" credit-card rate and then nudge you into a penalty rate that can be 500 percent higher. Simply bumping up your due date by a day or two will often do the trick. You didn't think these things were accidents, did you?

IV. What Is in This Book

So companies are using multimillion-dollar technology to confuse you with asterisks, mouseprint, marketing deception, contracts designed so you won't read them, pamphlets designed so you'll throw them out, and priceless goods. And you have better things to do than read every 28-page mailer sent to your home. That's why I wrote this book. I read the small print so you don't have to.

Gotcha Capitalism will shine a bright light on more than a hundred hidden fees that lurk within your monthly bills and big-ticket purchases. More important, it will offer you step-by-step instructions to win back your money, including sample letters you can write and phone call scripts you can follow. Follow just one of these strategies each month and you'll save hundreds of dollars each year.

This book is divided into three sections. First, this overview of the sneaky-fee economy and how it works. This is the "know your enemy" part of the book.

Section Two is the meat of the book: hidden fees by industry, and how to get your money back. In this section, we'll tackle your monthly bills in detail. Here's the industry list: credit cards and banks, cell phones and home phones, cable and satellite television, Internet access, travel, groceries, student loans, rebates, mortgages, retirement, and gift cards. In each chapter, you'll find an overview of the sneaky-fee culture in that industry, followed by specific fees and how to avoid them. The table of contents in this book is highly detailed so you can skip right to whatever fee irks you most and start there. Each chapter ends with a set of Gotcha-Stopping Strategies that you can follow and start saving money right away.

Finally, Section Three is a generic set of tools you can use to fight all types of customer-service battles. It includes sample letters and e-mails that work because they push exactly the right buttons. There are also sample scripts for dealing with those maddening customer-service phone calls (hey, they have scripts, why shouldn't you!). There are blank forms you can use to keep track of all these exchanges. You'll also find all the gory details of the Ponemon Gotcha survey. And finally, there are tips to defend yourself against the "nuclear" option—when you and your nemesis company get locked into a game of chicken, where you refuse to pay and they refuse to release you from the bill. It's a high-stakes game that can end up in a courtroom or in a fight over a credit report, and it's not for the weak spirited, but if you have to play, you can win. I'll tell you how.

Along the way, you'll learn the most effective way to allocate your precious time and complain wisely. Some companies and industries are much more willing to negotiate sneaky fees than others. We'll tell you which fights to pick. Then we'll pick apart apartment leases, invoices, bills, contracts, mouseprint, and asterisks so you are armed with the information you need to fight those battles. And we'll get inside the head of those customer-service agents at your various adversaries—so you are more persuasive and win more of those battles.

V. Shrouding, Reverse Coupons, and Other Tricks from the Dark Side

Now, let's get back to talking about what you're up against: Let's go back into the mouse hole and learn more about how the mice think.

We've already discussed the age-old tourist-local problem economists like to talk about. Remember, tourists always get cheated until they find a local to learn from. Two prominent economists, Xavier Gabaix of MIT and David Laibson of Harvard took the model and updated it for the "priceless" age in a landmark paper published in 2004. Gabaix and Laibson boiled the world of consumers down to two types: sophisticates and myopes.

Sophisticates are the coupon clippers of our age. They know exactly when to mail in the credit-card payments every month and take maximum advantage of what amounts to a free thirty-day loan. They even earn free plane tickets with frequent flier miles accumulated while using their credit card. They call to ask hotels about unexpected fees such as daily parking costs before they book that hotel. They might even attempt to consider the true lifetime costs of a computer printer before buying one.

Myopes, on the other hand, fail at all these tasks. They are tempted by new credit-card offers and forget to put a stamp on their bill payments. The penalty—their interest rate triples. Members of this group will be tempted by a $49 printer and never think to ask how much printer refill cartridges cost. They are busy, they are distracted, and they are easy prey for Gotcha capitalists.

The myopes pay for the sophisticates' free vacations and free loans. Credit-card revolvers—those who carry a balance and pay high interest rates—subsidize free loans for credit-card "freeloaders"—those who always pay their bill on time. And in between, companies skim off tidy profits.

Perhaps this doesn't sound like such a bad arrangement to you. Clever consumers are rewarded; stupid consumers are penalized. Darwin in action, you think. Economics is a game. Good players win. What's wrong with that?

Here's what's wrong: Corporations make the rules in this game. And they can change the rules whenever they want. That means they control exactly how many sophisticates there are at any given time. A simple, subtle rule change ("Starting today, we'll charge a $30 resort fee for all guests. Don't tell anyone!") throws a group of sophisticates overboard. Consumers who are sophisticates today cannot be sure they will be sophisticates tomorrow ("When did you start charging a resort fee at this hotel?"). He who makes the rules, wins the game.

A key law of Gotcha economics, with apologies to Las Vegas, is this: The house always wins. Credit-card companies will always invent new fees and make money. Supermarkets can always run out of sale items, or cancel discounts at odd times. Cable-TV firms can always move a few channels around and force you to upgrade. Whenever quarterly revenues look soft, companies can just turn the screws a little harder. The game, you see, is fixed.

One way companies do that, say Gabaix and Laibson, is by "shrouding" the price of things. Think back to the printer dilemma. When considering the cost of printing, the price label on the printer in the Office Max store tells only a part of the story, and not even the most important part. There is also the cost of operating the printer, largely driven by the cost of ink. How can a consumer assess the likely cost of ink for a new printer during its first year? During its lifetime? It sounds like a simple question, yet in reality, it can be impossible to answer. Buying a printer is the classic transaction in the Gotcha economy.

Theoretically, someone who hazards a guess at the number of pages they might print during a certain time span could guess their operating costs. A diligent consumer could guesstimate the number of pages that can be printed with each refill cartridge, and then calculate the number of cartridges that would need to be purchased each year. Similar mathematics could be tried for deducing a cost-per-page for each printer.

The equation, however, doesn't add up. Such mathematics can't give consumers guidance on the most critical question of all: Which printer is the least expensive in the long run? Ink cartridge makers don't use standardized sizes across printers. In fact, many cartridges don't even list their unit size on the packages. You don't know how much ink you're getting when you buy refill cartridges. That makes true price comparisons impossible. In short, there is no intelligent way for a consumer to buy a printer. The real price of the printer is entirely shrouded. There are no sophisticates, and no locals. At the printer store, we are all tourists. All myopes. And so, confusion reigns. Consumers make completely irrational printer choices because they have no other choice. They nearly always overspend. When you are in an information war, confusion is your biggest threat. Corporations love confused customers, because they always spend more money. Confused consumers are profitable consumers. That's why companies work so hard to confuse us.

THE BAZAAR

Now, imagine a densely packed bazaar in a foreign country where strangers yell and scream at you, even grab you, in an effort to get your business. A sign catches your eye: "Sale: Leather wallets!" So you decide to buy one. You ask how much. The first price you hear, you realize, is made up out of thin air. The last buyer paid perhaps half as much; the next perhaps twice as much. So you bicker for a while and settle on a price somewhere near the bottom end—500 garbanzos. Then, you reach into your wallet and hand over a bill that says 500 garbanzos. But the merchant says, "No, no, this is only worth 250 garbanzos today." So you hand over another bill. Then he says, "There's a 100-garbanzo fee for the bag." You decline the bag. "Well, there's a 100-garbanzo transaction fee." So you fork that over. But before you get your new wallet, there's one more gotcha.

"There's also a bazaar-rental fee of 50 garbanzos." Now what? Do you hand over the additional 50, knowing the tack-on charges could go on forever? Or do you begin the torturous argument to get back your 1,100-garbanzo investment?

To you, this exchange may sound ridiculous. Or it may sound eerily similar to a recent experience at an airport car-rental desk. Imagine trying to fairly compare leather wallet prices in our mythical market. Comparing car-rental prices isn't much easier, given the seemingly endless list of tack-on aftercharges. Among the fees you might encounter at a car-rental desk are:

- Peak season fee
- Concession recovery fee
- Facility usage fee
- Refueling surcharge
- Stadium surcharge
- Consolidated facility charges
- Highway use fee
- Vehicle license recoupment fee
- Frequent-flier miles fee
- Tire and battery recovery fee

Perhaps there are some consumers who pay the rock-bottom, advertised car-rental price, or the original 500-garbanzo wallet price. These are consumers who know the wallet price is only valid on Tuesdays, and consumers who know the magic words to decline the add-on car-rental insurance despite the apocalyptic sales pitch, and know where the gas station nearest the airport is. Myopes don't know any of this, and they pay, and pay, and pay. And remember, the most profitable companies are the ones that manage to make us all myopes.

FEES: THE ANTI-COUPON

Sneaky, hidden fees might be called anti-coupons. Today, rather than give discounts to the industrious newspaper clippers, corporate

America charges extra to those who miss the fine print and asterisks. It's not clear when this happened, but it wasn't a fair trade. Tracking down sneaky fees takes much more time and effort than cutting out coupons. Perhaps the corporations are writing the mouseprint, but we're the ones running around like rats when the light goes on.

Down there in the mouse hole, companies have lots of tools to trick us. They've even learned to team up against us to make more sneaky fees. In a market economy, competition is the key to keeping an economy moving. In our bastardized economy, new terms have to be invented to explain conspiracies against consumers, terms like shrouding. Here's another: reverse competition.

Almost anyone who's ever bought a home has been a victim of reverse competition. Your Realtor or your mortgage broker will almost certainly steer you toward one particular title-insurance company. Why? The agent can get a cut of the sale as a referral fee. That means title companies actually bid up the price of your insurance, since higher prices benefit both the insurer and the agent. There is no downward competitive pressure to keep costs in line; the only real price pressure is up. Similar upward price pressure can be found in other insurance arrangements, such as credit-card insurance programs. Economists sometimes call this a "trilateral dilemma," because three parties are involved in a transaction. Anytime an intermediary who is paid on commission is doing the bargaining for you, the price pressure always works in the wrong direction.

VI. How Did We Get Here?

Why do today's consumers find themselves in this incredibly precarious position? Why is the weather so fair for foul play? It's simple. What keeps players from cheating in any sporting contest? What prevents the strongest basketball players from simply tackling their opponents? Referees who call fouls. In America today, the economy's referees have all but disappeared. If you doubt this, turn on any television channel after midnight. The airwaves are awash in false advertising. There's misleading come-ons for free software that ends up costing $79; get-healthy-quick books that force consumers to pay for surprise website subscriptions to get the real health "secrets;" and of course, endless demonstrations for products that simply don't work as advertised. Unfair and deceptive (that is, illegal) trade practices are all around us. But the deceptive marketers seem to peddle their snake oil without any fear of reprisal. No one's doing anything about it. It's as if the league commissioner gathered the referees together and told them all to swallow the whistle and "let the boys play." You know what that means: a dirty game.

It's been open season on American consumers ever since the Federal Trade Commission—the chief federal agency devoted to protecting consumers—was targeted for dismantling by the Reagan administration. Some 30 percent of its budget was slashed in Reagan's first four years. Regional offices were closed. Adjusted for inflation, the FTC budget fell from $120 million in 1978 to $75 million in 1990. There was serious talk of folding the FTC, dumping its consumer protection activities, and sending its antitrust lawyers to the Justice Department.

"The burden the agency imposes on the consumer by raising the prices of consumer products and wasting the time of businessmen is staggering," said Senator Harrison Schmitt of New Mexico at the time. "A review of FTC actions is a chronicle of wasted money, costly litigation, silly regulations, and worthless government paternalism."

Despite this menacing talk, America's defender of consumers was saved, but it took a serious body blow. In 1979, there were 1,746 employees at the FTC entrusted with protecting the American consumer. In 2005, there were 1,019—a 40 percent reduction. That's like the police force in your town dropping from 100 to 60! Think what would happen to your crime rate. And today's FTC has far more responsibilities than it did in the late 1970s. Since then, the agency has picked up duties like managing the Do Not Call list, running the nation's effort to combat identity theft, and managing Internet security, to name a few. Thanks to population growth, the agency has about 75 million more U.S. consumers to defend. And then there's this: In the past decade, Congress has repeatedly passed laws that preempt state regulation, wresting authority away from statehouses and plopping it on the FTC—states generally cannot regulate the nation's credit bureaus, for example, only the FTC can. And yet with all that extra work, the FTC has about half as many employees as it did 25 years ago.

What keeps advertisers from lying? What keeps a wallet salesman from tacking on unfair charges? Government regulation. What ensures that national currency must be accepted at consistent values? Government regulation. What's the only way to achieve a fair, honest marketplace? Setting rules that everyone must follow, and penalizing those who don't. Despite Senator Schmitt's sentiments, regulation is not a dirty word—it is a necessary part of a functioning economy. So is a fully-staffed Federal Trade Commission. How many sporting events do you know benefit from having fewer referees?

And yet, Schmitt and others like him have bad-mouthed the refs so much that those who remain seem whistle-shy. The results have been disastrous. Companies have been given the message that they can get away with nearly anything. Beginning in the 1980s, consumer-hunting season was on. The rug was pulled out from under federal agencies devoted to consumer protection, and encouraged by the FTC's powerlessness, American companies have steadily stretched the limits of fairness ever since.

FREE CREDIT REPORTS? FOR A PRICE

Here's one example. It's impossible to avoid those FreeCreditReport. com ads that air repetitively on late-night television, promising what sounds like the annual free peek at credit reports mandated by Congress in 2004. Instead, the site is operated by credit bureau Experian, and there's nothing free about it. Consumers who visit the site must sign up for a pricey subscription service to get the report. Experian was sued in 2005 by the FTC for misleading consumers, and forced to refund much of the money it earned from the site— but yet the advertisements, and the sales, continue. The company admitted no wrongdoing in its settlement with the FTC. But it was only the most recent tussle in a decades-long struggle between the FTC and the nation's credit bureaus. They repeatedly misbehave, and make money off their misbehavior. The FTC repeatedly issues press releases and sues the companies, but little ever changes. Even companies that are directly in the sights of the FTC apparently have little to fear.

Weakened federal regulators is only one source of the problem, but something else, something even more subtle, has given corporations even more power over consumers—the privatization of the American court system.

You probably don't know this, but long ago you agreed to a contract—several contracts, actually—that eliminated your right to access the American court system. You pay taxes to fund these courts, but you can't use them. If you want to sue your cell-phone company, your credit-card company, even your auto dealer, you can't. Nearly all consumer interactions are now governed by hard-to-spot mandatory arbitration clauses, the ultimate mouseprint. This small print appears to signal an all-out assault on the Seventh Amendment to the Constitution.

The push to privatize our court system, to limit consumers' ability to sue for justice, is exactly what AT&T was trying to do with its contract designed for the trash that began this chapter. While Darcy Ting—who sued over AT&T's mouseprint—and consumer groups won that battle, virtually every other industry was busy getting consumers to agree to arbitration clauses in a myriad of sneaky ways.

Signatures are not required for you to find yourself bound by mandatory arbitration agreements. Often, simply opening a shrink-wrapped box with software inside is enough to put such an agreement into force. And once you open that box, you've agreed not to sue the company that made the software.

Instead, you must bring your complaints before an arbitration board. Nothing about arbitration hearings even vaguely resembles an American court of law. Adjudication before this board is secretive. The results of your dispute can't be shared, and they're not public, so consumers cannot reference prior cases. The arbitrators are chosen from lists that are essentially self-limited by the industry you are fighting. As we'll see with much more detail in Chapter 4 of the Toolkit section, arbitrators who rule for consumers don't stay arbitrators very long. There are no statistics on how often consumers win in these kangaroo courts, but one class-action lawsuit filed against a credit-card company revealed that the lender won well over 99 percent of the cases filed.

As a company, when you know an arbitration hearing is a consumer's last resort, you're not going to fret much about getting caught.

If you're wondering where the crazy idea for privatizing America's court system came from, look no further than the political movement that has pushed for privatization of every other government function in America—Social Security, schools, toll roads, and prisons. Karl Rove, President George W. Bush's former chief political advisor, is also chief architect of the "tort reform" movement in America, which traces its roots to the beginnings of Rove's career in Texas during the 1980s. Tort reform may have its place—we all know stories of class-action lawyers making millions while victims walk away with pennies. But tort reform has encouraged alternative dispute resolution—outside-of-court trials—as the answer to pricey trial verdicts. This has led to forced participation in mandatory binding arbitration, which virtually eliminates consumers' access to the traditional court system, and with it, consumers' ability to challenge bad corporate behavior. The results are clear: Corporations run amok.

Legal action fighting the mandatory arbitration clauses is popping up all around the country, and judges have occasionally ruled them invalid. But behind these clauses is an even more insidious trend companies have adopted in dealings with consumers—the habit of signing them up for what are known in the legal profession as "contracts of adhesion."

You know them by another name: an unfair fight.

Contracts of adhesion are struck by two parties where one has the upper hand, and the other has little say in the terms. These contracts are not negotiated. They are offered as "take-it-or-leave-it" deals. Most consumer contracts are now contracts of adhesion, as consumers have little or no ability to negotiate any of the terms. Because they are written entirely by the powerful party, unfair provisions they contain are not legally enforceable. To have a valid contract, both parties must be equals. Courts can and do strike down unfair provisions in a contract of adhesion—but only when someone files a lawsuit. Until a legal challenge is filed, companies can force consumers into contracts laced with $200-early-termination-fees all they want. And if you doubt these practices are one-sided, consider this: If your cell-phone company were to stop operating, could you demand $200 from it?

WON'T THE MARKET FIX THE PROBLEM?

There really isn't much debate about the problems of corporate misbehavior in our age. Companies like Enron and WorldCom taught us that corporate boardrooms often behave as if they are above the law. In the realm of consumer protection, ethics seem similarly absent. There is no debating the prevalence of sneaky fees and the dramatic impact they have on consumers.

But there is debate about this: Can't market forces take care of this problem? Won't consumers eventually leave the sneakier companies and stay with the fair companies, thereby creating a fair market?

Each question has an answer: no, and no.

Consumers who are stuck without choices can't quit their misbehaving companies. Research confirms this. Independent research conducted by the Ponemon Institute for this book shows most pay-television consumers don't quit over hidden fees because they can't—they have only one cable company available to them. So in many areas, normal market forces don't apply.

But even when they do, hidden fees can't be eliminated by normal consumer behavior. Instead, things often move in the opposite direction. Economists Gabaix and Laibson explain why in their paper on shrouding. Companies have little incentive to teach consumers about the world of hidden fees. Remember myopes? They are profitable, and often loyal. Sophisticates shop around. No business wants sophisticates. Any company that would spend marketing dollars saying, "Our prices are a little higher, but what you see is what you pay," would tend to lose customers. Gabaix and Laibson call this "the curse of debiasing." Those newly educated sophisticates would simply start looking around for lower prices. They would likely leave the honest company and pick the company with the lower prices and the tack-on fees, believing their new smarts would help them evade the aftercharges and ultimately get a better deal. No one wants to turn myopes into sophisticates. There is no incentive for a business to create more fee-wary consumers.

To wit: Credit card companies simply don't compete on fees. Ever seen an advertisement that says, "No overlimit fee MasterCard"? You never will.

To experience true free-market forces, markets require transparency. By definition, sneaky fees and transparency cannot coexist. So market forces alone cannot correct this problem. The prevalence of sneaky fees means we live in a broken market. Markets can only be fixed by rules, boundaries, and yes, regulation. We need to get to work rehabilitating our sick economy; we need to get over Senator Schmitt's fear of the R-word.

For help with that, let me conjure up another image for you. Remember the last time your family pulled out a board game? Now, remember the last time you dived into a game without first going over the rules. What happened? How many minutes before the first fight? Now, remember the last time one of the players decided to change the rules in the middle of a game. What happened then? That's the world of Gotcha Capitalism. We're playing a game but haven't been told the rules. Every one of us is, as Senator William Proxmire said in Congress while attacking hidden fees in real-estate transactions, a "babe in the woods." And the woods are full of wild animals.

VII. Fundamentals of Complaining Well

I've painted a fairly gloomy picture for you: Eroding consumer rights, massive computers, and consultants constantly dreaming up new ways to screw you, consumers so busy you can't be bothered to take on Goliath and so confused you don't know how. I see it with every *Red Tape Chronicles* column I write. There is an incredible sense of helplessness about all this, a learned helplessness that keeps consumers from fighting against this increasingly unfair system. People feel taken advantaged of, abused, and don't know what to do. The government is doing little to make new rules or enforce the rules we have, and in many cases, has just about signaled to companies that it's open season on customers. Many consumers, every day, simple cry uncle and pay up.

You don't have to.

Despite all these obstacles I've described, you can take on corporate America and win. You can get refunds from cheating companies. You can save hundreds, if not thousands of dollars, every year. Following the strategies in the book will let you keep much more of your own hard-earned money, and it will teach you how to get sweet satisfaction while doing it. You don't have to feel helpless and abused every time you shop for something.

We're not just talking about nickels and dimes. We're talking about saving enough money to stock a genuine retirement account. Getting back fees and surcharges can be the best, most lucrative part-time job you've ever had. Ridding your life of Gotchas is well worth your time. Consider this example: If you're paying $10 extra each month for premium cable channels you never ordered, you might think you are too busy to spend precious time on the phone fighting over the bill. Think again.

Let's say the customer-service fight might take you an hour. And maybe $10 isn't worth an hour's work to you. But we're not talking about a one-time $10 charge. We're talking about $10 each month, or $120 each year. Remember, you only have to fight that fight once. How many of us can turn our nose up at a $120-per-hour job?

Let me put it another way. In order to make $10 per month in interest earnings, how much do you think you'd have to park in a standard savings account? Assuming a decent 1 percent return, the answer is $12,000. Making that one phone call to your cable company is the equivalent of parking $12,000 in a savings account for a year.

So let's review: One hour of complaining to cable company = $120 in your pocket = $12,000 parked in a savings account.

Making money by earning interest on savings is hard. Keeping the money you've already made is easy. And boy, does it feel good.

This book is designed to make you an expert complainer. Not a whiney complainer, not a bitchy person, and not a penny-wise and pound-foolish consumer. A well-informed, successful, efficient complainer. For example, through extensive consumer research, I'll reveal the industries where complainers frequently get refunds—in fact, 50 percent of the time—and which industries are stingier than the Grinch. That's important. You're busy, so you might as well fight the easiest battles first.

Good complaining is an art, and it is a science. But it may not be what you think it is. It does not involve yelling or screaming or collapsing into a blithering mess (though you rightly want to do all those things sometimes). In fact, screaming often makes things worse.

The themes of good complaining are weaved within the fiber of every chapter of this book, but there are several principles that always apply. They are:

1. Know what you are talking about

You really want to scream, "That's not fair!" That might feel good (actually, probably not). But the goal is not to feel good; the goal is to be effective. That means gathering your thoughts, knowing the facts, and knowing your rights. This book will walk you through dozens of hidden fees so you know what's happening, and then explain all your practical and legal avenues for recovering that money. If you want justice, run for Congress. For now, you want money, so gather your facts and go after it.

2. Have paperwork, and ask for paperwork

This is the most annoying requirement, but it doesn't have to be. Knowing whom you talked with and when, knowing what you signed and why, and knowing when you paid what is all terribly important. Not every company listens to logical arguments, but any lawyer will tell you that "papering over" the opponent is an excellent strategy. The more you can back up your claims with data, the easier your discussions will be. At the same time, it's a really helpful (and effectively annoying) habit to ask your nemesis company for paperwork at every turn. When did you receive my payment? When did I sign that part of the contract? Can you please send me a copy of this, that, and the other thing? Some companies will surrender merely because it's cheaper than mailing you all these things.

Asking for documentation is also a good trick if you feel like you are losing an argument or don't know what to say next. Sending an agent scurrying for paperwork will give you time to think. The paperwork you get may help fill in some of the gaps in your own documentation.

This book contains simple worksheets that you can use to log your telephone calls and other interactions with companies. Once you realize you are in a dispute, it is vitally important that you take a moment to write down times, dates, and names for every conversation you have, along with tracking numbers or other company identifiers. The worksheets will help you do that.

3. Ask, ask again, ask again again

You don't have to be religious to learn from a famous Bible story found in the Gospel of Luke, sometimes called "The Persistent Widow and the Unjust Judge." In the parable, the judge is described as being so unfair and cavalier that he "neither feared God nor respected any human being." Sound familiar? And yet, a widow in the town where he worked was eventually able to win justice from him for one reason, and one reason only: She pestered him over and over again.

As one translation puts it, the judge ultimately relented, saying, "While it is true that I neither fear God nor respect any human being, because this widow keeps bothering me I shall deliver a just decision for her lest she finally come and strike me."

I don't recommend the threat to strike. But you must know that most company agents are trained to say no at first blush. After all, a few "nos" don't cost the firm anything. So you have to be ready to persist past the first few nos. As a general rule, keep this in mind: If you haven't been told no at least four times, you haven't really even started asking yet.

4. Don't take no from someone who can't say yes

Here's a related point. Many people are told "no" by customer-service agents who simply can't say "yes." Think about the key that grocery store clerks often need to get from a manager before they open the cash drawer to fix a mistake. Many companies are organized that way. Many front-line employees can't refund surcharges and fees because they don't have the authority, or the right computer code, to do so. But there is someone else at the company who can say yes. Your job is to escalate your problem to that person. During any confrontation, go ahead and ask the employee if he or she has the authority to fix your problem. They often tell the truth. That will prevent you from wasting your time hearing no from someone who literally can't say yes.

5. Have a Plan B

The most important negotiating tactic of all—always have a Plan B. You may not convince any given customer-service representative to give you what you want. You might not convince her supervisor, either. But there is always something you can do. The Toolkit section of this book offers you an endless set of Plan Bs. You don't have to get frustrated by a brain-dead agent who just won't work with you. You can always write headquarters, sue in small claims court, or call your attorney general's office. Knowing you have alternatives—and you do always have alternatives—will save you from that feeling of helplessness that leads to small-print rage. Knowing these alternatives well and sprinkling them into your conversations with your adversary company ("I have already picked out another cell-phone company," or "I've already written my letter to the attorney general. Should I just send it?") will often get you instant results, or at least instant respect. Some smart consumers actually spend their time waiting on hold with customer service by searching the Internet for the appropriate regulatory agency and beginning the complaint process. By the time an operator is on the line, they are just a click away from filing a complaint.

Having a genuine, dispassionate ability to get up and walk away from any business deal is your ultimate Plan B, the only foolproof negotiating tactic. Knowing you can do that will have an incredible, immediate impact on the companies you do business with. Most really don't want to lose you as a customer, so when you get up to walk away, suddenly refunds, better treatment, and other perks will come your way. You've heard of deathbed conversions? I call these "exit door" conversions.

6. Pick your battles

And finally, you must efficiently pick your battles. Decide how much your time is worth. Decide how much your sense of principle is worth. Understand, with help from this book, which fights you are most likely to win. And start with the highest returns, the "low-hanging fruit" companies often talk about.

That last point might sound obvious, but it's not always. Recurring fees, even tiny $2 fees, are a better target than a one-time $20 charge, for example—even though the $20 fee might stick in your craw a bit more. Bank fees are particularly confusing in this respect, since they are irregular. How much did you pay in ATM and overdraft fees last year? Few consumers know. But switching to a credit union and away from hefty deposit minimums, while obviously a hassle and time-demanding, may be the biggest fee-saver you ever accomplish.

Picking your battles also means asking for refunds from the firms most likely to cough them up. No, not all companies are created equal. In fact, the Ponemon Gotcha consumer survey conducted for this book reveals enormous disparities among industries and the likelihood they'll work with consumers who call to complain. The study also reveals that consumers waste a lot of time complaining to deaf ears. There is much more detail on this in Chapter 4 of the Toolkit section, but I'll sum up what you really need to know right now.

If you are busy, and only have time to complain to one firm, where should you fire that one complaint bullet? Answer: Your credit-card company. Consumers in our study who complained to card-issuing banks reported a 65 percent success rate, the highest in the survey. Airlines (60 percent) and grocery stores (57 percent) followed closely behind.

Those results might surprise you. Shoppers are less likely to complain about grocery store fees than any other industry surveyed, meaning the likely success of grocery store complainers must be a carefully guarded secret. Ditto for airlines: Only 15 percent of consumers said they complained about hidden flying fees, but three out of five who did complain said they got a refund.

Consumers rarely go begging to their bank for refunds, and that seems wise. Bank complaints rarely work (33 percent of the time, our consumers said).

On the other hand, pay-TV firms and cell-phone firms generate the most sneaky-fee complaints, and the lowest success rate—about 20 percent—a recipe for futility. Clearly, both industries have made the decision to slip in those extra charges and then hold the line.

These results don't suggest people should never complain to their cable company or cell-phone provider. But if you have only a few minutes a month to fight for fee justice (not to mention a limited number of minutes per month to talk on your cell phone), our study shows you are better off saving that precious time for fights with credit-card companies and grocery stores.

Remember, what we want here is money. Not a chance to vent. Not revenge. Just like companies with those big databases, you should judge your success strictly by how much money you make.

And you should use every piece of enemy intelligence you can get to plan your attack. After all, that's how companies do it.

In a world of information overload, the overlooked detail is a twenty-first-century malady. It's also corporate America's favorite weapon. Many commentators like to blame the victim, arguing that consumers who don't read contracts in full or read their monthly statements with a fine-tooth comb get what they deserve. Maybe so. But that does not give companies the right to intentionally abuse this overload. Besides, I've yet to meet someone who reads all the fine print in their lives. It's nearly impossible. Consumers now pay more than twice the monthly bills they used to pay. Once upon a time, rent, insurance, and electricity pretty much did it, but now there's cable, several cell phones, student loans, not to mention an average of ten credit cards. Who has time to watch each bill like a hawk? You'd have to be crazy—or perhaps a website columnist—to do that.

In *Gotcha Capitalism,* you will not find the tired, simplistic, and unrealistic advice you always hear: "Read everything carefully!" Instead, this book will teach you which details are more important than others, and help you pick the places to slow down and read up. I don't want to fill your life with more reading material—only more fairness. Now, let's get right to the gory details, to the more than one hundred sneaky ways companies separate you from your money, to the hundred or so places where I've read all the small print for you, and the hundred things you can do today, using my hundred Gotcha-Stopping Strategies, to get it back.

Sneaky Fees in Everything

1

Credit Cards

Wesley Wannemacher was the perfect credit-card customer. He was never quite able to pay his bills, but he sure tried. Exactly the consumer every card-issuing bank craves.

In 2001, Wannemacher got married. He paid for the wedding in tiny Lima, Ohio, by charging $3,200 on a new Chase credit card he'd received. He never used the card again. Soon after the wedding, Wannemacher's life got complicated, as often happens. He got a new job, he relocated, he was promoted. He had a child. She had emergency tonsil surgery. He had another child. Wannemacher paid his bills, but not always on time, and not always in full.

Wannemacher was in the industry's sweet spot.

He never wanted to declare bankruptcy. So Wannemacher regularly made payments of about $100, month after month, to pay off the Chase balance. When the collection department called, he paid more. But he was running in place. Six years after the wedding, Wannemacher had already paid Chase $6,300 on that $3,200 bill. And his February 2007 bill said he owed Chase $4,400 more.

After turning to a credit counselor, Wannemacher made an offer that Chase collectors accepted: He'd pay $130 each month for the next 47 months to get out from under that debt. If he completed that payment plan, his $3,200 wedding would ultimately have cost Wannemacher a total of $12,400.

In the credit-card industry, consumers who pay their bills in full on time every month are called "deadbeats." Wannemacher couldn't do that. He was a live one. He was a consumer who earned just enough to make regular payments, but not enough to get ahead, and he had a healthy dose of personal pride that kept him from taking the bankruptcy option. He was, card issuers say, a "revolver"— money comes in, money goes out, but the consumer keeps going around in circles, not getting anywhere.

How does a $3,000 bill become a $12,000 bill? Even usurious interest rates and revolving aren't enough to do that. To really screw consumers like Wannemacher, credit-card firms have devised a host of other methods for soaking them dry and keeping them in debt: penalty fees. The original credit limit on Wannemacher's card was $3,000. As a business courtesy, Chase allowed Wannemacher to exceed that credit limit when paying for his wedding—and charged for the courtesy. Card companies call this courtesy an over-limit fee. It's one of many sneaky fees card firms have invented to squeeze consumers.

Because Wannemacher was never able to get ahead of his debt, his balance was consistently over his credit limit—47 times, to be precise. Each time, he was charged $30, so by February 2007, he'd been socked with $1,500 in over-limit fees. And of course, that fee was added to the balance, which also incurred interest charges, making the real over-limit fee quite a bit more than $30. Naturally, Wannemacher fell behind on monthly payments, and was also charged a series of late-payment fees, too, totaling $1,100. These also incurred interest charges.

But Wannemacher was lucky.

In late 2006, he heard that Congress was investigating abusive credit-card practices and wrote to Senator Carl Levin, a Democrat from Michigan. Smitten by the story, Levin's staff invited Wannemacher to be the star witness in an explosive Senate hearing on the industry that took place in early 2007. Days before the scheduled hearing, Chase called Wannemacher and forgave his outstanding debt. A Chase executive even apologized to him at the hearing.

"In this case, we simply blew it," Chase CEO Richard Srednicki said at the hearing.

Unfortunately, there can be only so many star witnesses at Senate hearings. The rest of us have to face the wrath of credit-card firms with little or no help from Congress, federal agencies, the court system, or any general appeals to fairness. Your apology won't be coming anytime soon. I'm sure most of you wouldn't even hold out for an apology; you'd be happy just getting credit-card statements you can understand. Don't expect that anytime soon, either.

So I'm here to translate for you.

A TWENTY-SEVENTH-GRADE READING LEVEL?

If there were a hall of fame for sneaky fees, Visa, MasterCard, and banks that issue credit cards would all be first-year, unanimous selections.

It seems a simple proposition, perhaps even a good deal. You pull out your plastic, and a bank gives you a thirty-day interest-free loan. As long as you pay the money back each month, you are safely ahead of the game. Fall behind, and there's an extra charge. That even sounds fair. The problem is, we're hardly talking about simple interest here. No average consumer can possibly predict what that extra charge will be. And the terms of that penalty charge are changing all the time. Whatever the penalty is, as Wesley Wannemacher found out, the punishment rarely fits the crime. It does, however, swell profits.

That's why the industry shuns deadbeats (card companies make little money off of them) and covets revolvers.

Don't fret over card companies that serve a lot of deadbeats. They still make good money on the other side of the deal. Merchants pay banks a hefty fee for every transaction: In a typical contract, merchants pay 20 cents plus 2.65 percent of each transaction. Card companies are skimming about 2.5 percent of every sale in America, an astonishing take. That's why they can easily afford to mail eight billion preapproved credit-card applications to American homes every year. In case you're counting, that's 73 preapproved offers for every household in America!

But the real growth area for credit cards is in squeezing revolvers like Wannemacher for every last dime. In a perfect world for credit-card companies, every consumer would be paying just enough to stay out of bankruptcy. Every consumer would be a struggling revolver.

It only takes one late payment, as little as one day or even one hour late, to become a revolver. As a revolver, you've been pulled into what should be considered an alternate universe—suddenly everything is more expensive and rules of fairness don't seem to apply. Fees can come from anywhere, even fees that didn't exist when you signed up for the card.

Card companies often reserve the right to add fees and increase interest rates at any time for any reason. That's why you don't want to be lured into this alternate universe, a dragon's lair where the odds are against you in every battle. And yet, about half of American consumers don't pay their credit-card bills in full every month. Half of America is fighting a losing battle in that dragon's lair.

Of course, consumers do have options. They can pay with cash. If they chose to use credit, they have the responsibility to read their card-member agreements and understand what they're signing up for.

But while that's nice in theory, it's based on one very flawed assumption—that all consumers are capable of reading the contracts they are handed. They're not.

In 2006, the nonpartisan investigative arm of Congress, the Government Accountability Office, commissioned a usability study of credit-card member agreements. By analyzing the vocabulary used and the presentation methods, a consultant found that card agreements generally could be understood only by consumers who had completed a high school degree, even though federal agencies recommend such agreements be written to an eighth-grade reading level.

But that was only the beginning. The really important information, such as descriptions of annual percentage rates, balances, and fees, were found to require a fifteenth-grade education—just about enough schooling for a college degree. At one issuer, even that wasn't enough. Perhaps in an effort to target only the smartest consumers, this bank outdid the others. According to the government report, the description of interest rates for its card "were written at a twenty-seventh-grade level." It's hard to imagine what that would be—but think multiple PhDs.

The government's usability expert went on to perform the free service of rewriting some of the twisted language. After all, remember, this is a simple business—borrow money, pay it back in time, no charge. Pay it back late, pay extra. There's just the simple matter of explaining how much. Congress wanted to see what a straightforward credit-card bill might look like. So here's one text explaining interest charges in credit-card babble, and another translated into English by the usability expert:

> If at any time during any rolling consecutive twelve billing cycle period we do not receive two Minimum Payments by your payment due date or you exceed your credit limit twice, we may elect to automatically increase any and all of your standard APRs to the Penalty APRs. Your Penalty APRs on all existing and future unpaid balances will automatically revert to the standard APRs disclosed above if you make six consecutive Minimum Payments when due and you do not exceed your credit limit within the same time period.

Here's that same passage, once again, in English, thanks to the translator:

> If you pay late or go over your credit limit twice in a year, the interest rate you pay on most things goes up to the default rate, currently 30.49%. It will go back down when you pay on time and do not go over your credit limit for six months.

Of course, as we've already seen, confused consumers are profitable consumers. The more complex the writing, the more confused the consumers. Lawyers who write these poorly worded explainers are very valuable to credit-card firms. No doubt, they are much better compensated than bank-usability experts.

Contracts generally aren't enforceable if one of the parties can't reasonably be expected to understand the pact that's been signed. Nor can one of the parties unilaterally change the terms of a contract. Yet both are common practices by credit-card issuers. That's where most credit-card fees come from. Since 1996, card-issuing banks have set about inventing dozens of justifications for grabbing $10, $20, $30 a pop from consumers. Many were added after consumers had already signed cardholder agreements. Some to this day have never really been explained, and others have been explained due only to the enterprising work of consumer advocates.

The real trouble with credit cards began on December 18, 1978, a fateful day for consumers. While virtually none of us were paying attention, the United States Supreme Court ruled that card-issuing banks were subject to lending laws only in their home state—regardless of where their customers were. It essentially made card-issuers exempt from state usury laws. If you're wondering why banks that issue credit cards can charge such incredibly high interest rates, there's your answer. With Congress playing see-no-evil on the credit-card interest-rate issue, rate regulation had already been ceded to the states. Now it was left to a *single* state of the bank's choosing. To charge usurious rates, banks merely have to shop around and find a very friendly state government to be complicit in their game. That's why so many banks are located in the thriving business centers of South Dakota and Delaware, where state laws permit card issuers to do whatever they like. No matter where you live, your state legislature can't help you now. It has no right to pass a law limiting interest-rate charges on credit cards issued by nationally chartered banks.

The trouble with credit-card fees is much more recent. It came courtesy of another Supreme Court ruling, back on June 3, 1996. That decision declared credit-card penalty fees akin to interest-rate charges, thereby protecting fees from state regulation, too. Now, card companies were free to charge whatever fees they wished. The gold rush was on. The fate of Wesley Wannemacher and millions like him was sealed.

In 2006, a Government Accountability study showed that one in every three cardholders were issued a penalty fee in 2005, and the fee averaged about $34. When one-third of all customers pay a penalty, it's no longer a penalty—it's an arbitrary price, a trap designed to catch the maximum amount of people.

And why not? Fees are the fastest-growing profit center for credit-card firms. In 1995, the average late fee was $12.83. Ten years later, it was $33.64. Even adjusted for inflation, that's a 160 percent increase. Add up all those fees, and R. K. Hammer Investment Bankers, a California credit-card consulting firm, says banks collected $17 billion in penalty fees during 2006, a whopping 15 percent increase from 2004.

Don't be a part of that statistic. Here's how.

THE "FALL FROM GRACE" AND OTHER INTEREST-RATE GAMES

You probably know you have about a month to pay off your credit-card bills. That's the bargain you make—card issuers offer a free monthlong loan, and those who pay each month stay in their good graces.

What many consumers don't understand is this: You don't always get that monthlong loan. In fact, about half of Americans don't. Anyone who doesn't pay their bill in full each month becomes a revolver, and revolvers don't get these free loans. No grace for you. The moment you don't pay your bill, you have fallen right into the trap laid by the first preapproved credit-card application you received. From that moment on, every charge you make incurs interest from the moment you make it until you pay your balance in full.

Here's a subtle charge you might miss. If you don't pay your balance in full, the interest charged is often retroactive for the entire past month. If you have a $5,020 balance and pay $5,000, your balance is only $20, but your finance charge will be almost double that amount. Why? Credit-card math means you don't pay interest on just $20—you pay interest on the entire $5,200 balance. Your entire grace period is revoked. On the next month's bill, you'll owe $35 in interest on that $20 balance, assuming an interest rate of 17.99 percent. The extra money you owe is called "trailing interest" or residual interest, and the practice is called "double-cycle" billing. The fall from grace is swift and the penalties are unforgiving. Congress found that one-third of credit-card firms used double-cycle billing to compute interest charges.

Remember, this is a game and you don't make up the rules. So ignore the rest of the unintelligible card-member statement you receive. Here's all you need to know:

Pay your balance in full every month by the due date, or else the card company can have its way with you.

That's the only way to play. Now remember, the credit-card company doesn't actually want you to pay in full each month. So what's their move in this chess game? Play with the English language, of course. So let's translate the part of that sentence that comes from the banks: "Pay your balance in full every month by the due date." We'll parse it bank-style, starting with "Pay your balance." Simple enough, yes?

No. Banks have a number of ways to encourage you to fail to do this. Here's a fun game. Call up your credit-card company and ask what you owe. The answer may surprise you. I recently called my card company after I had received a new card, but not a new bill, to ask how much I owed. I was told, "No payment is due." Isn't that grand! No one mentioned that if I took the operator's advice and believed no payment was due, I'd have to pay $26 in interest charges.

In fact, my account had *already* been charged about $24 in interest. The operator never got around to mentioning that. I had to hang up and call back to get that information.

Even then, it took quite a while before I stumbled on the true magic question, which is, how much do I have to pay to pay my balance in full and avoid any possible additional interest charges? Even then, the advice the operator gave would have cost me an extra $20 or so, because she urged me to pay in full at the due date listed on my second month's bill, which would have given the card company another 30 days to ding me.

When paying your bill, make sure you don't confuse "Minimum Payment" or "Payment Due" with "Balance Payment." Always ask the right question when calling your credit-card company, always use the phrase "in full," and don't trust the first answer you get.

Now, on to the next part of the sentence: "Due Date."

Remember the deal we discussed? That free one-month loan? Well, card-issuer largesse has started to shrink in recent years. Those thirty-day loans, the grace periods, have quietly become twenty-eight-day loans, twenty-five-day loans, even twenty-two-day loans. The best way to turn a steady deadbeat consumer into a re-volver is to creep up the payment date a smidge. If your payment was always due on the tenth of the month, but suddenly it's due on the fifth of the month, you're likely to pay late. Gotcha.

Banks don't play just with the due date; they also play with the clock. Many firms now require that payments be received by a cer-tain time on the due date—often 1 P.M.—and consider anything ar-riving later than that time as late. The policy is designed to "trick you into a fee, even if you have good payment behavior," says Consumers Union senior attorney Gail Hillebrand. Because you have no control over when the U.S. Postal Service delivers the mail, you have no control over what time your payment arrives. Gotcha.

A word of caution here for those who use online billing to make electronic payments. While the payment appears to disappear from your account instantly and electronically, many banks still issue these payments slowly and on paper. Check with your bank; online payments can take five days or more to arrive at your credit-card company. Proof that your account was deducted by 12:59 P.M. on the payment-due date means nothing to the card company, and won't save you interest charges or late fees. Gotcha! In many cases, you'll need to make online bill payments a full week before the due date to be safe.

Once you fall into the late trap, no matter how you land there, you become a revolver, and a lot of things work against you. When you get the following month's bill, it will include penalty interest charges, late fees, and the payoff amount. But remember that fall from grace? It still applies. Now, every new purchase you make incurs immediate interest—right up until the moment when your account is paid in full. That means your account may not be current until two billing cycles have passed.

Note: Once you have a fall from grace, for any reason, you should stop using that credit card immediately and use another one that's current. If that's simply not an option, you should pay the balance as soon as possible, and not wait for the due date on your statement. Otherwise, the following statement could still show interest charges, even though you believe you've paid the balance in full on time.

PAY TO PAY

We all stumble, of course, and run behind on bills or run out of stamps or just plain forget. And we pay the credit-card bill late. When that happens, smart consumers pay off their bills as soon as they discover the error. One would think the fastest and best way to do that is to call the company and arrange payment. Not so. To remind you how small and insignificant you are to Big Bank Credit Card Issuer Inc., card collection departments charge steep fees—from $5 to $15—just for paying your bill by phone. Senator Carl Levin calls this, "Pay to Pay."

I call it a final insult.

Whatever you call it, paying by telephone is generally a bad idea. Mail a check instead.

PENALTY INTEREST RATES AND UNIVERSAL DEFAULT

Of course, the real money comes from playing games with the interest rate itself. Banks sign you up with promises of low interest rates—teaser rates of 7 or 8 percent, and sometimes, no interest at all. They hope you screw up so they can bump you up to a 30 percent "penalty" interest rate. In more English-language chicanery, even "fixed rate" cards can jump from 8 percent to 30 percent.

While the large print promises your rates will never go up, the small print tells you the fixed-rate promise doesn't apply to "penalty interest rates." See how they play with language? What could "fixed rate" possibly mean?

But even if you don't screw up, even if you pay your balance in full every month, even if you never miss even one minimum monthly payment, the bank will go looking for a screwup. It will hire a financial hit man—the nation's credit bureaus—to spy on you and look for any transgression.

Called "universal default," this is Gotcha Capitalism's winner of the Least-Fair Fee Award. Card issuers ping your credit report often, sometimes every month, looking for mistakes. They're looking for evidence that you paid some other bill late—auto loan, another credit card, you name it. Card users who slip up anywhere in their financial lives are at risk of slipping up everywhere, the argument goes—at risk of universal default. And so, they deserve a penalty interest rate.

Put simply: If your car payment is late, your credit-card interest rate may jump from 8 percent to 30 percent. I call that kicking someone when they are down. Or perhaps piling on. Or maybe just looking for trouble. But fair? Hardly. And in fact, after congressional scrutiny, some card issuers have abandoned the practice.

WHAT RATE APPLIES?

If you think that's confusing, consider this: Some consumers pay penalty interest, normal interest, and zero interest *at the same time on the same card!*

The high-stakes game of serial balance transfers from one card to another, which can lead to temporary interest-rate relief, can create these kinds of sticky situations. Some card companies offer to take on a big credit-card balance from another card for low or no interest, but normal rates apply to new purchases. And higher rates apply for cash advances, and of course, kick in if you are late on any of this. Some cards offer tiered percentage rates, meaning the interest rises as your balance rises.

Now, here's the fun part. When you send in a payment that is something less than the entire balance, the card issuer can decide where to apply that balance—to the part of your bill accruing 19 percent interest, or the part accruing 8 percent, or the part that's interest-free. Guess how that decision is made! Banks pay off the cheapest part of the loan first, keeping the high balance as high as possible for as long as possible.

Quick *Gotcha* quiz: What's the interest rate on the cards in your wallet right now? If you're not sure, the card companies have you right where they want you.

WHAT'S YOUR CREDIT LIMIT? NOT WHAT YOU THINK

You probably believe your credit card comes with a built-in credit limit. After all, that's what it says right on the piece of paper you get with your bill every month. But there really is no such thing as a credit limit anymore. Where once there was a limit, there is now only a "fee trigger." It is not a ceiling, just a squeeze play.

A consumer with a credit card that has a stated limit of $500 and a balance of $451 might think an attempted $50 purchase would be rejected. After all, such a buy would pierce the credit limit ceiling.

Not anymore. Years ago, card companies realized they don't make any money by rejecting transactions. So as a "courtesy," they now gladly allow consumers to zoom right through the limit, and tack on a fee of $30 or so—the over-limit fee. As we saw with Wannemacher's forty-seven over-limit fees, breaking the credit limit ceiling has become an excellent source of revenue for card issuers. In 1995, the average over-limit fee was $13. Today it's nearly triple that.

And remember, as Wannemacher's case demonstrated, an over-limit fee is not a one-shot ding. Consumers are not charged for buying beyond the limit, but rather for maintaining a balance above the limit during any given month. A consumer who runs into a debt trap will find that in addition to the $550 balance they owe, and the interest charges they are paying, a $35 over-limit fee will appear *every month* until the balance is brought down below the limit. Often, consumers who pay only the minimum balance will not tuck themselves back under their limit, because the fee and the interest charges are higher than the minimum payment. So the fee is self-perpetuating.

Believe it or not, there is even a bigger trap here; credit-card firms sometimes lower credit limits for consumers they perceive as risky. Even a consumer who is paying down their debt may find they are chasing a moving target, and continue to incur over-limit fees even as they pay their balance down below their original limit. In fact, such lowering of a credit limit can trigger a fee on its own. Consumer attorney Michael Donavan says he has counseled clients who ended up facing over-limit fees for one reason, and one reason only—their credit limit was lowered below their outstanding balance.

And then there's this double-whammy—consumers who are near but not over their credit limit can be pushed over by a late fee, which in turn triggers an over-limit fee. Total cost of this double whammy: $70, not including interest.

How is all this possible? Over-limit fees should be, by definition, impossible. After all, how can a consumer buy beyond the stated credit limit of a card?

The answer: There are actually two limits to every credit card—a nominal limit and an effective limit. The nominal limit is the one disclosed to consumers in the mail. The effective limit is a dynamic amount generated by a computer that determines a favorable risk/reward ratio for the credit-card company. It's higher than your nominal limit, perhaps by 10 percent or more. It can change month to month.

It's also a secret. You're not allowed to know what it is. Gotcha.

Many consumers take their nominal limit literally, of course. They assume they cannot spend more than their credit-card limit would allow; they are often pleased that a purchase is approved, then are surprised to see the fee. In fact, no rational consumer would perform a transaction that would incur such a fee. In the earlier example, a $50 sweater purchased by a consumer who is $50 from their $500 credit limit suddenly becomes an $85 sweater. Sending even $1 to the credit-card company before the purchase would keep that sweater at $50. Or, more practically speaking, an informed consumer could put that $50 sweater back and pick a $45 sweater instead, which would ultimately cost nearly half the price. But without that information, kept in the dark by the credit-card company, the consumer is, as has been said before, a babe in the woods—an easy target.

Meanwhile, the card-issuing bank knows that this one purchase will exceed the limit and trigger the fee. The entire transaction-processing system was built to detect exactly this situation. And yet, no warning is given, no advisory, no opportunity for the consumer to accept or decline the consequences of that suddenly expensive sweater purchase. Perhaps it's fair to offer consumers a "courtesy" increase to their credit limit. Perhaps it's even fair to charge something for it. But it's never fair to do that without warning, which is what every card company does. It's not fair for the price of the sweater to nearly double. And it's never fair to keep the effective credit limit a secret.

Precisely when the over-limit determination is made varies from company to company. Some only charge the fee for consumers who are over their limit when their monthly billing cycle ends and their bill is generated. Others charge the fee the moment the limit is exceeded, and in every month where the limit is eclipsed for even an hour. When the Government Accountability Office studied this issue in 2006, fourteen of the twenty-two most popular credit cards took the lowest road, imposing the fee even for a momentary piercing of the credit limit.

SAME AS CASH? NOT EXACTLY

Consumers encounter voluminous opportunities to get bank credit cards—eight billion chances, thanks to U.S. mail—but the offers don't stop there. You can't buy anything from a major retail chain without being pushed to sign up for store-brand cards. That one-time, 10 percent discount might sound like a good deal, but you know the retailer has done the math, don't you? A 34.99 percent interest rate is likely in your future.

Note: Store cards always have the worst terms.

As if there weren't already enough credit crack pushers in the world.

All the rules and Gotchas in this chapter apply to these store cards, but they offer a few of their own twists. The most sinister is the same-as-cash shell game.

All electronics-store shoppers are familiar with tempting "same-as-cash" deals. These are essentially free loans with no interest for a predetermined amount of time, as long as eighteen months. Who can pass up a free loan? All that's required is for you to get a store-brand credit card. Filling out the application only takes a moment, you're told. Even if you have the money for that new plasma TV, why wouldn't you take the free cash? Let me tell you.

For starters, you'd better not miss the payoff date when it arrives. Talk about a fall from grace. Interest charges really do accrue while you are enjoying that allegedly interest-free period. They are simply set aside—the interest is "deferred" for those who pay the entire bill before the due date. But if you are even a day late when the full payment is ultimately due, you will pay a hefty fee—you'll pay all that back interest. On a $1,500 purchase with an eighteen-month same-as-cash deal, that can easily add up to $300 or more, making a good deal into a very bad deal very quickly.

Now, I know you think you are smarter than that. But so did Steve Monteith, a consumer who thought he had avoided these hefty interest charges by paying in full on time. An engineer at North Carolina State University, Monteith wrote in to the *Red Tape Chronicles* after he paid off a same-as-cash loan, but ended up facing one more bill with a shocking bottom line: It added about 30 percent to the price of his big-screen TV. Monteith had purchased a $1,500 LCD TV at a Best Buy electronics store in 2005, and he missed a bit of fine print when he signed up for his credit-card-based, same-as-cash loan.

When the monthly bills started coming, complete with the expected zero balance due, Monteith ignored another line on the bill. It read "debt cancellation—$5.34." He ignored it, assuming it was some optional service. Given that he was assured he didn't have to pay anything for eighteen months, he just discarded the bills. That seems a reasonable course of action.

But it cost him nearly $500.

Monteith had been enrolled in a kind of insurance policy called a "debt forgiveness policy." It ensures that credit-card debt will be paid if the buyer cannot pay under certain grave circumstances. For example, buyers who die before that $1,500 TV is paid off have the debt forgiven, at a price of $5 to $10 a month.

This is a terrible deal for consumers, because it's really an insurance policy for the retailer, not you (you'll be dead, what do you care?). And yet, many consumers sign up for the policy, particularly electronics consumers. Why? Because the enrollment can require only one signature, placed in a box on the same form that's required for buying the TV. Consumers who are all jacked up about getting that new wall-size screen in the living room just in time for the Super Bowl are unlikely to notice the small print.

An electronics retailer worker who wrote to the *Red Tape Chronicles* said he was trained to pass the form by excited consumers as quickly as possible, in the hopes that they'd sign before realizing what they were signing.

That's how Steve Monteith's trouble began. But it didn't end there.

After eighteen months, he'd accrued $168 in debt forgiveness bills. He did pay off the entire LCD TV bill in plenty of time to avoid interest charges. But he ignored the $168 in debt forgiveness charges. You can guess what happened the following month.

He got a bill for $168 in insurance and $304 in back interest on the TV. By not paying the debt forgiveness bill, he had triggered the interest rate on the entire eighteen-month, same-as-cash loan. His free $1,500 loan now cost him nearly $500.

When I called to find out about what happened, Best Buy sent me to HSBC Retail Services, which handled Best Buy's credit-card programs. An HSBC spokeswoman told me the company was aware of complaints and working on new training strategies for checkout clerks. It did forgive Monteith's debt after my call.

But as we learned at the beginning of the chapter, not everyone can become a star witness in a congressional hearing or a star character in a national network news story. So the simple lesson for you: Be very skeptical of same-as-cash offers, and handle payments to those companies as potentially radioactive. After all, lenders don't make money for giving away money.

Credit Cards
GOTCHA-STOPPING STRATEGIES

1. Always pay your bill in full a few days early.
2. Always look at the bill's due date to make sure it hasn't changed.
3. Use online bill pay and automatically send $50 or $100 early every month to your card firm so you'll never face a late fee. Late fees are usually more expensive than a few days' interest, so by automatically paying a minimum payment each month, you will always avoid them. But pay it early—online payments can take a week before landing at your credit-card company.
4. If you do "fall from grace," stop using that card immediately and switch to another card with no balance. That way, you won't continue to rack up interest charges.
5. Also, if you fall from grace, don't wait for next month's bill to come. Pay your balance in full as soon as you can, to avoid additional interest charges.
6. Pay off same-as-cash cards very, very early to avoid huge fees.
7. Always have one card with no balance on it, and make sure you keep it current. That way, if you run into a temporary financial glitch, and can't pay your bills one month, you will still have "grace" you can use.
8. Don't be shy about negotiating over fees with your bank. Credit-card firms were among the most likely to issue refunds to complaining consumers in our sneaky-fee survey. Also, tell the bank you really will switch companies if they won't work with you. It's a competitive industry, and taking your business elsewhere is the one piece of leverage you have.
9. Be ready to complain to regulators, including:

- **The Federal Reserve**
  (Board of Governors of the Federal Reserve System/Division of Consumer and Community Affairs/20th and C Streets, NW, Stop 801/Washington, DC 20551)
- **The Office of the Comptroller of the Currency**
  (customer.assistance@occ.treas.gov)
- **Your state attorney general**
  (Google your state attorney general's consumer affairs office.)

10. Also complain to consumer groups like Consumers Union or the Center for Responsible Lending.

Banks

It began as perhaps the most mocked new fee of all time. Charge $3 just for a conversation? The idea conjured up images of *Peanuts'* Lucy and her "5 cents please" therapy booth. Politicians threatened legislation; comedians were relentless. And yet, on April 25, 1995, First National Bank of Chicago held its nose, covered its ears, and began charging for conversations with its tellers.

Jay Leno's punch line at the time: "For $3 you can talk to a human teller, and for $4, they'll talk dirty to you."

Analysts predicted a massive customer exodus and a huge revenue hit. In one survey, 54 percent of consumers said they'd switch banks if forced to pay a $3 teller fee. Surprise! Just the opposite happened. Within a month, ATM usage doubled. Within a year, a few customers had left, but as for the rest, 80 percent of their transactions were performed electronically. Profits jumped 28 percent.

Retail banking changed forever. First Chicago provided an important principle that has guided banks ever since: Driving customers away is good business.

Banking is an incredible industry. Banks manufacture nothing, other than pretentious buildings. They simply take your money, and keep some of it for themselves. Profits too low? Simply push a few levers, or change a formula on a spreadsheet, and keep more of the money. Mortgage interest rates going down? Lower the passbook-savings rate. Loan profits down? Raise the fee structure. Yes, profitable banks are good for the country because the availability of credit for consumers is generally a good thing, but hidden costs are not. They are the enemy of transparency, and hidden banking costs eat away at the national savings rate. Bank fees—not including credit-card fees—take a $32 billion bite out of Americans' savings, according to research firm SNL Financial. The FDIC says fee income has soared 44 percent in the past decade. To put it bluntly, about half of bank income now comes from fees, according to R. K. Hammer. Wondering why a "free" checking account can cost you $100 or more a year? And why some banks need to advertise "truly" free checking? Sneaky fees are the reason.

Fees are so critical to bank bottom lines now that at some banks, fee profits exceed profits from credit cards, mortgages, and all other lending combined. Take TCF Financial Corporation in Wayzata, Minnesota. According to *BusinessWeek,* fees brought in 76 percent of profits in 2004 at TCF, up from 52 percent in 2000. And banks sure don't make it easy to decipher where the next fee will come from. At Wells Fargo & Co., the fee schedule in 2005 was fifty-five pages long.

Even the most enterprising consumer faces a nearly impossible task when shopping around for the best fee-free account. In 2005, the Consumer Federation of America surveyed thirty-three large banks in an attempt to produce a fee-comparison chart. It had to abandon the effort, because most banks don't disclose fees on the Internet until *after* consumers have signed up for an account.

WHAT THE #%$& IS THIS FEE FOR? THE QUEST FOR MORE INFO

Even after you open an account, tracking down the source of hidden fees can be a mammoth challenge. Andy Gallagher of Washington D.C., an MSNBC.com co-worker, complained to me in the hallway one day about a $3 fee he found while dutifully checking an online bank statement at Wachovia Bank's website. Next to the line that read "Service fee—$3" was the helpful hyperlink "more info." So Gallagher, a 33-year-old market researcher, clicked on it, expecting—what else—more information. Here's what he saw:

"Service Fee. Quantity: 1. Total $3."

I called the company to ask the simple, obvious question, "What good is a link that promises 'more info' when clicking on it reveals absolutely no more information? The $3 charge, it turned out, was a monthly maintenance fee—but there was no way to learn that from the online banking page. Wachovia eventually told me it was reconsidering its website design.

If all these fees seem mysterious and manipulative, that's no accident. One anonymous tipster told me a bank he works at has a division that's devoted to creating sneakier and sneakier fees. He writes:

> [They work] down the hall in a room with a sign on it saying "Danger—Think Tank." These folks stay up all night devising ways to create and sock fees at customers . . . If you think the military is bad on the "don't ask–don't tell" policy, banks are 100 times worse. [The company] actually has "data miners" in that dark room . . . searching for customer usage patterns and pricing fees according to statistical analysis or a probable "hit rate." They basically study "human nature" and create and price fees according to how profitable they can be!

Another bank employee offered a similar tale from the dark side.

> They are quite aware of the money that they are making out of NSF (non-sufficient funds or bounced check) fees, unexplained service fees and ATM fees. Unexplained fees are deliberate because they know that a high percentage of customers won't give it a second glance. They know that a small percentage will complain. However, the majority won't and thus that's why they do it. Managers have meetings on how much money will be made in NSF fees. It's in the billions!!! They also have automated phone systems that make it impossible to talk to a live person because again they know that a large percent will give up trying to ask questions. Even their concierge is set up outside on the platform so that way customers will feel embarrassed to ask for NSF refunds. This concierge/manager desk was not created to help customers but rather to make them shy away from requesting refunds (management explained that to us). It works ef-

fectively. Trust me, I have seen the numbers. Our focus is to get you to start using the debit cards so you can charge up those NSF fees, because the purchases that you make will not show in your account until many days later.

PISSING OFF CUSTOMERS IS GOOD

This is why people hate banks. They are a necessary evil, but generally, consumers have a very negative impression of those big buildings where their money is hidden away, and they have a constant, nagging sense that something unfair is going on in there. You might think banks would work hard to improve their image. Doesn't image matter? After all, this was the industry that once filled American kitchens with free toasters. How did the free toaster turn into $3 teller-talk fees? How can a business that is so willing to piss off its customers be so profitable?

To understand this world, you must shed your notions of traditional business practices. You must understand that customer satisfaction is not the goal. Rather, satisfying the *right* customers is the goal, but pissing off the *wrong* customers is equally important.

In a computerized world where every single customer is graded on profit potential, banks have systematically set out to chase away their worst customers. It all began with First Chicago's teller fee in 1995. Of course, depositors with large accounts were exempt from such fees. The result of the teller fee was straightforward: Only irritating customers with tiny bank accounts who asked a lot of questions went elsewhere. Before the teller fee, only 33 percent of First Chicago's customers produced an "adequate return." In the year following the teller fee, that number jumped to 44 percent. Analysts were shocked that an "anti-loyalty" strategy could work so well. Chasing away undesirable customers with outrageous fees has been an important element of the banking business model ever since.

Of course, if you can't chase them, you can gouge them. The First Chicago model has been enhanced during the intervening decade (First Chicago eventually became Bank One, which dropped the teller fee in 2002, but some other banks still charge for teller talk).

You'll notice all the fees discussed in this chapter cluster around undesirable behavior such as low-balance accounts or asking that your canceled checks be mailed to you. And allowing your balance to hover near zero? Well, that's a bank bonanza. Rich customers would never find themselves in such unsavory situations.

Even if you are not the type to ever bounce a check, don't consider yourself safely outside your bank's crosshairs. Banks are constantly fine-tuning the formula that tests the boundary of how much they can piss off customers, which ones they want to retain, and at what "adequate return" level. They go to great lengths to do this, even instructing their ATMs to lie to you! More on that in a moment.

OVERDRAFT PROTECTION

Any discussion of bank fees has to begin with old-fashioned bounced checks. Every depositor knows you're not supposed to write a check for more money than you have in your checking account. In some harsher quarters, doing so is considered the moral equivalent of stealing. There is often little sympathy for consumers who are charged fees for bouncing checks, no matter what the circumstances. Into this morally charged arena, banks have set loose their most creative fee designers.

Now, banks offer products with friendly-sounding names like "courtesy overdraft" or "bounced check protection." These are hardly acts of banking largesse; in fact, they are short-term loan instruments with an effective annual interest rate as high as 1,000 percent or more. Of course, you'll never see that interest rate published anywhere, because overdraft services are not covered by the Truth in Lending Act. As we'll see, banks try hard to offer services not regulated by the Act, because they don't have to provide those pesky annual percentage rates that might scare off customers. This makes these kinds of offerings much less comprehensible and much more profitable. Consider it your bank's way of competing with those seedy paycheck-advance loan shops.

Here's an example. *BusinessWeek* tells the story of NYU student Chris Keeley, who bought seven Christmas gifts during one weekend totaling $230 using his debit card. All seven transactions were approved, even though his account was overdrawn. He was charged a $31 overdraft protection fee for each purchase—totaling $217 in fees! Keeley, like many consumers, thought his transactions would be denied if he didn't have the money. Simply swiping his credit card instead of his debit card would have saved him $217 in fees. Instead, just because he pulled out that cash card, his $230 Christmas shopping trip cost him nearly double that.

Overdraft fee structures can be even more complicated. Some banks pile on a daily $5 fee for every day the account is overdrawn, in addition to the $30-something charge for each purchase. Other overdraft protection plans involve linked credit cards that automatically transfer money—in the form of a pricey cash advance—from a credit card to a debit card. While this is cheaper than courtesy overdraft protection, banks figure out how to make the most of this loan, too. A $4.32 overdraft can result in a $100 cash advance, and the resulting interest charges on $100. When asked, the bank will inform you it can only offer credit-card transfers in $100 increments. This deck is stacked against you in many ways.

Perhaps you still don't have any sympathy for people like Keeley, who could have done a better job of knowing he was perilously close to a zero balance in his account. Without much trouble, he could have checked his balance at a nearby ATM, for example, to make sure he didn't overdraw.

That's assuming that ATMs tell the truth. Sometimes, they don't.

ATMS THAT LIE

Courtesy overdraft protection will allow consumers to withdraw $100, $200, even $300 more than the available balance in their accounts. This means consumers can bounce a check just by withdrawing cash from an ATM. Once upon a time, ATMs would clearly say "insufficient funds" when such a transaction was requested, and deny it. Clever bankers realized they don't make any money by denying withdrawals, however. So now, many ATMs allow the withdrawals to sail through, allow the account to go negative, and allow the bank to collect big fees.

You might think consumers who are close to the edge still have no excuse. They can ask an ATM for a balance before withdrawing money, to make sure they're not in danger of bank "courtesy." Not so fast.

When consumers ask an ATM how much is in their checking accounts, some banks automatically add in the courtesy overdraft cushion into what's described as an "available balance." Then the available balance—not the actual balance—is displayed. This is practically an invitation to overdraw.

Here's how it works. When a consumer with an $80 balance and $200 courtesy overdraft protection asks for a balance, the ATM indicates "$280 available balance."

Regulators have warned banks about this not-so-subtle form of encouraging overdrafts, but have so far stopped short of telling them to stop.

Here's one example, provided by a *Red Tape Chronicles* reader:

> My bank . . . instituted a $200 overdraft protection in basic checking accounts. This protection showed up on the balance on both their drive-through ATMs and any other ATM you checked your balance through. Unfortunately, they did not inform any of their customers that the only way to check the real balance before they received their next statement in the mail was directly calling a bank employee during business hours. They also failed to alert any of their customers of this overdraft protection in the first place. I ended up generating about $200 in overdraft fees in that first month, mostly from buying a $4 sandwich or smoothie in between classes. Luckily I was able to smooth it all out and delete the fees. But my final conclusion is this . . . the Banks don't care. It's not their money.

The industry response?

"We've heard from customers that they'd prefer to be assessed a fee [rather] than face the embarrassment of having a purchase declined," Bank of America spokeswoman Alexandra Liftman told *BusinessWeek*. Plenty of people would rather pay $31 for a $5 hamburger than face the mortification of being forced to pull out a different piece of plastic, Liftman seems to believe.

Here's the truth: Banks prefer to collect the fees, which total about $17.5 billion every year, according to the Center for Responsible Lending. And while old-fashioned bounced checks are still a frequent, and perhaps less sympathetic, transgression, debit card swipes and ATM withdrawals now account for most "bounced check" fees.

There's a good reason for this: Check writing is a dying art. In 2003, an important line was crossed—there were more electronic payments than paper-check transactions. In fact, check writing has been on the decline since 1995, with more consumers now opting for debit card and other electronic payment forms. Bank fees had to keep up with the times.

"Overdraft" charges are cast by banks as an appropriate penalty for someone who has tried to steal, but that's not what they are. Instead, they are a systematic attack on consumers, designed to take advantage of the most fragile depositors and to replace the disappearing revenue stream of bounced-check fees.

SHIFTING MINIMUM BALANCE

Still, you might be the kind of person who thinks no one should ever allow their balance to dip so close to zero. Then consider this: If you are lucky enough to maintain a high minimum balance, one that's $1,000 or more, then you are probably lucky enough to enjoy a checking account with no service fee. But you may not know that if you dip below that $1,000, even for an afternoon, you will end up paying a $5 to $15 charge for that month anyway.

What if you are so perfect that you never come close to your minimum balance? The bank can make its money from you by changing the rules along the way. Banks sometimes raise the required minimum balance and send only a perfunctory note home to consumers. If you don't notice the minimum balance has jumped from $1,000 to $2,000, you're out $8 per month.

Consumers like Keeley might consider leaving in protest after a bout with six or seven overdraft charges. But that's OK by the banks. Remember, we're talking about unsavory customers, such as college students who aren't bailed out by their parents' credit cards. Keeley and others like him may end up as churn, but banks don't mind that kind of churn. The overdraft game drives away just the right kinds of customers.

WHO ARE THE WRONG CUSTOMERS?

Who are the customers most likely to get caught up in the overdraft game? That shouldn't come as a surprise. Consumers earning below $40,000 annually are 37 percent more likely to overdraw their accounts than those with higher incomes. Blacks and Latinos are twice as likely as whites to overdraw, according to the Consumer Federation of America.

Meanwhile, the bad publicity you might imagine would be generated by such misbehavior hasn't hurt banks' marketing efforts at all. Consumers do not select their banks based on penalty fees. Remember that fifty-five-page fee schedule at Wells Fargo, and the researchers who simply couldn't find fee schedules?

"These are not things that are subject to price competition," says analyst Greg McBride of Bankrate.com, an independent firm that studies bank and credit-card fees. "No bank is going to advertise low bounced-check fees."

BIGGEST CHECKS CLEAR FIRST, CAUSING MORE BOUNCES

Here's something else banks don't advertise. Banks cash your checks and clear your other transactions once a day, from largest to smallest. That might sound like an insignificant detail. Gotcha! Clearing large checks first nets a sizable chunk of change for the bank, because your account will overdraw much more quickly and much more often this way. Here's an example: If you have $500 in your account, and you write checks for $72, $98, $28, and $410 on the same day, you'll bounce the first three checks, and pay about $100 in fees. Were the bank to process them in the order I just typed, you'd bounce only the last and pay about $30 instead. Regardless of when checks arrive during the day, banks process them largest to smallest, and pocket the fees.

Banks defend the practice by saying customers prefer to have the largest check cashed first. No one believes them. But who is going to stick up for the rights of consumers who bounce checks?

CHECK 21, FLOAT, AND CANCELED-CHECK FEES

There's one simple principle when it comes to dealing with money flowing in and out of your account when you are hovering near a zero or minimum balance: Expect the worst. Banks will devise formulas that take advantage of the situation as best they can. That's what they do. Take Check 21. In the early part of this decade, banks appealed to the Federal Reserve for the ability to clear checks electronically—at the time, they were still flying handwritten canceled checks around the country, back to their originating bank, and mailing canceled checks home to account-holders each month. Grounding these endless flights seems a sensible, twenty-first-century upgrade. With Check 21, also called the Check Clearing for the 21st Century Act, passed in October 2003, Congress allowed this. Now, digital images of the checks, made available online and at bank branches, replace actual canceled checks.

Unfortunately, the law was essentially a gift to the banking industry. Congress packed the legislation with several other advantages to banks, balanced with nothing for you. Banks save millions in costs, now that they don't have to move all those paper checks around. More important, they can also clear checks much more quickly. Check 21 meant, for the most part, the end of consumer "float."

What's float? Check writers used to live with the added cushion of knowing that—because of all those checks flying around—it might take a few days for the amount written on a check to actually disappear from their checking account. Of course, people living on the edge used float to make ends meet during tough months. Check 21, which shrank the check-clearing process from days to hours, virtually eliminated float.

Correction: It eliminated float that benefits consumers. The other kind of float—the kind that lets banks hold on to your deposited checks for five days before disbursing funds—lived on after Check 21. Now banks get float, but don't give it.

Electronic check cashing also spelled the end of other consumer advantages. Most banks don't mail home canceled checks anymore— unless you pay. Bank of America now charges $3 a month to folks who want to continue carefully balancing checkbooks with old checks in hand, and file them away, as they were trained to do for years. Suddenly, that most diligent habit of personal financial management—balancing checkbooks while manually inspecting canceled checks—costs $36 a year. Gotcha!

ATM FEES

The poster child for twenty-first-century banking fees is the ATM fee. Getting $20 at the wrong ATM costs you around $4. Banks rake in about $4 billion a year in wrong ATM fees.

ATM fees are much more visible than all the other dirty bank tricks we've mentioned already, so they've received a lot of publicity. There's even been legislation proposed to end the fees. But of all bank fees, ATM fees have this going for them—at least they are disclosed. The warning page on each ATM indicating the fee you'll pay for using the machine is a model of informed disclosure.

Of course, that's not to say consumers really know how much their money costs when they withdraw from a wrong, or "foreign," ATM. In fact, account holders are only shown the amount being levied by the machine they're standing at; their own bank's tack-on charge is buried in some fine print in the monthly statement. For the most part, a wrong ATM withdrawal will come with a warning of a roughly $2 fee. The other $2 fee is still hidden. It's a curious thing that the actual surcharge can't be shown, isn't it?

The ATM network is a remarkable, sophisticated piece of technological wonder. Think about it: In virtually an instant, a machine at a gas station in the middle of Death Valley can check your balance and verify your PIN code stored at your home bank thousands of miles away. The PIN trick is even more impressive when you consider the crucial transmission with your PIN code has to be scrambled with complex cryptographics and kept secret all along the way, through numerous switches and computers.

It's amazing that this incredible system, perhaps the world's most sophisticated network, cowers at the idea of adding up the $2 local charge with your home bank's $1.75 charge. The ATM in Death Valley will know if you just spent $3.21 on gum at a gas station nearby, and that purchase can be reflected in your balance immediately. But Bank of America's $1.75 charge, a figure that remains constant for months? The Death Valley ATM can't compute that.

Why? Because some consumers would sometimes stop in their tracks if they knew exactly what they were paying for their own money. The $2 now plus $2 later disclosure is much more palatable.

Most palatable of all? Banks and credit unions that allow "truly" free ATM withdrawals anywhere. These institutions don't charge foreign ATM fees and they refund other banks' fees. It effectively makes every ATM a "local" ATM. This is no small victory—two foreign ATM withdrawals each week will cost the average consumer $300 every year, according to Bankrate.com. Many credit unions offer truly free ATM withdrawals; so does USAA Federal Savings Bank. It should be no surprise that USAA was cited by *BusinessWeek* in March 2007 as America's customer-service champ.

ATM DENIAL FEE

Still, using an ATM is a tremendous convenience, and it's fair for the bank to collect a nominal amount for letting you get access to your money at any time from anywhere. And most consumers understand by now that taking money from an ATM can cost money. But did you know that it can cost you money even when you *don't* get money from an ATM?

I found this out the hard way when I was sent to Houston with twenty-four hours' notice to cover Hurricane Rita, which struck Texas only days after Hurricane Katrina in 2005. Reporters who were in the Katrina zone had told me getting cash there was nearly impossible, so on my way to the airline gate, I stopped at the nearest ATM—no time to hunt around for a Bank of America machine. I tried to grab $400, which I believed was my daily limit. Too much, the machine warned me, spitting back my card. I then asked for $300, grabbed the cash, and was on my way. I thought nothing of it.

A month later, my bank statement included this line: "ATM Denial: $1.50." That's in addition to the $4 I was charged for the successful $300 withdrawal.

When I called to inquire, Bank of America censured me for not reading its mailings more closely. The bank had months earlier begun charging consumers anytime they used a foreign ATM and tried to exceed their daily ATM cash-withdrawal limit. Processing out-of-network transactions was expensive, I was told (It could cost the bank $5 to $7, the customer-service agent told me. Later, I found the real cost was more like 25 cents). So actually, I was getting off easy. My $1.50 denial charge was reversed, but not before I endured a minilecture and a warning not to let it happen again.

WANT IT BOTH WAYS

Banks often justify ATM fees by saying the machines are costly to operate. In fact, despite all these $4 fees, they lose money on most machines. ATMs cost $1,000 or so a month to run, when electricity, maintenance, and secure cash restocking charges are added up. Since depositor withdrawals are fee-free, each ATM must attract hundreds of noncustomers each month just to break even. Most analysts concede this point to banks. And in fact, the number of ATMs in the country has actually flattened out; independent entrepreneurs have abandoned the ATM business because it's rarely profitable.

But ATMs were not designed to be little bank cash registers or profit centers. They were designed to get you out of the bank. Remember the talk-to-teller-fee, where we began this chapter? Each time you use a machine and not a teller, the bank saves big—nearly $5, the average cost for banks to hire someone to smile and take your deposit. Banks want it both ways—they want the cost savings *and* the sneaky fees.

MORE SOLUTIONS

There are ways to beat the bounced-check game, the ATM fee game, and all these other fees banks charge. But they require a bit of personal discipline.

First off, talk to your bank (even if it costs $3!) and opt out of courtesy overdraft protection. If your account balance is low, you want your transaction to be denied. It's that simple.

Online banking is your best ally for tracking account balances and fees. A couple of times each week, you can glance at your account to make sure you have a solid grasp of your real balance—not a bank fabrication. The balance shown online won't necessarily reflect recently mailed checks, of course, but banks are clearing checks quicker and quicker now (thanks to Check 21), so you won't be far off the actual balance.

If you want extra insurance, you can sign up for true overdraft protection, which links your checking account to another account, a credit card, or a line of credit. These products might come with various names, but here's the distinction to watch for—if you are using the bank's money to cover the cash gap, it'll really cost you. Use your own money (through a linked account) instead. It will cost you a few dollars, but far less than courtesy overdraft protection.

Go small. Credit unions often have remarkably better deals than banks. Many refund ATM fees, for example, and have much lower overdraft fees. You can always visit a bank lobby and grab a lollipop or play with the chain-linked ballpoint pens if you miss the warm, fuzzy, Big Bank atmosphere.

Finally, be a good customer. The only way to really win this game is to be—or at least appear to be—the kind of customer your bank wants. Today, that often means leaving $1,000 to $2,500 as a minimum balance. Going along with these rules is usually your best insurance policy against extra fees. For example, when you finally have a bad cash-flow month, dipping below that $1,000 balance might cost you a one-time $10 monthly service fee, but you won't hit cascading overdraft fees. If you can't afford that kind of buffer in your financial life, building up such a buffer should be the first thing you do. And when you look at the account and feel terrible because you are earning a microscopic interest rate, consider that the average American family is paying $300 a year for banking fees. If that $1,000 is actually earning you truly Gotcha-free checking, then that's a nifty return in itself. It's also an important headstart toward the most basic rule of personal finance, having three month's living expenses in easily accessible, liquid form, in case of an emergency like unemployment or a health crisis. A frightening amount of Americans—four in ten, according to an HSBC study in 2005—don't even have one month's living expenses on hand, so a $1,000 kitty would put you toward the top of the personal finance heap.

There is one possible exception to this $1,000 checking account rule: If you need the money to rid yourself of $1,000 high-interest credit-card debt. A $1,000 credit-card balance paying 20 percent interest will cost you close to $17 in interest each month, so the money would be better spent there, even if you end up paying a few $10 checking account monthly service fees to the bank. But be careful with this strategy: Many consumers who are dancing with the credit-card devil end up spending one-time cash infusions like this instead of truly applying them toward debt relief. You may very well be better off keeping the $1,000 liquid as your financial insurance policy.

But before resigning yourself to parking that kind of cash in your checking account just to avoid the fees, check with your institution. It might offer other fee-avoidance provisions; many banks will waive fees for those who sign up for direct deposit through their employer, for example. Or perhaps your bank quietly offers a cheap, limited-feature account, and you are confident enough in your ability to keep an accurate check register that you are willing to take the risks associated with such a bare-bones account—that you'll never need to write more than five checks in a month, for example, or you'll never need to talk to a teller. This high-wire act is only for the most fastidious accounting types—one mistake each year could easily cost you $100 in fees, tilting the risk–reward ratio for most consumers.

Bank Fees
GOTCHA-STOPPPING STRATEGIES

1. Opt out of courtesy overdraft protection.
2. Link your savings or credit card to your checking to prevent pricey overdraft protection from kicking in.
3. Use online banking to keep track of your balance.
4. Consider a credit union, where fees are almost always lower.
5. Find a bank that refunds foreign ATM fees.
6. Maintain a minimum balance to avoid monthly fees.
7. If you do overdraw, replace the money as soon as possible to avoid per-day charges.
8. Assume any deposit will take several days to clear—even your paycheck. Build in this buffer before you spend the money to give yourself the float banks no longer give you. Meanwhile, know that banks cash your checks almost immediately now and debit your account, so you can't count on float anymore to cover checks you write.
9. Be ready to complain to regulators, including:

   • **The Federal Reserve**
     (Board of Governors of the Federal Reserve System, Division of Consumer and Community Affairs, 20th and C Streets, NW, Stop 801/ Washington, DC 20551)
   • **The Office of the Comptroller of the Currency**
     (customer.assistance@occ.treas.gov)
   • **Your state attorney general**
     (Google your state attorney general consumer affairs office.)

10. Also complain to consumer groups like Consumers Union or the Center for Responsible Lending.

Retirement/401(k)s

If we had to disclose fees, half the people in this room wouldn't have their jobs.

Wall Street money manager

Little things can mean a lot. Two dollars here, three dollars there, it just doesn't seem like such a big deal. But if you are still unconvinced of the cumulative impact of Gotchas, a discussion of retirement accounts should cure you of that notion.

Sneaky fees are flat-out killing your retirement plans. They may very well force you to work an extra four or five years before retiring. They are stealing roughly one out of every three dollars you expect to have in your old age. The younger you start, the worse the sneaky-fee effect is: A twenty-year-old who invests today can find Wall Street has stolen 80 percent of his or her return when age eighty-five rolls around!

And yet, virtually all Americans don't even know they're paying any retirement fees. That's because the fees are so hidden there is virtually no way to know how much you are paying.

Welcome to a discussion of the biggest swindle Wall Street has ever pulled on Main Street. Only a generation ago, most Americans planned for retirement by budgeting with that monthly pension check from their employers. Fixed-payment pensions have virtually been eliminated now, replaced by personal investment plans—401(k)s, and their cousin, 403(b) plans. These cost employers a tiny fraction of the price of pension plans; the vast majority of the money in your retirement account is your money. You supply the funds, you take the risk by investing it (and as Enron employees learned, you can lose it all). But the rewards? They go to Wall Street. Right now, a huge chunk of your 401(k) is slowly siphoned off by Wall Street money managers, and you don't even know it.

At this point, perhaps you are thinking about your most recent 401(k) statement. If you look at it closely every quarter, you might notice a tiny, fractional charge labeled with words like "administrative costs." They might be as small as $40 or $50. That's the only fee you've ever noticed. And you are probably thinking, "No way that's costing me 33 percent of my retirement."

And you'd be right. This debacle has nothing to do with the fees that are clearly disclosed in your 401(k) plan. Instead, it has to do with the fees paid to those who manage the mutual funds in your 401(k) plan, fees you've probably never noticed. That's because they aren't called fees at all. They're called "expense ratios." They never appear as a line item on your statement. Instead, fund managers simply help themselves to the money you invest in the fund, taking their cut by fractionally reducing the number of shares you buy. Because you are constantly buying fractional shares in your funds through regular payroll deductions, there's never a noticeable ding in your shareholdings as a result of expense ratios. You could easily invest your entire career in a 401(k) mutual fund and never know you've been paying through the nose for them.

Expense ratios generally vary from about 0.25 percent to 2 percent—a wide range. In general, the more actively managed a fund is, the more expensive the expense ratio. An index fund, which requires only a computer program to make sure the fund neatly matches the composition of a stock index like the S&P 500, is usually rather cheap. An "aggressive overseas high-growth fund," which theoretically has a supergenius investor constantly pulling and pushing stock-trade levers to help make you rich, could cost you 2 percent or more each year. Plenty of studies show actively managed funds aren't worth the money you pay for them (computers, monkeys, and people using dartboards often do as well as fund stock pickers). But let's set aside that age-old investment debate for a moment. No matter how talented your fund manager might be, expense ratios are killing your retirement.

Perhaps you are still wondering how I could claim that a tiny 2 percent fee could end up costing you years off your retirement.

But I'm not the one making that claim. The U.S. Labor Department is. And so is Congress's investigating arm, the Government Accountability Office.

In a study conducted during 2006, Congress found that a 1 percent increase in fees works out to a 17 percent decrease in retirement funds after 20 years. Here's the example it used: $20,000 parked in a 401(k) earning a reasonable return for 20 years would be worth $70,500 if mutual-fund fees were 0.5 percent. Increase those fees to 1.5, and the kitty sinks to $58,400.

As time goes by, the impact gets much worse. Using similar numbers, the Labor Department found that after 35 years, the same one-point difference in fees can shrink a $227,000 kitty all the way down to $163,000—nearly a 30 percent punishment. A difference like that can genuinely impact your quality of life at retirement—or simply force you to keep working. If you save a respectable $10,000 per year into your retirement, you'd have to work an *extra five years* to make up for the loss caused by that 1 percent fee difference.

Who gets hit the worst by these fees? Those who follow Wall Street's advice and begin investing as soon as possible. Let's go back

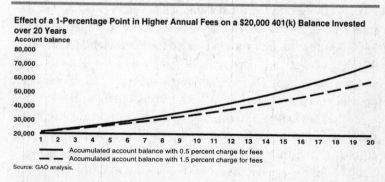

Effect of a 1-Percentage Point in Higher Annual Fees on a $20,000 401(k) Balance Invested over 20 Years
Account balance

—— Accumulated account balance with 0.5 percent charge for fees
– – Accumulated account balance with 1.5 percent charge for fees
Source: GAO analysis.

SOURCE: "Changes Needed to Provide 401(k) Plan Participants and the Department of Labor Better Information on Fees," Government Accountability Office report GAO 07-21, November 2006.

to that precocious twenty-year-old we've already mentioned, who began investing even before she could drink. Taken cumulatively, a twenty-year-old who makes a one-time investment and then lives to the ripe old age of eighty-five will find that fully 80 percent of the money generated by that investment goes to Wall Street, with only 20 percent left to our judicious investor. John Bogle, founder of Vanguard, tells this tale by using simple numbers: $1,000, invested at age twenty, and never touched through age eighty-five, assuming an 8 percent return each year, nets the investor $160,682 after 65 years. But subtracting a 2.5 percent cost of investing each year, the return shrinks to $34,250, with Wall Street taking $126,432—that's 79 percent to Wall Street, 21 percent to the investor.

Bogle calls this, fittingly, "The Tyranny of Compounding Costs."

I call it a scam.

So far, all these examples have assumed a static amount saved for multiple decades to simplify the math. That's not realistic, of course, as most people continually add to their 401(k) all through their working years. Here's a more realistic example: Say you have $50,000 today in a 401(k), and you are thirty years from retirement. With each paycheck, you dutifully save enough to get the full matching benefit from your employer (often 6 percent of your paycheck, with the employer kicking in an extra 3 percent), and a little extra, so you sock away the maximum allowed by law. Say you get a solid 8 percent return each year. A 1 percent fee difference will cost $450,000 toward your retirement, says attorney Jeff Robertson on 401khelpcenter.com. That's nearly half a million dollars. Forget about shaving years off your retirement—most people simply could not work enough years to make up for that kind of lost return.

It's hard to believe the cumulative power of retirement fees over time, but think of it this way. Compounding interest often works against you, particularly in your home mortgage. That's why a $200,000 mortgage can cost you $500,000 during the life of your loan. As you save for retirement, compounding interest should be working for you; instead, it's seriously blunted by these "expense ratios"—the tyranny of compounded fees.

Now, consider about how much time you spent shopping around the last time you bought a home, trying to lower your mortgage interest rate by 0.25, or even 0.125 percent. You visited websites, you talked to friends, perhaps you even hired a mortgage broker. You were probably proud when you thought you saved yourself a fraction on interest charges.

Well, I have bad news. That was all a waste of time if you're getting socked in retirement-account fees. That same quarter-point difference in a 401(k) expense ratio will cost you more than the interest you saved on the cheaper mortgage, thanks to the tyranny of compounding costs. And you're probably overpaying by much more than 0.25 percent.

Still, the mystery of compounding interest can muddy the discussion of 401(k) fees, so here's a simpler way to look at it. That swanky overseas fund you've invested in, the one with the "1.5 percent expense ratio"? Imagine it grew a respectable 4.5 percent last year. Forget the confusing 1.5 percent expense-ratio description. The fund manager actually took 25 percent of your returns. Without any fee, you would have made 6 percent.

You never see this deduction—it's just slurped right out of your returns. The thought that 25 percent of your retirement growth is going to a money manager instead of you twenty five years from now should make your blood boil. But that's precisely why a 1 percent fee difference can cost you 20 or 30 percent of your retirement kitty over time. Now consider this: Some year, that swanky overseas fund you invest in will lose 4.5 percent. But the fund manager *still* makes 1.5 percent. This is your retirement, yet you are obligated to take all the risk. Wall Street has guaranteed returns. Your only guarantee: You'll be working awfully hard, awfully late in life, to make money for Wall Street.

401(K)S EVEN MAKE YOUR CEO RICH

Without any real societal debate, we've allowed corporate America to divorce itself from obligations to help workers retire with dignity. Silently, the burden has been shifted entirely to workers. And the sinister plot only begins there. This Teutonic shift—today 50 million Americans have $2.4 trillion socked away in 401(k) plans—has allowed Wall Street to buoy the mutual-fund industry and raid this huge personal retirement fund for countless billions in fees. Along the way, companies like Enron have used the incredible power of these huge investing plans to manipulate their own stocks by urging workers to invest all their retirement funds in company stock. This keeps stock valuations artificially high and rewards executives who have received extravagant stock-option grants. Now there's a Gotcha. But as Enron showed, investing in your own company can ultimately cripple your retirement account.

Switching from pensions to private retirement accounts has left a generation of Americans perilously unprepared. The average American *who holds a 401(k) account* has a paltry kitty of about $62,000 for retirement. That amount wouldn't even generate $500 a month for old-age living expenses, assuming the worker knows how to put the money into a safe income-generating investment. Or, more to the point, it will barely pay for the first serious illness a husband or wife will suffer after retirement.

And you thought you were doing well because you are getting 3 percent extra each year through your company's matching contributions.

THE END OF PENSIONS

The origins of this societal outrage date back to the early 1980s, when an IRS ruling opened the door for private individuals to save a little extra for their retirements, tax free. The 401(k) tax advantage was born of humble beginnings, as an IRS ruling in 1981 concerning deferred bonus payments to employees. But corporate America quickly seized on it as an opportunity to push off an enormous cost of doing business onto average workers. During the next two decades, defined-benefit pensions were dismantled. They've largely been replaced by 401(k) plans, which cost companies a tiny 1, 2, or 3 percent payroll-matching payment and some overhead—and that cost is generally passed along to workers anyway.

About half of all workers don't really know what to do with their 401(k) plans, and many still don't even bother to sign up. Those who do join the plan are given a paltry set of investment choices, a tiny fraction of the choices available to the general public through standard brokerage accounts. There's usually just a handful of funds to pick from in a 401(k) plan—a useless money-market fund that generates measly interest earnings, a couple of high-risk funds, and perhaps an index fund and a bond fund.

Even conscientious employees who want to take charge of their retirement, who want to know exactly what their 401(k) plans are costing, don't stand a chance. Fees for these funds can be found only by reading the annual prospectus or digging around some investing websites. The actual cash amount the investment costs the investor is never disclosed. Since the amount invested in each fund is constantly changing due to regular contributions, only half-crazed, spreadsheet-obsessed employees could possibly generate the formulas necessary to compute precisely how much each fund's expense ratio dings their retirement accounts every year.

There is no practical way to know how much richer you are making Wall Street by trying to invest in your retirement.

That in itself is unconscionable. But this story gets even worse.

401(K) STANDS FOR KICKBACK

Ever wonder why you can't use 401(k) money to invest in any company or fund you wish? After all, isn't it your money? Why does your 401(k) come with a seemingly random, even cryptic, set of fund choices?

Someone gets paid off, of course. Someone gets a kickback.

Of course, on Wall Street, they're not called kickbacks. They are called "revenue-sharing payments."

Corporate human resource departments don't manage 401(k) plans and pick the slate of mutual funds you get to pick from. Instead, your company contracts with third-party administrators to do this work. It's very likely your company genuinely believes it's secured a great deal on your behalf. The fund administration work might even be free! After contracting with a provider, your HR manager slaps her hands, gets a pat on the back for setting up the benefit, and moves on to other chores.

Meanwhile, you have a seemingly odd set of 401(k) plan choices. And if you are really enterprising and dig deep, you might find the expense ratios on these funds are pretty high. Sometimes, they are even higher than the fees on similar funds sold to the general public. How could that be?

Well, someone has to get paid for all this work. You didn't think it was really free, did you? Administrators make sweet deals with your company because they get paid on the other side of the deal. A lot.

Mutual-fund companies trying to shop their plans to 401(k) administrators have the greatest marketing tool of all at their disposal: money. They pay administrators huge fees to get them to include their funds in your slate of 401(k) choices. It's worth it for the funds, of course, which in turn get huge accounts of employees' money to play with.

Think your plan is immune? Probably not—90 percent of 401(k) plans use revenue sharing.

The kickbacks—er, revenue-sharing payments—that administrators get can be enormous. They can make up half of your funds' hidden fees, or more.

Who pays for the kickbacks? You do. They are buried into your funds' expense ratios. As we've been discussing, the money is simply siphoned out of the retirement gains you should be accumulating. You thirty-five-year-olds out there who are losing a half-million dollars of your retirement to high fees? Probably half of that half-million is lost in 401(k) kickbacks.

Retirement-plan kickbacks are now finally getting the attention of regulators. The Securities and Exchange Commission began investigating revenue-sharing agreements in 2005. In 2006, New York State's then attorney general Eliot Spitzer reached an agreement with investment firm ING, in which the firm agreed to pay $3 million to the state's teachers and to more clearly disclose fees for the teacher's retirement fund, a 403(b) plan. ING had paid $3 million per year to the New York State United Teachers union so it would recommend ING annuity plans. In 2007, Congress began holding hearings on the subject of retirement-fund kickbacks. Still, the problem of 401(k) expenses has a long history and won't disappear easily.

So for now, what should you do? Corner your human resources director at the next company gathering and ask the uncomfortable question, "How much do we pay in fees for our retirement plan?" When he or she says, "nothing," whip out a copy of this chapter and gently offer your new knowledge. Then ask when was the last time your 401(k) plan was "put out to bid," giving other administrators a chance to pony up lower-fee proposals. Competition is the best medicine for fat-cat fee plans.

Then, be sure to analyze your own investments. Spend an hour digging through your available funds to find out what the expense ratio is for each one. You can simplify this task by figuring out what the five-letter ticker symbol is for all your plan funds—mutual funds have ticker symbols just like stocks. Then punch the symbols into your favorite investing website, such as Yahoo Finance or MSN Money. These sites do what a fund prospectus often doesn't do: They break out expense ratios in obvious, black-and-white terms. If you own any funds with expenses of more than 1 percent, you should seriously consider dumping the fund for a cheaper one. Your plan's index fund likely has the lowest ratio, probably about 0.25 percent or less. Park your money in there and you won't be sorry, as it will track the larger stock market no matter what it does, and you won't be making a fund manager rich. If you do decide to stay in a high-priced fund, make sure you have a good reason—some inclination that you are getting your money's worth, that the fund will far outperform the rest of the market. Remember that most experts don't believe that's possible; last year's top fund is often next year's dog.

Finally, don't be so scared by mutual fund fees that you overcorrect and take the only fee-free option that's likely available to you in your retirement plan—purchase of your company's stock. Enron workers learned this lesson the hard way. As your company pays you your salary, your financial life is already tightly bound up in your company's success or failure. You want diversity in your retirement account. In general, you want to stay away from buying your company's stock in your 401(k).

And don't avoid your 401(k) because of this fee issue. The free, temporarily tax-free money your company gives you is still the best retirement deal you've got. It's just important for you to understand it's nowhere near the good deal you think you're getting. It's a crime that while your company may give you 3 percent extra each time you put money into your retirement, fund managers can take about half of that. Still, in the end, you will come out ahead with sensible investing choices. You'll just have to work much harder, and much longer than you realize, thanks to the hidden Gotchas of retirement investing.

If you are supplementing your retirement savings with other private means, such as an Individual Retirement Account (IRA), the problem of hidden expense ratios also applies. There is a marked difference, however. IRA users are free to invest in the entire market, including stocks, so you are not hamstrung by limited mutual-fund choices. Also, many funds actually sport cheaper expenses when purchased independently rather than through a 401(k) plan. That puts IRA investors ahead of the game, and it should make you seriously consider what you're getting for all those 401(k) fees you're paying.

Retirement
GOTCHA-STOPPING STRATEGIES

1. Meet with the person in the human-resources department responsible for 401(k) plans and discuss hidden fees and expense ratios.

2. Ask about the last time your plan was "put out to bid." If it's been a while, encourage your human-resources department to ask for bids again. The industry is getting more competitive, and a new third-party plan administrator might offer cheaper funds.

3. Find expense ratios at independent investing sites by using mutual-fund ticker symbols. Consider dumping funds with expenses over 1 percent.

4. If your company's human-resources department is not helpful or transparent enough for you, consider joining with fellow employees and hiring an independent consultant to assess the expenses of your current 401(k) plan.

5. Avoid company stock, even if the fees are low. Never use more than 10 percent of your 401(k) money to buy company stock.

6. Invest in your 401(k) anyway, at least enough to get your company to match.

7. Apply the same principles to 403(b) plans and IRAs. Mutual funds in both should be scrutinized for high fees.

8. Annuities should be handled with extreme care. The promise of a steady check is reassuring, but because they are so confusing, they can be easily packed with high up-front fees that eat away at your principal. And in the end, your principal is all you have.

9. Reverse mortgages: See annuities. These can be a solid alternative for elderly folks who have a lot of equity in their home but not much retirement savings. Still, in this growing mortgage sector, the deals can be confusing. Banks can walk away with 10 percent of a home's value after day one, in up-front fees.

4

Mortgages and Rentals

The whole thing is something of a tragedy.
Jack Guttentag, the Mortgage Professor

I. Mortgages

Money magazine conducted an amazing experiment during four months in 2006. It picked a single block in a suburb of Minneapolis and visited every home that had been sold in the past six years. And it sent out longtime real-estate writer Stephen Gandel, a veteran who's also worked for the *Wall Street Journal* and Crain's *New York Business,* to canvass the block. He convinced home buyers to share with him their home-sale settlement statements. Gandel then had experts pore over them looking for hidden fees and charges. The sad findings: Homeowners on Aquila Lane in St. Louis Park, Minnesota, paid an average of 23 percent more than they should have. Some overpayments were small, junk fees labeled with terms like processing, administration, application, commitment, document preparation, and the like. But some were devastating. Thanks to the experts, an Aquila Lane couple named Nikole and Josh Didier found out they overpaid by nearly $3,400. The mortgage on their $165,000 home funded a $3,398 referral payment to their mortgage broker. They had no idea.

"We thought we had paid our mortgage broker up front," Josh Didier said to the magazine when given the bad news. He had. But he also paid out back, too. The bank also paid the broker. It then turned around and charged the couple a higher interest rate to recoup the payment.

Welcome to the murky, dirty world of home purchasing. Consumers pay $110 billion buying and selling homes each year—not including the price of the home. The most important purchase consumers make in their lives is the one they know the least about—and the one where they get cheated the most frequently. That's because the system for buying and selling homes is hopelessly flawed. In fact, when the federal government did a thorough examination of home buying in the early 1970s, it concluded that the only way to fix the system was to blow it up and set fixed prices for home transactions. Instead, Congress settled for middling reform. We've been paying billions more than we should ever since.

Jack Guttentag is a retired Wharton School finance professor and home-buying expert who goes by the moniker the Mortgage Professor. His website, which is full of free calculators and home-buying advice, helps thousands of people cut through the confusion of getting a mortgage each year. He doesn't mince words when talking about the industry.

Government regulation of mortgages is an "invitation to abuse," Guttentag says. Consumers who shop around for mortgages are given Good Faith Estimates of their cost by mortgage companies—but these, Guttentag says, only provide "legal sanction for lenders to cheat." The estimates are not binding in any way. Both brokers and lenders can charge anything they want when closing day comes. The Real Estate Settlement Procedures Act (RESPA), Congress's feeble attempt to clean up the industry in 1974, permits—even encourages—such deceptions.

"It could not do this more effectively if it were deliberately designed for that purpose," Guttentag says.

We can all agree that in a market economy, competition is a good thing. In fact, that's the foundation of capitalism. It stands to reason, then, that reverse competition would be bad. And yet, reverse competition is exactly what you'll find in the fees attached to the largest purchase you probably will ever make. Here's a taste of it.

Buried in that closing settlement statement—the one you might not see until 24 hours before you close on your home purchase—is one of the biggest hidden fees, in dollars, you'll ever pay: "Title Insurance." A bit of a relic in today's time of sophisticated databases and electronic records, title insurance simply guarantees that the person selling a property has the right to sell it, and that there are no other claimants to the house or land, such as a long-lost relative. Thanks to computers, the work of a title search becomes easier and easier each year. And yet, title insurance might be the most profitable fee any company ever charges any consumer. If you live in a place like Washington D.C., for example, you'll likely pay nearly $2,000 for title insurance that could cost you as little as $110 elsewhere.

Title insurance is a massive business. It's much bigger than medical malpractice insurance, for example, and much more profitable. Most insurance firms, such as those that write auto or home policies, tend to pay out in claims about 80 percent of what they collect in premiums. Title claims are so rare that title insurance firms pay out an average of just 5 percent of premiums as claims, and some pay as little as 1 or 2 percent.

Title firms rode along with the housing bubble like so many other home-sale support industries. In 2005, title firms took in $17 billion—double what they took in for 2000, and four times the revenue of 1995.

Much of the money collected is pure profit for everyone along the food chain—the chain of resellers and referrers who create the reverse competition.

How does this thievery happen in a world where it seems there is so much competition? Well, in home buying, competition runs backward.

When lenders compete, you win. Unless they are competing for the right to charge you fees. Then, you lose. That's exactly what happens when you pay for title insurance on your new home or condo.

"Reverse competition" is an anomaly, a rare circumstance that occurs when the buyer of a product is not the shopper for the product. When intermediaries or resellers who are paid for referrals get involved, they profit when prices go up, not down. Any time the person being marketed the product is not the person actually paying for the product, you end up with a lack of downward price pressure. If that middleman benefits from higher prices, there is actually upward price pressure—that's reverse competition. Economists sometimes call this a three-cornered transaction or a trilateral dilemma, and it always results in high prices for the buyer, unless a government regulation is inserted into the process.

Title insurance is often the largest single line item on your home-purchase closing statement, other than the purchase price itself, but most consumers have no idea what it is. They only know their lender requires it.

Buyers certainly don't know enough to shop around for title insurance, but even if they did, they wouldn't find much choice. Five companies ultimately own more than 90 percent of the market. So consumers usually take the recommendation of their real-estate agent, lender, or home builder.

Those five companies, and their various resellers, compete fiercely for your business. But they don't compete by lowering prices. They compete by raising referral fees to the agents who steer consumers their way. Thanks to reverse competition, the price pressure is up, not down. By raising prices, the title company makes more money and the referring agent makes more money. Consumers pay through the nose. The mortgage business is rife with these referral payments, but here's the funny thing about them: They're not legal. RESPA makes third-party referral fees illegal if they exceed the value of the services provided. Under-the-table payments, however, are widespread, as the Department of Housing and Urban Development rarely enforces the rules. More reputable financial institutions create a system of affiliates to channel the payoffs and stay on the right side of the law. But either way, consumers are forced to buy into a system that is clearly broken, putting them at the mercy of Gotchas—and we haven't even looked at the mortgages themselves yet!

Hopefully at this point, you've managed to find your statement from your most recent home purchase—it's also called a HUD-1 Settlement Statement. Think of it as the grand master hidden-fee tip sheet. Anyway, if you've found it, you've found line 1108, which indicates how much you paid for title insurance. Now think about what your closing costs would have been if you lived in Iowa, where title insurance was long ago declared illegal. Instead, the state government there guarantees all titles, for a flat cost of $110. Compare that to title insurance on a $500,000 home in Washington, D.C., which can cost you $1,800, or 16 times more. Perhaps that doesn't sound like a lot when you are spending half a million dollars. But real closing costs hover roughly around $10,000, and most consumers fight to assemble the cash they need at closing, making a $1,800 line item on your settlement sheet a very big deal.

There are various estimates from experts about just how much title insurance is overpriced, but there is little disagreement that it is. Several states are investigating title-insurance sales practices and class-action lawyers are milling about. There are proposals in Congress to reform the industry and some consumer advocates argue for doing away with it.

But until that happens, the best way to protect yourself is to do something virtually no one does—between your accepted offer and your closing, ask your Realtor for a list of title insurance companies and call each one, asking for a price quote. You can't avoid title insurance, but you can save a few dollars in title-related fees such as "title search" or "document preparation." And you might save a few bucks on title insurance, too. Now you can begin to dwell on all the other entries in your HUD-1.

YIELD-SPREAD PREMIUMS AND OTHER BROKER TRICKS

As a general principle, consumers get screwed when buying homes because it's hard to tell friends from enemies. Often, people trust their mortgage brokers and Realtors too much, believing the agents are working on their behalf, not realizing that both can benefit when the home buyer overpays. This allows these too-trusted agents to steer consumers into too-expensive products, as we've just seen with title insurance. Still, ultimately title insurance costs tend to cluster around the same price, because the market is so concentrated, making it hard to save big money on that fee. But another kind of pricey kickback, the kind that killed Nikole and Josh Didier at the beginning of this chapter, is much easier to attack: It's called a "yield-spread premium."

When Congress took a serious crack at regulating the messy mortgage business with RESPA, mortgage brokers weren't widely used. That industry was born largely in the 1980s, and it thrives today thanks to the increasing complexity of the mortgage business. Now, some 70 percent of mortgages originate with a mortgage broker.

Consumers know they are paying something to their mortgage broker, who allegedly shops around and gets the best interest rate on their behalf. But many consumers don't know that banks sometimes also pay the brokers. That gives brokers mixed motivations.

To make matters worse, the fee that brokers receive from banks has a cryptic name—a yield-spread premium. Put simply, it's a tack-on added to the loan's interest rate. The broker gets a cash payment at settlement from the bank, and the consumer pays the bank back through higher interest rates. The higher the loan rate, the greater the kickback to the broker. Consumers who are tricked into paying above-market interest rates are profitable to both broker and bank, and the two share this premium rate profit—the yield spread.

The yield-spread premium does appear on that HUD-1 Settlement Statement. But consumers only get those a few hours before they are about to close on their home loans. That's long after the purchase contract has been signed, the price has been negotiated, and the loan papers are readied—at that point, it often seems impossible to stop a house deal. Time pressure is nearly always immense. Switching lenders would almost certainly mean losing the house.

Like Nikole and Josh Didier, many consumers don't realize they have funded a yield-spread premium because the cost is rolled into the loan. It adds a tiny fraction to each monthly payment, so it's easily overlooked. In fact, that's the strategy employed by most of the people who grab at your wallet on house-closing day—roll fees into the loan balance. Consumers rarely notice the trick.

There has been intense debate on the ethics of yield-spread premiums in recent years, and if federal regulators ever do act to clean up the mortgage business, these will be under the microscope. The Center for Responsible Lending said in 2004 that American families spend $2.9 billion more than they should on loans each year, thanks to yield-spread premiums.

But there's no need to wait for Congress. There is a surefire way to avoid the yield-spread-premium problem: Get your broker to put their total fee in writing, and agree to pay them up front. Some brokers already operate this way—they go by the obvious name "upfront brokers." Most brokers will operate under upfront conditions if you ask, Jack Guttentag says, *but make sure you get that in writing*. A simple form indicating "The total compensation to [the broker], including any rebates from the lender, will be," signed by both parties, should protect you. On Guttentag's website there is much more about selecting upfront brokers.

SAVED BY KISS

Mortgage loans are full of many other hazards that can and do fill entire books—prepayment penalties, appraisal fees, and so on. Then there's the exotic loan instruments that really hurt consumers during the recent housing boom, loans that leave consumers owning less of the house in five years than the day they closed on it (negative amortization loans), teaser-rate loans that claim 1 percent introductory rates (that's a lie, there is no such mortgage), and interest-only loans with payments that can suddenly jump 50 percent or more when principal payments kick in and the loan resets. In each case, consumers are usually fooled by looking at monthly payments rather than overall cost of the house and the money it takes to buy the house.

That's why old-fashioned advice here works well: KISS, or Keep It simple, stupid. A thirty-year fixed loan is still the right product for most people. It's the easiest to understand, and the easiest to compare.

Generally, the consumers' best tool while mortgage shopping is the Good Faith Estimate, which banks and mortgage brokers will provide on request. This form details the lender's best rate and closing-cost fees—a bit like the estimate you might receive from an auto repair shop. But the estimates are not legally binding, making them a great tool for scams and hidden fees. Former mortgage broker Carolyn Warren, author of *Mortgage Rip-Offs and Money Savers*, says sleazy lenders would brag to her at lunch about their tactics for slipping in thousand-dollar surcharges at the last minute before loans closed. She says no consumer should ever get a home loan without first obtaining at least three Good Faith Estimates, generally one from a bank and two from mortgage brokers. Since mortgage rates change daily, it's important to get the estimates on the same day. Also, to make them easy to compare, make sure the estimates are for precisely the same kind of loan (for example, thirty-year fixed, no points).

The sad news is this: Mortgage estimates have less legal weight than auto repair estimates in most states. According to federal law, lenders can lie on their Good Faith Estimates. They are not legally bound to honor anything on the term sheet. Only upfront brokers and lenders will guarantee their closing costs in writing. Even if an upfront broker is a tad more expensive, you might be better off taking the guaranteed price over the closing day roulette.

On closing day, lender fees are just one segment of the closing costs. Your HUD-1 mixes in a host of other fees: courier fees, notary fees, documentation fees, overnight delivery fees, credit report fees, tax service fees, flood determination fees. It's a long list. After all, the HUD-1 form has 1,400 lines. Some, but not all, are foretold in the Good Faith Estimate. Others just appear, since the bank and mortgage broker are within their rights to change prices at any time. Some people call these junk fees. And in fact, Warren describes in

her book mortgage brokers who quite literally add $1,000 or more to
the closing costs on closing day in a practice I've heard called a
"dumb-ass fee" or other similarly crass name. These can appear virtually anywhere on the HUD-1.

You have the right to question every one of these fees, but realistically, you can't. There are just too many. That's why you're better off
asking a lot of questions before closing day, and focusing intently on
the bottom-line closing cost when the big day comes. Some above-
board lenders will actually provide an estimated HUD-1 form several days before closing. Ask for that. An early estimated HUD-1
statement is your best defense against Gotchas. It'll give you several
days to pull out your magnifying glass and hunt for junk fees, giving
you a much better chance to catch anything that's amiss.

One other crucial point about fees. Many lenders advertise fee-
free loans. Of course, that's ridiculous. There's no such thing as a
free loan. The lender or broker is just encouraging you to roll the fees
into the balance of your loan. Bad idea, for several reasons. Here's
one: It's a lot more expensive. If you take an interest rate that's 0.5
percent higher to avoid $2,000 in up-front closing costs on a
$100,000 mortgage, you'll pay an extra $11,520 on a thirty-year loan.

But more important, it's a recipe for abuse. If you roll up the fees,
you are much less likely to pay attention to them on closing day, because they will be much less painful for you. Another reason that
postponing financial pain is often a bad idea.

FIRST-TIME HOME BUYERS

Conventional wisdom says buying a home is the smartest financial
decision you can make. Generally, that's true. Most people stretch to
get their first mortgage, then start building equity and find it gives
them all sorts of new life choices (trading up to larger homes, taking
out home-equity loans, etc.). Much of this has to do with the incredible bias in our federal tax code toward home ownership. Generally,
for young people, mortgage interest is the only meaningful tax deduction you'll get, which means you need it.

But despite what you may have heard, and despite the tax advantages, there unquestionably are times when renting beats buying. We've just lived through one of those times. In a scary, on-fire real-estate market, renting can help you sleep at night. Renting is clearly superior to buying when you are near the top of what might be a bubble market, or if getting a mortgage is just too far out of sight.

Also, property-tax considerations can tip the scales in favor of renting. In areas where property taxes are oppressive, like New Jersey (where some buyers need second mortgages to pay $1,000 a month for local taxes), renting often beats buying. The threat of mountainous property tax hikes easily outweighs the threat of rental increases, particularly where rent controls are in place.

Still, most are lured to buying, if for no other reason than the right to paint the bathroom any shade of purple the owner desires. If that's you, there are some special considerations for first-time home buyers.

For starters, you are in luck. Despite the mystery of the process, generally the first home someone buys is far and away the easiest home purchase. Most home shoppers find themselves squeezed by an awful game of leapfrog, where they've got to sell the home they're in so they can buy a new place. Timing in these situations is incredibly critical, and can lead to premature gray hairs and domestic strife. It also leads to lowball home offers. Things usually work like this: Shoppers find the place they want to buy long before they sell their own abode. That makes sense, considering the reverse would leave you homeless. But the minute you sign up to buy home No. 2, the clock starts ticking on the sale of home No. 1. As the initial closing date gets closer and closer . . . the buyer/seller usually ends up caving some on the sale price just to close in time to buy No. 2.

But not you. You are a clean buyer. You can shop without time pressure. That patience will serve you well.

Another advantage: You don't have to pay your real-estate agent. The seller will do that. Of course, in reality, you do pay through a higher sale price—this hidden fee was once invisible, but now you see it in Craigslist.org advertisements listed by sellers who offer a 2 or 3 percent discount for buyers who show up without agents.

Agents, you've no doubt heard by now, generally get 6 percent of the house sale as commission—your agent gets 3 percent, and the seller's agent gets 3 percent. Increasingly, consumers are using For Sale By Owner (FSBO, or FiSBO) sites to get around real-estate agents, with mixed results. Real-estate agents have many tools for gaming the system, such as keeping the prime-real-estate sellers and homes away from unrepresented buyers. But the good thing about the FSBO phenomenon is it's given home buyers and sellers some negotiating leverage. First-time home buyers will find agent commissions are negotiable, and you might find an agent who will work for 2.5 percent, or even 2 percent. That will let you reduce your sale price offer without reducing the offer to the seller.

It's important to understand that while there are many, many professional and caring real-estate agents, they are not legally bound to work in your best interest. Agents have all sorts of mixed motivations, which were explained eloquently in *Freakonomics* by Steven D. Levitt and Stephen J. Dubner. For starters, both buyers' and sellers' agents really have one goal in mind: to close deals. The price you pay, or the price the seller gets, is of minimal interest to Realtors. As a buyer, you probably understand that because your agent gets a cut of the final sale price, he or she makes more money as the price goes up. That clearly creates incentive to negotiate badly on your behalf. ("Sorry, they won't budge a dollar below $400,000."). The seller's agent also gets a cut, giving that agent incentive to shoot for the highest price, right? Not as much as you'd think. There isn't an agent in the world who wouldn't take a quick deal for a few thousand dollars less than a protracted negotiation that results in a slightly higher buying price. Why? Consider this: On a $400,000 home, one agent's standard commission is $12,000, which is usually split with a home office, for a net of $6,000. Holding out for a $405,000 sale price only adds another $150 to the commission (and in reality, more like $75). What numskull wouldn't take a $6,000 commission today and move on to other buyers rather than $6,075 next week, or next month?

First-time buyers need to understand this dynamic because it plays out long before any discussion of closing costs arises. Deep inside, that very nice agent—be it a stranger, a friend of a friend, or your cousin—is secretly rooting, every time you open a lockbox on a front door, that this is the house. They get nothing from you until the day you sign a deal, at which point they get a lot. Therefore, you will undoubtedly find agents who can't help but paint an oh-too-rosy picture about that home with the questionable furnace or the loud neighbors next door ("They sound like fun!"). Again, patience is your best ally.

Once you settle on the home, you and your agent will submit an offer. It will include the price you are willing to pay, proof that you can pay it (generally, your prequalified lender letter), and a check toward the down payment, called "earnest money." The seller can accept or reject the offer. Expect offer No. 1 to be rejected. But if it's accepted, the deal is legally binding, and you must begin the process of buying the home.

It is never smart to submit an open-ended offer. Always put a time limit on it; the quicker the better. Otherwise, the seller will simply use your offer to try to shake other offers out of the trees. Generally, twenty-four hours is an acceptable time period. There's nothing wrong with asking for an answer by the end of the business day, however.

You will likely receive a counteroffer, which instantly voids your first offer. Now, they are on the legal hook. If you accept, you get the house. You can make another counteroffer. Then, a few more counteroffer rounds may follow.

Either way, the offer will have contingencies connected to it. These can put the brakes on a deal even after an offer has been accepted. The most common involves a home inspection. Houses have flaws that are invisible to the untrained eye. No one should buy a home without getting it inspected by a professional. That can cost up to $500, and the buyer pays, but it's always worth it. Even if the inspector turns up nothing wrong, inspection reports always form the foundation for a great list of small, worthwhile projects to take on (for example, the gutter should be turned away from the foundation, or the roof probably only has five years left).

Of course, if the house is fundamentally flawed, you can back out of the deal, or demand repairs before you continue with the purchase. That $500 inspection fee is nonrefundable, but if it keeps you from buying a piece of junk for $500,000, it'll be the best $500 you ever spend.

In the red-hot housing market of the early part of this decade, many buyers were willing to waive their right to a house inspection because there was so much competition to buy new homes. That was crazy, and hopefully, those days have passed and are not to return. No one should invest thirty years' worth of money on something without an inspection, particularly someone who's never purchased a home before.

If you are buying a condominium, you should also receive background materials on the building association at this time. The most important is probably the building's annual budget. Look immediately at how much surplus the building has in the bank. If it's less than one year's worth of expenses, you will likely face some kind of unplanned assessment within a few years—say, when the roof starts to leak. The stronger the building's bank account, the less risk there is of a sudden spike in condo fees.

Many buildings now have websites and e-mail lists for residents. Joining these, and pawing through archives, will give you a good idea about the building's heartiness and the neighbors' neighborliness.

Once you have survived the inspection stage, and you haven't found anything suspicious in those condo documents, you will be eagerly headed toward closing. That means finalizing your loan with your bank, picking a title-insurance company, and dealing with all the other potential mortgage-related Gotchas. For those, refer to the beginning of this chapter.

One other thing to look for: In the condo/single family home debate, you should know that for every $500 you pay each month in association fees, you could afford roughly another $80,000 in home price. For example, a $400,000 condo with $500 fees will land you roughly the same monthly bill as a $480,000 single-family home (assuming $80,000 down in both cases and a 6.5% interest rate. Things are slanted a bit more in favor of the home, actually, because the extra mortgage interest is tax deductible while the condo fee is not. Of course, you might not have time to mow the lawn on your new yard, given the second job you'll need to pay the mortgage, in which case, opting for the condo might be smarter.

II. Apartments

You renters out there might think these fees have nothing to do with you. And while your renting experience offers nothing like a HUD-1, you have little reason to let down your guard. Once upon a time, people picked apartment living because they didn't have to worry about things like garbage and water expenses. No more. Tack-on fees are now standard fare at apartment complexes across the country. These fees make it easy for complexes to tease you with lower-than-real monthly rent prices—and they can make it nearly impossible to compare two apartments, unless you know what to look for.

The biggest fee-sucker for apartment hunters is the deposit that's not really a deposit. Increasingly, apartments are calling something a deposit which is really just an upfront fee. Pet owners know this well. Rover can easily cost you a $500 "nonrefundable" pet deposit. You'll want to read your lease over carefully before you sign it, and make sure your deposit is really a deposit (as opposed to a gift to the landlord) when comparing rentals.

Some complexes now have the grace and dignity to just call their upfront surcharges "apartment fees." That's more honest than "non-refundable deposit." Renters will be surprised to find them—but perhaps even more surprised to find that they have to pay a fee for garbage (it's not like that's optional!) or water (ditto!). Why wouldn't such services be included in the price? Because then the complex couldn't advertise that $995-a-month special.

Electricity, telephone, and Internet monthly fees are to be expected, of course. But you should also keep your eye out for exorbi-

tant, disproportionate late fees. No one ever thinks they're going to
pay the rent late, but it happens. And when it does, you are better off
knowing what to expect.

And finally, many complexes are now mandating renter's insurance, and of course, they offer a great deal with an insurance part-
ner. Renter's insurance is a fine idea, but it's easy to overpay. Don't
accept the first offer you get. For a quick comparison, call your auto
insurance company; it might offer you a cheaper plan.

Mortgages
GOTCHA-STOPPING STRATEGIES

1. See a HUD-1. Before you ever start talking to a lender or broker, take a
   look at a sample HUD-1 form. They're all over the Internet, but you can
   get one from the horse's mouth at the U.S. Department of Housing and
   Urban Development. Familiarize yourself with what's coming; that will
   make you much better at asking questions.
2. Get several Good Faith Estimates. When you do, make sure the loans are
   as similar as possible (an easy rule of thumb: compare loans with identical interest rates and lengths—that will immediately betray variations in
   closing costs). For more peace of mind, select a firm that guarantees
   Good Faith Estimates, called an upfront broker or upfront lender.
3. Shop around. Get several bids for title insurance, often the single largest
   cost associated with your closing.
4. Ask your broker. If you are using a mortgage broker, ask them about yield-
   spread premiums. You want to know if the broker has a financial interest
   in getting you to pay higher interest. Upfront brokers, who guarantee their
   commissions in writing, will offer you peace of mind.
5. No overlap. When you get a HUD-1 Settlement Statement, look for overlap in closing fees, particularly if you use a mortgage broker. You don't
   need to pay for two appraisals, two origination fees, or two courier fees.
6. Know who your real friends are. Real estate agents and mortgage brokers
   aren't legally required to act in your interest in many cases, and they may
   be profiting from you in ways you don't understand. Always keep them at
   arm's length and know their suggestions could be very profitable—for
   them.

7. Web help. Visit Jack Guttentag's mtgprofessor.com website. It has the best general mortgage information and a list of upfront brokers and upfront lenders.

8. You can also ask an expert. For $45, the National Mortgage Complaint Center (866-714-6466) will review your HUD-1 statement and call out too-large fees.

5

Cell Phones

Cell-phone companies have locked in profits with ironclad contracts for services that don't work and complicated and inaccurate billing that no one understands.

Janee Briesemeister, Consumers Union

At any given time, most Americans are in cell-phone jail.

You know the feeling. You talk to a friend with a snazzy new handset that does amazing things. Or you see an advertisement for a great deal on a monthly plan. Then what do you do?

You sigh, wistfully wishing you could shop for a new phone. If you are really on top of things, you call your provider and ask when your current cell-phone contract expires. And then you wait.

One thing you don't do: You don't act like a rational consumer in a normal, functioning market economy. You don't go buy the new phone, or get the cheap new plan. You don't reward the more efficient company with your business. You can't. You're in jail.

Imagine if you couldn't switch coffee shops or grocery stores without paying hundreds of dollars in penalties. Preposterous? No—not in the world of cell phones.

From the start, wireless providers have worked hard to lock you up into losing situations, constructing walls with cancellation fees, service-specific phones, and the loss of your phone number.

Worse yet—cell-phone companies can, and do, change their side of the contract unilaterally. Consumers seemingly have no options to decline the higher prices. In other words, they can raise prices, and you can't quit. Consider this note of complaint, filed with the Pennsylvania Public Interest Research Group by a consumer named Kerry:

I'm currently in the middle of a two-year contract with Verizon Wireless. They just notified me that they are dramatically increasing the charges I pay for receiving each text message from two cents to ten cents. When I called to complain, they left me with a few choices, and I was unhappy with all of them. I could simply accept the increase in charges. Alternatively, I could sign up for an unlimited text-messaging plan for another $5/month but only if I renew with Verizon for another two years. Or, I could end my contract and pay an early termination fee of $175. If I don't pay the fee and change my plan to get the best rate for text messaging, then I'm locked in with Verizon for even longer than I originally would have been had they just kept the rates the same. And since the new plan also has an early termination fee, I'll face the same problem if they decide, without my agreement, to change the plan again to suit their needs.

Make no mistake about it—like Kerry, most cell-phone users are captives. In 2005, Ipsos North America surveyed 1,000 U.S. adults and found that 47 percent would consider switching services if termination fees were eliminated. Fully 36 percent said fees already had forced them to stay in a higher-priced plan against their will.

This, it should be obvious, is economic lunacy. And it certainly explains why U.S. residents suffer from what is remarkably among the world's least reliable cell-phone service. After all, what's the incentive to fix the U.S. network? *NBC Nightly News* anchor Brian Williams, on his personal blog, mentioned wistfully once that he often enjoys "crystal clear, uninterrupted" cell-phone conference calls to New York while on the road in faraway, "middle of nowhere" places like the highway from Amman, Jordan, to the Dead Sea. But on his daily commute into New York City? That's another matter. In fact, cross-country drivers on Interstate 90, the main east–west highway in the northern United States, will learn this sorry fact: They can't make a reliable phone call all the way from Chicago to Seattle.

It's an embarrassment, but it's completely predictable. Captive consumers are bad for everyone, consumers and businesses alike. Why would anyone start a new cell-phone company in this environment? Why would anyone invest in customer satisfaction?

Consumers have managed to tear down one wall in this jail. In 1996, the FCC ruled that consumers who switched providers didn't have to surrender their phone numbers, mandating what's called number portability. Of course, it took nearly eight years of legal battles to force wireless carriers to play along, but finally, in November 2003, consumers were allowed to switch carriers without switching numbers.

There was an immediate impact. About 367,000 consumers abandoned AT&T Wireless during the first quarter of 2004, an incredible number given that cell-phone carriers were enjoying unprecedented subscriber growth at the time. Like dogs suddenly let off their leashes, consumers began a mass exodus from the notoriously unreliable provider as soon as they could. The exodus eventually brought the company to its knees, and it was forced to sell out to Cingular (who has since reinstated the name AT&T). Competition works. That's capitalism. Bad companies don't deserve to be propped up by bad regulations or supportive government agencies.

The wireless providers who watched the demise of AT&T learned quickly, and the wall that was knocked down—number portability— was rebuilt even taller. In 2004, most carriers extended typical contracts from one year to two years. Nothing portable about that! By 2006, the cell-phone jail was more fortified than ever.

And in the ultimate irony, cell-phone firms found a way to profit handsomely off number portability. Beginning about a year before portability kicked in, cell-phone firms began charging customers roughly $1 per month for number portability—at one point collecting nearly $100 million per month, according to the Center for Public Integrity! The fees were hard to spot, often lumped into a line item called "federal recovery fee" or something similar. Collectively, the industry took in more than $1 billion before the practice was curbed.

TERMINATING EARLY-TERMINATION FEES

Bottom line: Firing your cell-phone company will cost you $150 to $200, at least. A family of four that wants to cancel service can pay $800 to do so.

The argument you will hear incessantly from mobile-phone providers is this: Consumers pay far below cost to buy their cell phones because the price is subsidized by carriers and the termination fees are merely a means to recover some of that subsidy for consumers who bail early. Callers should be happy they can buy a cheap phone, and accept the consequences if they quit early.

Of course, if that were true, the cancellation fee wouldn't be the same for consumers who quit after three months as it is for consumers who quit after nineteen months. Verizon Wireless conceded this point in 2006 when it announced it would begin prorating early-termination fees. Unfortunately, other carriers didn't follow suit.

Consumers who don't want to pay early-termination fees do have options. They can use prepaid, disposable cell phones, a small but growing part of the industry that doesn't require contracts with termination fees. Or they can pay full retail price for the phone up-front. They can try to pawn their phone and plan off on someone else (cell-phone contracts allow transfers at places like Cell-TradeUSA.com). Or they can throw themselves on the mercy of a customer-service representative. Having a good story to tell apparently helps. Internet websites are abuzz with hints on how to get a firm to waive the fee. The most common recommendation is to use a firm's coverage map to find a zip code that isn't covered, then call and claim to have moved there. Results to that one seem to be mixed; many providers require proof of address.

Another popular tip is to become an expensive customer. Start making calls outside of your cell-phone firm's coverage area, which will force your provider to pay for time on another provider's network (we're assuming here that you don't pay roaming charges). After a few months, you'll likely receive a polite letter strongly inviting you to find another cell-phone company.

Once in a while, cell-phone companies themselves open up a window of opportunity for early cancellation. In 2006, when most carriers upped their text-message prices, they had to send new agreements to users. Some consumers used these as an opportunity to decline the agreement and attempt to void their current contract. Because a change in terms could be interpreted as a change in the contract, the change constitutes a termination of the original pact, the argument suggests. Cell-phone firms fought back, but often relented, when consumers used this tactic.

A popular myth holds that lack of adequate service—a poor signal at home, for example—is enough to void your cell-phone contract. This might seem crazed (doesn't the contract imply that the cell-phone provider is bound to provide you with cell-phone service for two years?), but that's not true. Service quality is not part of the contract. Poor service gives consumers no right to cancel.

Dying, however, seems to work. Carriers will release you from your contract when you reach the great beyond. Only a few carriers require copies of death certificates to prove you're dead. Others will take your word for it.

PICKING YOUR PHONE'S LOCKS

Termination fees are not the providers' only trick to win forced loyalty, however. In fact, they have become a bit of a red herring in the cell-phone-jail debate. With monthly bills creeping up toward $100, a $175 cancellation fee doesn't sound so bad. Increasingly, cell-phone jail is much more a function of hardware than contracts. Paying a $175 fee is one thing; throwing out a fairly new $500 handset is quite another.

Isn't it amazing what phones can do today? They can pull up Web pages in a moving car. Take pictures and videos. Schedule appointments. Even give directions. It's a wonder these smart phones can't be used to make dinner or launch rockets. And yet, there is one thing these technological marvels can't do. They can't work with anyone else's network.

A T-Mobile phone usually won't work on Cingular's network. Ver-

izon phones won't work on either of those networks. The lack of inter-
operability might remind old-time techies of the days before the Internet, when you'd never imagine trying to make an Apple computer
talk to a Microsoft-powered PC. That language barrier is a relic now.
How can these incredibly sophisticated cell phones be so unsophisticated in this one way?

Well, it's intentional. Cell phones are locked down by cellular
providers with special software that prevents them from being used
on other networks. In this realm, there isn't even a pretense by cell-
phone providers about their intentions. The software is called "locking" software. With consumers now paying $500 or more for these
not-so-smart-after-all smart phones, locking software is the best tool
yet cell-phone companies have invented to lock up consumers. Even
after a consumer's contract has run out, even after a consumer finds
a competitor with a much cheaper per-minute plan, or much more
reliable coverage, phone locks are still a major deterrent. You have to
swallow hard to throw a fully functional $500 phone into the trash.

With that kind of money at stake, clever engineers (hackers! But
good hackers!) have jumped in and worked up a work-around. There
are ways to trick phones into ignoring the locking software. Internet
sites sell such services for as little as $5.

Naturally, cell-phone providers have spent a lot of time and killed
a lot of trees trying to argue that use of unlocking tricks is illegal.
Specifically, their lawyers have argued that unlocking software vio-
lates the Digital Millennium Copyright Act of 1998, which was designed to keep thieves from circumventing software used to prevent
pirating of movie DVDs, music CDs, and software.

Let's look at this argument more closely. According to the industry, you paid $500 for a phone, but you're not allowed to type a small
string of characters into the handset that allows you to use the
phone as you wish.

Jennifer Granick, a high-profile lawyer based at Stanford University who often defends computer hackers, took on this argument in
2006. She suggested that courts had already rejected a similar argument from computer-printer maker Lexmark, which fought to stop

generic ink cartridges from working in its printers. Courts had also ruled in favor of generic garage-door opener makers.

In late 2006, the federal government sided with Granick, deciding that unlocking a phone was not a violation of the Digital Millennium Copyright Act. By then, some companies were already starting to give in and give unlock codes to consumers who were clever enough to ask for them. Other firms were still stingy about it, but couldn't prevent would-be unlockers from buying the software. Consumer advocates claimed victory. So did environmentalists, who saw new hope that fully functioning phones wouldn't end up in landfills quite so often, as they could now be resold and reused. Many hoped that cell phones had been set free.

Not quite. The phones, as sold, are still hamstrung with locking software by default. Only those who know enough to ask ever consider using their phones on a competitor's network. Despite the fanfare surrounding Granick's case in techie circles, the vast majority of Americans still think cell hardware is limited to use with a single carrier. But now you know better. From Gotcha to Got Them!

FEES FOR SWITCHING, FEES FOR STAYING

With all this Herculean effort to keep customers under contracts, all these penalties for leaving, and all these incentives to stay, you'd think cell-phone companies would at least reward loyal customers. Nope. There's a fee for being loyal, too.

Jessica Persson's house near Wilmington, Delaware, burned down in January 2006, and she lost almost everything, including the family cell phones. After a frustrating go-round with Nextel's customer service, she wrote in to the *Red Tape Chronicles* to warn other consumers about hidden fees she'd found.

Jessica and her husband Colin went to Nextel to see about getting a new phone, and were surprised to learn that because they were in the middle of a new contract, and no discounts were available, even a basic phone would cost her several hundred dollars. She reluctantly forked over the cash and signed up.

But that wasn't the only kick in the teeth Persson received. Two months later, while digging through her cell-phone bills, she discovered that the normal $150-a-month bottom line had become nearly $190. So she looked more closely and found a line that read, "Handset update: $36."

Now, there's a Gotcha.

Confused, Persson called Nextel customer service.

"I said, 'What is this thirty-six dollar charge?'" The customer-service representative gave her a blasé answer.

"It's because you bought a new phone," she recalls the operator telling her.

"But I paid for the phone already!" she barked back. "And I paid a lot."

They argued for some time over whether she had been warned about the fee at the Nextel store; either way, she was told, the warning was right there on the paperwork Persson had signed to get the new phone.

Upgrade fees became standard during 2006 as yet another way for providers to recoup the cost of subsidizing new phones. Buried deep within a phone bill, they can appear as late as two months after initial sign-up. They are not chump change—a typical upgrade fee can nearly double the price of a new phone advertised at $39.99.

Providers say there are costs associated with registering new phones on their back-end networks. That may be true, but since the cost is directly linked to the new phone, it's misleading for the price to appear anywhere other than on the sticker that's placed on the phone in the store.

You'll also hear from some providers that consumers shouldn't complain about the fee, as they are getting new phones at well below actual cost. Well, Persson's case certainly rules out that argument, since she paid full retail price for the phone.

Instead, upgrade fees are simply the latest industry adjustment to the changing winds of cell-phone jail. Each time one unreasonable wall is knocked down, a new one is erected. Each time the marketplace is opened, by number portability or unlocking of phones, another door is shut. Upgrade fees arrived as a direct response to the challenge the industry faces from number portability. But in this case, upgrade fees seem particularly egregious, since they might accurately be called a loyalty fee.

The good news is this: Persson got her $36 back by complaining. She had to spend a good hour on the phone with Nextel, and she had to demand to speak to a manager. Consumers around the country who notice the fee often received refunds by registering firm complaints.

"PREMIUM" TEXT MESSAGING, AND OTHER SURPRISE CHARGES

You might think text messages cost 10 or 15 cents each—even less if you're signed up for a monthly plan. But not all text messages are created equal. Some cost $1, $2, or even $30 a month.

Many cell-phone users have never heard of premium text messaging, but it's an exploding side of the business. Late-night TV game-show hosts solicit 99-cent premium text messages from watchers, offering a chance to win big prizes—a game that sounds an awful lot like gambling. Prime-time TV shows like *Deal or No Deal* also charge watchers a buck to get in the game.

Premium texts that lead to monthly subscriptions are much more costly, however. Plenty of websites and TV commercials offer consumers "free ringtones" or other free services in exchange for sending a simple text message to a marketer's phone number. Cartoon-style ads that entice children with phones to send text messages are the most troubling of all. Of course, many don't read the small print, and only months later discover they've signed up for useless joke-a-day-style services that cost up to $30 each month.

Avoiding premium text messages can be easy: Some carriers allow users to block premium texting altogether. Call and ask your provider. Otherwise, you've got to study your bills carefully to see if you've been trapped in an unwanted premium text scheme. If you spot such a charge, call your carrier and complain. Most cell-phone firms will work to get you a refund; they don't make a lot of money off these third-party services and the negative publicity isn't worth the trouble.

OUT OF THEIR CONTROL: TAXES

There is another reason many consumers dread opening their cell-phone bills: taxes. Cell-phone providers have almost no control over the taxes that appear on your monthly bill. I say "almost," because there is this exception: Sometimes, what's called a tax isn't really a tax, a common telecom industry trick.

But first, let's look at greedy local governments and their assault on your cell-phone bill. You'd think cell phones caused cancer, or intoxication, the way cell phones are taxed by local, state, and federal governments. Outside of the sin taxes on cigarettes and alcohol, cell phones are perhaps the nation's most heavily taxed consumer good or service.

In Nebraska, fully 22 percent is added to every consumer's bill in taxes. New Yorkers pay 22 percent, too. And it's not just Uncle Sam or your statehouse that's sneaking into your wallet. Your county seat, and even your hometown likely dips into your cell-phone bill every month, too. Baltimore levies a $3.50-per-month tax on phones. Alexandria, Virginia, charges $3 a month. San Franciscans pay 7.5 percent of their bill. Los Angelenos: 10 percent.

It's not just big cities, either. To show just how loopy local cell-phone taxes have become, tiny South Sioux City, Nebraska, proposed a 4 percent cell-phone tax in October 2006—on top of the 22 percent state residents already pay!

"In recent years, policy-makers have viewed wireless as a way to raise taxes without leaving fingerprints," said Joe Farren, spokesman for CTIA, the cell-phone lobby group. He's right. Sneaky taxes are the government fund-raising tool of our time. On average, 17 percent of each cell-phone bill goes to some government kitty. On a $50 phone bill, consumers pay an average of $9 in taxes, according to CTIA.

This isn't a book about government agencies pickpocketing consumers; it's a book about corporate America pickpocketing consumers. But cell-phone taxes are so out of line, and so much a part of that complicated cell-phone bill you can't understand, that they contribute mightily to your cell-phone bill bottom-line shock.

Here's how out of line cell-phone taxes are: 17 percent is 2.5 times the average taxation U.S. consumers pay for other goods and services that don't come with a sin tax. The trend accelerated in 2003, when the Pennsylvania state legislature began this gold rush by approving a 5 percent gross receipts tax on all wireless phones. Other local governments decided this sounded like a good idea and followed suit. During 2003 and 2004, taxes on wireless skyrocketed at nine times the rate of other goods and services.

Here is an abbreviated list of taxes you might find on your phone bill:

- State 911 Tax
- County 911 Tax
- City Gross Receipts Tax
- County Sales Tax
- State Sales Tax
- Federal Universal Service Fund
- Regulatory Programs Fee
- Second Tuesday of the Month Fee

OK, I made that last one up. But you get the idea. Consumers take a jab from the left, then a jab from the right, at every turn. Gross receipts taxes, for example—what are those? They are a tax on the price of goods sold. Kind of like a sales tax. But they are levied using separate names, so they are separate lines, allowing state governments to levy both taxes and collect twice the amount.

Then there's the federal excise tax, which was enacted to help pay for the Spanish-American War. Of 1898. You know, Teddy Roosevelt, the Rough Riders, William Randolph Hearst, Fredric Remington, and the excise tax.

The excise tax is an example of a small victory for consumers, as it was finally dropped in 2006 after the federal government lost no fewer than six lawsuits challenging it as illegal. But to be sure, there's plenty more taxes where that came from.

WINNING THE CELL-PHONE TAX GAME

While this whole maddening world of cell-phone taxes might make you feel helpless, you aren't entirely so. *Forbes* magazine editor Scott Woolley—a devoted hidden-fee seeker—stumbled on an inventive way to escape exorbitant cell-phone taxes in 2005. To borrow from our litigious friends in the legal profession, let's call it "venue shopping." Woolley moved from New York to Los Angeles, and like many consumers, kept his old well-worn phone number. Big mistake. That meant he kept his New York taxes, too. New York's tax rate—22 percent—is among the highest. Verizon told him taxes were based on area code, not home address. So he turned this injustice to his advantage. He got a new cell phone from a store in Idaho, where the taxes were a little more than 2 percent. His taxes shrank to $1.15 a month. The legality of Woolley's cleverness is in dispute, and your mileage may vary. Still, it's nice to know someone escaped an exorbitant cell-phone tax bill.

HOW TO GET YOUR MONEY BACK

Ah, would that it were this easy to get sneaky fees removed from your cell-phone bill. It's not. Cell-phone companies are notoriously unresponsive to consumer complaints because they are incredibly well-insulated from government oversight and regulation, and from the natural forces of competition. In our Ponemon Gotcha survey, only one in five consumers who complained received refunds.

Cell-phone firms are exempt from review by state utility boards and other local agencies. That gives them quite a bit of moxie. The industry has to answer only to the Federal Communications Commission (FCC), which is generally too distracted by wardrobe malfunctions to notice any sneaky behaviors. So, if you want to recover money from your cell phone provider, you can go to the fcc.gov website and file a complaint, but you should know that it will probably get you nowhere.

Your strategy should be much more practical. Your best bet is a calm, tenacious, well-informed conversation with a customer-service representative. Oftentimes, you can get a fee refund through sheer persistence. If the phone call route doesn't work, a thoughtful one-page letter to company executives often gets action. Look up the company's headquarters address at a place like Hoovers.com.

That's what Jill Kurz did after her run-in with Cingular. A single mom living outside Chicago with three daughters, Kurz, 47, left a retail store feeling happy after buying four new phones in June 2006. But a month later, she discovered the store sales rep had signed her up for a series of services she'd never asked for, such as roadside assistance. She also discovered four surprise handset upgrade fees on her bill. After having no luck calling customer service, and no luck revisiting the store, Kurz pulled out her letter-writing skills and drafted a complain-o-gram (not a nasty-gram!) to the senior vice president of Cingular customer service. After some investigating at the Hoovers.com website, she found the officer's fax number and faxed the letter.

Within weeks, Kurz received a credit for almost every surprise charge.

"My letter was very brief and to the point," she said. Kurz wrote to the *Red Tape Chronicles* to give a bit of hope to frustrated readers, offering her success story as a suggested model for others. "You have to not only complain, but you have to complain with a purpose. . . . There is always someone at the company who realizes that without consumers, there is no company."

Letters that rant "It's not fair" rarely work. Letters written with serious consideration are much more effective. And missives that show you are willing to appeal to higher authorities are better still. Your higher authority, however, should be your state attorney general's consumer affairs office, the only agency I've found that will act on your cell-phone complaints.

You can also consider sending letters to the Better Business Bureau, which sometimes manages to settle complaints, or your state's utility board, which may compile useful data that at some point can be used in a lawsuit.

And finally, get involved in the politics of cell-phone fees. States around the country are right now trying to pass model legislation called a Cell-Phone Users' Bill of Rights. Central to these laws is a measure that would give state utility boards oversight of cell-phone firms. That's imperative. Only when someone local can investigate your complaints will you start to see meaningful results. The next time you are frustrated by a sneaky cell-phone fee, your first call should be to customer service, but your second call should be to your local state legislator.

Cell Phones
GOTCHA-STOPPING STRATEGIES

1. Negotiate your way out of termination fees and upgrade fees.
2. If you can't, swap your phone and your plan online using a trading site like CellTradeUSA.com.
3. Use unlocking software to switch carriers and keep your phone.
4. Make sure you aren't overpaying taxes because you're using an old area code.
5. For most people, a stable bill is better than a surprise; sign up for monthly text-message plans and high-minute plans that you know you won't over-shoot. For you very disciplined callers, a low-minute, free-weekend, low-cost plan might save you money. Make sure you ask specifically for the company's cheapest plan—many firms don't advertise these basic, rock-bottom-price plans, for obvious reasons.
6. Use your cell-phone firm's website regularly to check on your monthly minutes usage. Sign up for text-message warnings that you are near your limit, if your provider offers them.
7. Ask about return policies when you sign up. In the first week after buying a new phone, make sure to make calls in your backyard, on your commute, at your parents' house, anywhere you really need the service to work. Return the phone within the fifteen-day window if you have doubts.
8. Don't leave the store without getting an answer to the question: How much will my first bill be? Get it in writing.
9. Always keep your eye out for better plans from competitors. Even if you can't switch, you can use these plans as a negotiating tactic with your carrier.

10. Resist extending your contract for a trivial upgrade, such as fifty more free minutes per month. There is great value in being a cell-phone free agent. It allows you to get the latest phones and the best deals. Don't tie yourself up unnecessarily.

11. Each time you call your cell-phone firm, it will attempt to extend your contract—even if you just ask a question about your plan. Don't allow that. Before you hang up, ask when your current contract expires to make sure an "accidental" extension isn't in force.

12. If you reach an impasse, threaten to quit the company, even if you must pay the termination fee. You're still more valuable as a customer, so you might get better treatment. Many cell firms have special retention departments to deal with this situation, which can offer you better deals to keep you. Of course, don't threaten to quit if you aren't really prepared to do it.

13. Support a Cell-Phone Users' Bill of Rights in your state.

6
Home Phones

Reach out and take some money.

I'll bet you know someone like Aunt Ethel, who's lived in the same New York City apartment since 1980, and had the same telephone number the whole time. During this span, telecommunications has taken almost miraculous leaps forward. The grand AT&T monopoly was dissolved, broken up into many smaller pieces, inviting competition in the local phone market. Millions of cell phones have flooded the country, providing an alternative to the dial tone. We can use our cable-TV lines to make phone calls now, and calls over the Internet can even be free!

And yet, in this age of great advancement, what benefit has Aunt Ethel seen? Her monthly plain old telephone service bill has risen 426 percent during that time. Now there's progress.

It's true that long-distance calling rates—particularly international calling rates—have plummeted in the last two decades. And yet, something fishy is going on. Think about the check you write every month for your home phone. Has it gone up or down?

While cell phones have become little cash registers we all carry around in our pockets, ever decreasing the distance between our wallets and our wireless companies, providers of POTS—plain old telephone service—haven't sat idly by. Home-phone bills may be the most incorrigible documents consumers must face every month, and as we've seen many times, confusion is usually an expensive problem. So now we turn from the wonders of wireless to the old-fashioned scams that are buried in plain old home-phone bills every month.

Bruce Kushnick has been a thorn in the side of telephone companies for nearly twenty years. Once a consultant to the industry, in 1992 he founded a company named New Networks Institute to investigate the impact of AT&T's breakup. He didn't like what he found, and later formed Teletruth, which exposes hidden fees and sneakiness by old-fashioned landline providers. His plainspoken, wry humor, evidenced by the annotated image of a phone bill on page 17, tends to embarrass the telecom industry and those who regulate it.

Kushnick likes to talk about his Aunt Ethel's home-phone bill, as an example. In 1980, her bill was $7.63 per month. And that included telephone rental and some free directory assistance calls. By 2006, the same bill was more than $40. But even that doesn't tell the whole story, as Ethel was actually getting less service. She had to supply her own phone hardware, for example, and dialing 411 cost her 80 cents.

Meanwhile, she paid $3.45 as insurance that her telephone wires wouldn't short out. The wires aren't even worth that much.

Landline providers will say that phone bills have remained under control since the divestiture of AT&T. Some will even claim that their home-phone rates have stayed flat for decades. But what about Aunt Ethel? One or the other must be lying, right?

Not quite. More like sleight of hand. The base rate for home-phone services has remained relatively constant; it's the sneaky fees and aftercharges that make Aunt Ethel's bill—and yours, too—400 percent higher.

Here's how telcos do it: What was once a normal cost of doing business has become a line item, a fee, or a surcharge tagged with names like "regulatory," "administrative," or "mandated." Many of these labels are misleading, and in the words of the National Association of State Utility Consumer Advocates, "do nothing more than soak consumers for the carriers' ordinary operating costs." That's

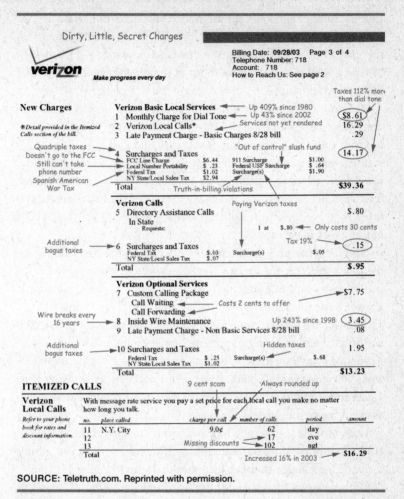

Dirty, Little, Secret Charges

verizon *Make progress every day*

Billing Date: **09/28/03** Page 3 of 4
Telephone Number: 718
Account: 718
How to Reach Us: See page 2

Taxes 112% more
than dial tone

New Charges

Verizon Basic Local Services ← Up 409% since 1980
1 Monthly Charge for Dial Tone ← Up 43% since 2002 $8.61
2 Verizon Local Calls* ← Services not yet rendered 16.29
3 Late Payment Charge - Basic Charges 8/28 bill .29

*Detail provided in the Itemized
Calls section of the bill.*

Quadruple taxes
Doesn't go to the FCC
Still can't take
phone number
Spanish American
War Tax

"Out of control" slush fund

4 Surcharges and Taxes 14.17
   FCC Line Charge $6.44   911 Surcharge $1.00
   Local Number Portability $ .23   Federal USF Surcharge $ .64
   Federal Tax $1.02   Surcharge(s) $1.90
   NY State/Local Sales Tax $2.94

Total   Truth-in-billing violations.   **$39.36**

Verizon Calls   Paying Verizon taxes
5 Directory Assistance Calls $.80
   In State
   Requests: 1 at $.80 ← Only costs 30 cents

Additional
bogus taxes

                                       Tax 19%
6 Surcharges and Taxes .15
   Federal Tax $.03   Surcharge(s) $.05
   NY State/Local Sales Tax $.07

Total   **$.95**

Verizon Optional Services
7 Custom Calling Package $7.75
   Call Waiting ← Costs 2 cents to offer
   Call Forwarding ←

Wire breaks every
16 years

8 Inside Wire Maintenance   Up 243% since 1998 3.45
9 Late Payment Charge - Non Basic Services 8/28 bill .08

Additional
bogus taxes

                                       Hidden taxes
10 Surcharges and Taxes 1.95
   Federal Tax $ .25   Surcharge(s) $.68
   NY State/Local Sales Tax $1.02

Total   **$13.23**

ITEMIZED CALLS   9 cent scam   Always rounded up

**Verizon
Local Calls**   With message rate service you pay a set price for each local call you make no matter
how long you talk.

*Refer to your phone
book for rates and
discount information.*

no.	place called	charge per call	number of calls	period	amount
11	N.Y. City	9.0¢	62	day	
12			17	eve	
13		Missing discounts	102	ngt	
Total			Increased 16% in 2003		**$16.29**

SOURCE: Teletruth.com. Reprinted with permission.

why the first page of Aunt Ethel's bill includes thirteen different line items.

Typical phone bills are also full of optional service fees like call waiting and three-way calling. Consumers who overpay for such services don't garner much sympathy—after all, they are optional. Still, prices for these services seem a bit out of whack. When the

Florida Public Service Commission researched the real costs of tack-on phone services in the late 1990s, BellSouth admitted that the cost to offer call waiting was less than a penny, yet many customers pay $4 a month or more for it. That's an impressive 50,000 percent profit margin.

Tack-on, obligatory fees are more my target here. Consumers don't have a choice but to pay those. And pay those, they do.

Grab your most recent bill, if you can, and give it good look. For starters, you'll see a set of line items that would rival a medical bill you'd receive from a hospital after a cancer treatment stay. You'll see fees that are called taxes and taxes that are called surcharges and taxes that are levied on both fees and surcharges and just about nothing that makes sense.

The fee structures are incredibly effective—at being unintelligible. Back in 1993, Kushnick's New Networks Institute conducted a survey and found that literally zero percent of the consumers could answer basic questions about the line items on their phone bills.

Things have only become more complicated since then. In 2003, Kushnick conducted an experiment—he attempted to find an explanation for every line item on typical Verizon phone bills in New York and New Jersey. He failed. But he did succeed in showing this: Taxes and surcharges on the average bill were 112 percent as much as the price of the service. Sound familiar?

Look again at your phone bill, and just try to answer this question: What do you pay for your landline each month? I'll bet you a Subscriber Line Charge that I've just stumped you.

With between fifteen and thirty line items on each bill, it's virtually impossible to say how much the phone line actually costs. A recent BellSouth advertisement in Florida promised phone service for $11 a month, but the actual bills sent home—before telephone call charges—dinged customers more than $27 a month. Only a naïve American consumer would expect to pay the actual advertised price for phone service (think about *that* for a moment). But more than double?

It's not just mega-conglomerate telcos misleading consumers, however. Here's a sample list of charges provided by the small Ohio-based Toledo Telephone on its website in 2006:

BASIC RESIDENTIAL SERVICE CHARGE

Residential Line	$10.94
State E-911 Excise Tax	$ .20
County E-911 Excise Tax	$ .50
TRS Fund/Tax	$ .14
WTAP	$ .13
Federal Universal Service Charge	$ .70
Subscriber Line Charge	$ 6.50
Total	**$19.11**

The list is clear enough—but the explanations are not. At the bottom of the list, the site informs visitors that "most of the charges that appear on your bill are either a federal or state mandate." Is that assertion true or misleading?

Well, that depends on your definition of the word "most." If "most" means the most line items, well, that's true. Five of the seven items on this list are government mandated, such as state and county 911 taxes. But all five only add up to $1.67. The two largest items—"residential line" and "subscriber line"—go directly to Toledo Telephone. The total: $17.44.

Most consumers would say that $17.44 represents "most" of a $19.11 bill, making the phone company's claim mostly misleading.

FCC LINE CHARGE

The confusion—intentional or not—really stems from that last line item, the subscriber line charge, which is one of America's most prolific, valuable, and sneakiest hidden fees. It comes by many names . . . so many that I can't tell you what it's called on your bill. But here's a few to look for:

"FCC Charge for Network Access," "Federal Line Cost Charge," "Interstate Access Charge," "Federal Access Charge," "Interstate Single Line Charge," "Customer Line Charge," or "FCC-Approved Customer Line Charge."

Whatever the name, the price is nearly the same everywhere: about $6.50, adding perhaps 50 percent to the price of basic phone service. What is it? With a name like FCC Line Charge, it sure sounds like a tax that goes to the Federal Communications Commission, doesn't it?

It's not. Rather, it's a mandatory tithe to corporate America. That $6.50 fee is simply revenue that goes directly to your home-phone company. It just has a funny name. The fee has risen about 600 percent from the day it was first instituted 20 years ago in the wake of the AT&T breakup. That's *just a bit* higher than the rate of inflation. Believe it or not, the subscriber line charge, the FCC says, helps keep your telephone bills low.

When AT&T's monopoly was broken up in 1983, the FCC mandated that the resulting smaller phone companies, called Baby Bells, open their telephone lines to alternative long-distance providers. These outsiders had to pay a fee, or a toll, for their traffic to ride over Baby Bell lines. That fee was seen as anticompetitive, because the local phone companies could price the long-distance newcomers right out of business if they wanted to. So, the FCC forced local telcos to lower the toll, but allowed them to recover the expense directly from consumers through the subscriber line charge. The result: You are paying a subsidy to your phone company so it can subsidize your long-distance company. Even if you don't use long-distance service on your home phone.

Successively, the FCC has raised the amount phone companies can recover from consumers through the FCC line fee, each time promising lower long-distance rates as a result. In 2003 the fee went from $3.50 to $6.50, a startling 86 percent hike. Consumers pay about $100 a year for this fee when taxes are added in—yes, the $6.50 is taxed by federal, state, and local governments. The sharp hike in FCC line charge fees is one reason companies like Verizon can claim their home-phone prices have not risen in decades—when in fact, Aunt Ethel's phone bill, and yours, too, has soared.

The formula used to determine this amount is nearly incomprehensible, and the fee is set during FCC meetings essentially conducted at the whims of the phone companies. Even the name for the fee itself—FCC line charge—is intentionally oblique, designed to give consumers the idea that it's a tax.

There is only one way consumers can avoid this charge. Don't have a phone. Not as crazy as it sounds. More and more consumers are dumping their home phones and going mobile-only, dumping the subscriber line charge with it. That's a good thing. But don't pat yourself on the back and think you've left landline hidden fees behind forever. Because, in fact, they're coming to get you.

And they're doing it in the name of poor schoolchildren.

UNIVERSAL SERVICE FUND

Another familiar line item on phone bills is the Universal Service Fund fee. Americans donate $7 billion each year to this fund, which pays to subsidize Internet access at schools and to wire remote communities with telephone service. Between 1998 and 2005, the size of the annual contribution doubled. But now that most schools are wired and the number of unserved rural communities is approaching zero, what are the chances the tax will be dropped?

Zero, of course. There will always be a school that needs better Internet access, or a poor, downtrodden rural area that's in desperate need of telecommunications services.

Like Hawaii.

There's a project right now to string a Hawaiian island with some 1,500 miles of fiber-optic cable to give residents there state-of-the-art connectivity. Honolulu-based Sandwich Isles Communications is stringing up the homes—about 1,800 properties on land that once was part of a royal estate.

Because the properties are considered rural enough, Sandwich Isles is getting millions in subsidies from the Universal Service Fund to pay for the project, all from the kitty designed to help poor kids have telephone service. How much? About $13,700 per home. When complete, island residents will have perhaps the best connectivity in the country, with enough bandwidth at each house to perform telemedicine—which can even involve surgery over the Internet. That, some might say, is overkill. Alternate technologies, such as state-of-the-art satellite phones, would cost a fraction of the price, but were rejected in favor of USF-funded fiber.

Universal Service is certainly a noble concept. All Americans should have good-enough access to telephones and Internet services. But it should be obvious that this "tax" is just another form of corporate subsidy. The money collected by the government goes right back to telecom corporations in the form of projects ordered by companies like Sandwich Isles Communications in Hawaii.

To make matters worse, the tax that appears on your bill every month—it might be called the Universal Service Fund, USF, or FUSF—hasn't always gone into the Universal Service Fund. Telcos used to keep some of it for themselves. They collected the USF from you in advance, intentionally overcharged, paid into the government-managed fund, and pocketed the rest as a tip. In other words, telephone companies were essentially reselling donations to America's poor schoolkids, and skimming a profit off the top—*without disclosing the markup!*

Universal Service Fund markup is not a consumer-advocate conspiracy theory. Here's what the FCC said in December 2002 about this practice:

> We acknowledge that carriers in the past may have marked up their universal service line items above the relevant assessment amount for uncollectibles and other factors. We are concerned, however, that the flexibility provided under our current rules may have enabled some companies to include other completely unrelated costs in their federal universal service line items.

The FCC has now barred phone companies from padding USF charges this way (what critics call "gaming" universal service line items), so the practice isn't legal anymore. Instead, phone companies found a new way to do the same thing. They broke out a new line item onto our bills and take their chit that way. You'll see it listed as the FUSF administrative recovery fee or something similar on your bill. The recovery fee is often less than the markup that telcos had been hiding earlier this decade, which shows the value of shedding a bright light on hidden fees. Nevertheless, your telco is still pulling off the incredible—the equivalent of an electronics store charging you $5 for sales tax on a television you buy and then an additional 50 cents as a "sales tax collection recovery charge."

CUT-THE-CORD? NOT OUT OF THE WOODS

At this point, all you hip "I've-cut-the-cord-and-gone-all-wireless" or the "I-make-my-calls-over-the-Internet crowd" might be feeling smug. Wireless-only users pay very little into the Universal Service Fund, for example, and no FCC line charge. If you're in that crowd, you might imagine you've outsmarted the system. Fat chance. Those Hawaiian islands are on to you. The FCC and the telecommunications industry is well aware that the tax base for Universal Service slush money is in danger of eroding. There are multiple proposals for increasing USF fees on cell phones to compensate. And Internet-based services? The FCC lumped them in with the USF-paying crowd in 2006.

And those who only keep a home phone for emergencies, who exclusively use cell phones to make long-distance calls—the phone company is on to you, too. In 2007, Verizon began levying a $2 (plus tax) "shortfall fee" on customers who don't make any long-distance calls. That's like paying a gasoline tax for taking the bus instead of driving your car! It's true—customers are genuinely paying something for nothing. That's how home-phone bills work. To avoid this charge, simply turn off long-distance access to your phone altogether. Keep a calling card with a toll-free number handy for emergencies. Because the Universal Service Fund only applies to long-distance calling, you'll avoid the monthly USF fees with a local-only phone, too. But there is one caveat. Some phone providers are now charging a one-time fee for turning off your long-distance access!

LINE-ITEM-ITIS

Perhaps you're starting to understand how a simple phone bill can grow to nineteen line items *on page 1.* Don't think it's gone unnoticed. This line-item-itis led the National Association of State Utility Consumer Advocates—a consumer interest group—to file a landmark complaint with the FCC in 2005, alleging widespread Truth in Billing abuses by the telephone industry. The complaint cited practices like this: "New line items with generic names like 'Carrier Cost Recovery Charge' allow the firms to lump together and pass along costs like relay services for the deaf, number-portability charges, universal-service-fund collection costs, and even property taxes."

In its complaint, the consumer-advocate agency called for a stop to the lunacy of tack-on charges of nineteen-line home-phone bills. It argued that telcos should be barred from tacking on lines for items like property taxes, which are considered part of the cost of doing business in most other industries. The agency argued that consumers cannot realistically compare surcharge-based expenses, as such fees distort the marketplace and reward companies that offer lowball advertised prices and charge high, hidden fees—For example, BellSouth's $11 monthly service that really costs $27.

The petition was still awaiting action in 2007. But telephone companies mounted a vigorous defense. Among their arguments: Limiting sneaky-fee levees would violate their First Amendment free-speech rights. More specifically, they argued the fees were "political speech."

That's right. The right to charge hidden and confusing fees is akin to free speech and freedom of religion, the way the telcos tell it.

SLAMMING, CRAMMING, AND STUDYING

Consumers navigating the phone bill line-item minefield don't really have a lot of choices for shedding these quasi-government-tax-fee-surcharges. Complaining to the FCC for clarity is certainly a good step, but it won't save you any money. The best habit to get into regarding home-phone service is to ask very specific questions when choosing services. One: "Are there any other fees?" or simply, "What will the exact amount be at the bottom of my monthly bills?" Don't accept the first, "no fees, sir" answer. Ask it a few different ways before you sign up for one of those discount long-distance plans or change providers.

But after you sign up, there are plenty of ways to save money. Chief among them: Spend an hour every few months deconstructing your statement. Phone bills are often riddled with errors. Research firm Gartner says that 12 to 20 percent of business phone bills have errors in them, and 95 percent of those errors just happen to be in the telco's favor. There's no reason to believe home bills are any different. The phone company is not above charging for services that don't exist. In 2006, Verizon settled a class-action lawsuit that the firm made millions by continuing to bill customers for phone lines that were no longer operational. These were special, "nonswitched," or nonvoice phone lines used for burglar alarms and other similar services. Verizon agreed to offer consumers up to two years' worth of refunds, without admitting any wrongdoing.

Another reason to carefully inspect your bill: cramming. Third-party companies can cram small fees and additional services onto your bill that you don't need and you never asked for—services like "enhanced" voicemail or enhanced 411 services. It's an illegal practice, but it's an easy scam to pull off because local phone companies must allow third-party companies to sell you services, and they usually just take the third-party company's word for it when told you've agreed to the charge. A simple call to your local phone provider will rid your bill of these charges, but you have to make that call.

Slamming involves similar billing shenanigans related to your long-distance company. It is possible for your long-distance provider to change without your knowledge, and that can lead to big bills. Don't overlook the long-distance portion of your home-phone bill, even if it's small, or else you can easily be victimized by this illegitimate practice. You can even be an unwitting accomplice if you fill out the wrong piece of junk mail. Don't be tempted to endorse those authentic-looking checks or fill out those sweepstakes forms sent to your home promising you long-distance discounts. You never want to switch long-distance providers under those terms. If you do, you will end up paying far too much.

Of course, your local phone company is hardly immune from making mistakes involving long-distance charges—costly mistakes. There have long been allegations that phone companies play with telephone-call lengths, rounding them up generously to generate more revenue. There are also accusations of convenient computer glitches that work in the telco's favor. Here's one that's more than an accusation: In May 2000, California resident Linda Roark looked at her bill and saw a pricey one-minute phone call—$3.57. The call apparently had been billed through the wrong long-distance provider. Eagle-eyed, she asked for a review of her past bills by the company and unearthed $840 in mistakes.

She wasn't offered a refund for that amount, however—she was offered a credit against future bills. Roark eventually became the lead plaintiff in a class-action lawsuit against her telco. Both over-billing and credits-instead-of-refunds were apparently common practice for her phone company. Lawyers readily found other consumers with similar stories. A victim named Valerie Zamarron said she called Ventura, California, on July 4, 2000, and was charged a rate of fourteen cents per minute. The next day, July 5, she called the same number and was billed $3.63 for one minute.

The defendant, GTE California (now Verizon), ultimately agreed to refund about $14 million to California consumers for the alleged overcharging—while admitting no wrongdoing.

If you do spot overbilling charges, be persistent. Allegations made by Roark's attorneys in an article in the local *Santa Barbara Independent* newspaper accuse GTE of telling customer-service reps to give customers like Roark a hard time when they first call. Internal memos warned staff not to be too "customer friendly" when consumers complained, Roark's lawyers said, and customer-service agents routinely offered credits of 10 percent or less on the first pass. Persistent customers were rewarded, however. One manager told Roark's lawyers that when customers balked at the initial lowball credit offer, "then we're to rerate it to the proper amount, whatever it is."

Persistence, in the world of Gotchas, usually pays.

Home Phones
GOTCHA-STOPPING STRATEGIES

1. Look for unwanted services crammed onto your bill.
2. Make sure the right long-distance discount plans are in effect.
3. If you cancel your phone, remember to cancel local and long distance separately. Local providers are supposed to cancel long distance for you, but often they don't, and you are liable for the continuing monthly long-distance bill fees.
4. Make sure your long-distance provider isn't suddenly changed, a practice called slamming.
5. Ask for refunds when discounts aren't honored. If denied, ask again.
6. Never endorse sweepstakes checks mailed to your house. These are often shady telco marketing plans.
7. Go wireless to avoid some fees, like the FCC line charge.
8. Include monthly fees when comparing prices on those all-you-can-eat discount calling plans.
9. Don't think Skype and other Internet-only calling plans will be fee-free for long. Users already pay into the Universal Service Fund and other fees are on their way.
10. Always assume there are errors on your bill. Studies show up to 20 percent of bills have them.
11. If you never make long-distance calls with your home phone, turn off long-distance access. You'll save on taxes and fees, and avoid newfangled "shortfall" charges assessed to those who don't make any long-distance calls.

Pay TV

Unfortunately, the FCC appears to have little interest in reining in cable operators, since Michael Powell, who chairs the agency, insists that rising prices are not a consumer problem.

Mark Cooper, Consumers Union

I. Cable

Television, from the start, has always been addictive. And there's nothing easier than stealing from an addict. To the cable industry, you are not a customer. You are an "average revenue per user," or ARPU. Understand that, and you will understand why this group of companies does everything it can to sign you up for the most basic service and get that coaxial cable churning. Then, it's all about squeezing more and more out of your wallet, enrolling you in more services, and making you a bigger and better ARPU.

To that end, cable is king . . . of misleading come-ons. For example, I challenge any reader who picks up an ad for a cable-service bundle to find the real price. Take Comcast's Triple Play, an attractive bundling of TV, Net access, and telephone service rolled up with a tidy price tag—often $99. But how big were buyers' monthly checks to pay their bills? And how much was the price six or twelve months later? Here's a typical consumer experience:

> I have a Comcast service plan for cable/Internet/phone package that totals $120.93/month. I received a call from a Comcast representative indicating that my promotional period has ended for the bundled

package and my rate will go up to nearly $148.00/month. First, when I decided to go with the bundle package of service, Comcast did not tell me this was a promotional rate. I specifically asked the sales representative if the prices would go up on the bundle as it had with cable and the representative said it would not. But here now a year later it is going up 23 percent and there's no alternative broadband cable available in Attleboro to contact for a competitive service.

That come-on price didn't last long. In fact, it doesn't make it to the first bill, which can be 20 percent higher than the ad, thanks to taxes and fees. Worse yet, the base price was a teaser rate. It was advertised even lower than $99 in some areas, such as Seattle, where the customers could sign up for as low as $85 each month. But on mailers sent to Seattle-area residents in 2007, the introductory period was not defined. When did it end? Whenever Comcast called. And despite the abundant small print on postcards sent to Seattle-area TV watchers—which numbered 300 words or more—the real price of the service never appeared once.

There's only one term for this: legal false advertising. And if you think small print on cable advertisements is bad, advertisements targeting Hispanics can be even worse. There are full-page cable advertisements in Hispanic publications where the large print is in Spanish, but small print is in English. Of course, I can read English and the Comcast small print didn't make much sense to me, so maybe the language barrier is the least of our worries.

The bottom line: their bottom line. If you're wondering how your average cable bill (their ARPU) soared from around $22 a decade ago to $60 in 2006, look no further than legal false advertising and small print.

Don't just take my word for it. Here's how the Massachusetts state attorney general described Comcast's advertisements in a 2006 out-of-court settlement between the company and the agency.

Comcast, and its predecessor, AT&T Broadband, engaged in a series of unfair practices in the advertising and sale of its cable-television services, including advertising limited-time offers of free or reduced-rate digital-cable packages without adequately disclosing to consumers what the actual price of those services would be during and after the promotional period.

The attorney general also accused Comcast of "hiding material terms and conditions from consumers in difficult-to-read fine print, in violation of the attorney general's advertising regulations."

The hits don't stop there. Here's a few other Comcast ARPU-enhancing tactics, pulled from the attorney general's memo:

- Promoting Comcast's higher-priced digital packages, like its "Digital Gold" video programming, without disclosing to consumers that they could purchase less expensive digital cable packages.
- Overstating the number of channels available on digital-cable packages by failing to distinguish among video, music, and pay-per-view channels, and overstating the capabilities or benefits of Comcast's "On-Demand" and "Digital Video Recorder" services.
- Charging a $5 monthly rental fee for a converter box and remote control, even for consumers who did not need the converter box and remote to get their programming.
- Advertising "free" installation, but then charging consumers for installation and requiring them to redeem coupons or vouchers to receive an installation credit. In some cases consumers were unable to receive the "free" installation as advertised.

There's no need to pick on Comcast, however. Time Warner Cable had a similar run-in with then New York attorney general Eliot Spitzer just a year earlier. Spitzer's office found that Time Warner offered three-month teaser rates to consumers without disclosing that they had to keep the service for twelve months to get that price.

In another instance, the company offered "free Digital Cable TV and free HBO for one year." But there was a Gotcha. Consumers received free HBO, and free digital equipment, but still had to pay extra for monthly digital access. And in another case that might sound familiar to many subscribers, Spitzer's office found consumers who signed up for a "$24.95 for four months" special who were actually charged higher prices during those four months. Finally, Road Runner Internet broadband customers who signed up for a promotional discounted Internet service later found out they had to also order cable TV from Time Warner—or else the Internet discount was forfeited. Such bundling is great for ARPU, but bad when a state attorney general notices.

CABLE'S HUMBLE BEGINNINGS

The first cable-television subscriptions cost about $3 a month. Cable's unceremonious invention is often credited to engineer Ed Parsons, who in 1948 rigged up a crafty community antenna and married it with long cables to bring television to his home in remote Astoria, Washington. Parsons simply wanted to let his wife watch the new Seattle TV station, which had gone on the air a few months earlier. At the time, no one could have imagined he was inventing a multi-billion-dollar industry that would become a king of sneaky fees. In fact, cable came simply because the Parsonses, and millions of other Americans, didn't live close enough to broadcast stations to receive a signal. CATV, the most familiar abbreviation for cable, actually stands for community antenna television, and literally means sharing access to a superpowered antenna. Parsons discovered an area where signal strength was particularly strong, atop a nearby downtown hotel, erected an antenna, and then strung wire—coaxial cable—to his apartment across the street.

The addictive power of cable was clear from the start. As Parsons tells the story, from the moment he flicked the switch on cable TV in his apartment on Thanksgiving Day, 1948, he said the couple "literally lost our home."

"People would drive for hundreds of miles to see television. We had gotten considerable publicity. . . . And when people drove down from Portland or came from The Dalles or from Klamath Falls to see television, you couldn't tell them no."

To get the crowds out of the way, Parsons strung a similar cable into a nearby hotel lobby and turned on a TV there. Soon, he had to shut the service off because the lobby was so full of visitors that guests couldn't check in to the hotel.

Parsons turned his hobby into a business, stringing wire to area homes for $125 and charging $3 a month. The price seems quaint now, but even in the early 1990s, when cable prices were controlled by regulatory agencies, decent plans could be had for $20. An activist Federal Communications Commission regularly kept cable companies in line, resolving 18,000 complaints involving 5,700 communities, ordering $100 million in consumer refunds to 40 million cable subscribers from 1993 to 1998.

Then, quite suddenly, cable prices exploded—rising at three times the rate of inflation in the next five years. What happened? The sweeping Telecommunications Act of 1996 deregulated cable rates, effectively killing the FCC's ability to act as a price watchdog. The deregulation took effect in 1998. The ARPU race was on. You lost.

And what are you getting for this pricey service? Cable television consistently ranks near the bottom of most customer-satisfaction surveys. In 2002, the American Customer Satisfaction Index found that cable companies "now rank among the worst rated businesses in . . . history." The Ponemon Gotcha sneaky-fee survey is no exception. Cable firms were essentially tied for the bottom with credit-card companies as purveyors of hidden fees.

And yet, despite skyrocketing prices and widespread dissatisfaction, two-thirds of Americans subscribe to cable, clear evidence that real market forces are not at work in the world of cable television. There is the occasional discomfort of competition from satellite television or new fiber-optic TV delivery services, but cable firms still enjoy sizable monopoly power in many places. And that's how they get away with so much. They know most of us would still crowd into Ed Parsons's living room to watch if we had to.

TEASER RATES

The single biggest problem facing cable consumers is the fact that cable companies have learned far too much from credit-card companies. Introductory price "teaser" offers, with their fleeting discounts and unpredictable bottom lines, are the bane of cable-TV watchers. Consumers who are enticed by $50 or $100 teaser prices can easily end up writing checks for twice that amount by the time the real rate kicks in and the digital video recorder starts piling up episodes of *Lost*.

The only way to avoid bottom-line shock is to ask the right questions—repeatedly—when you sign up. What will my bill be six months from now? One year from now? Never sign on the dotted line until you get a solid answer to those questions, preferably in writing.

Some consumers endeavor to play the teaser-rate game with cable firms. If you are the type of person who stays up on your bills, you can try this, too. Some people call this the "Just Ask" strategy, and it's amazing how few customers actually try it.

Sign up for a low rate, and then call and cancel just as the teaser rate is about to expire. Or if the higher price has already kicked in, call and ask for the low advertised price offered in a newspaper ad or flyer. Ignore the line that says, "for new customers only."

Key to the success of this conversation is that you've got to be willing to drop your cable service. You must convince the cable-firm operator that you are a customer who deserves special "retention" treatment. Obviously, this strategy works best when you are in an area where there is genuine competition for your business. If you can call and say, "I'm thinking of going with another cable firm because they are offering this price," and you are telling the truth, the odds are good you'll get a better deal. Ditto if you have done your homework and can drop into conversation the possibility that you are going to have a little dish installed on your roof if the cable doesn't cough up a better price.

Bluffing might work, but it might not. And remember, you might have a term commitment and face early termination penalties if you do switch. Never sign up without fully understanding the cancellation terms. And of course, if you play this game, you've got to keep playing it, because every six months or so, the lower rate will expire, and you'll have to start over again.

One advocate of the "Just Ask" strategy is Jeffrey Strain, a freelance personal finance writer who contributes to a fabulous pennypincher blog at pfadvice.com. Here's how he used "Just Ask" to save his mom 50 percent off her cable bill:

I don't know why people don't like to call the different companies that give them services to try and get a better price, but there are a lot of people out there. My mom is one of them. I wrote last September that we shaved my mom's cable bill from $65 to $39.95 a month last September. After doing so, I specifically told her that she needed to call back every three months to get a better rate, which she promptly failed to do. Even worse, she decided to upgrade her account to a silver level to get some of the premium movie channels and I found she was paying $79.20 a month for cable.

That was ridiculous when there were other competing firms offering a free month and $29.95 a month after that for similar service. So I gave a call to the cable company today to see if we could get a better deal for her. I simply called like I always had done in the past and went directly to the cancel-service option.

I explained I had a better deal from one of their competitors (they asked which offer and I gave the company name and the offer), but really didn't want to go through all the hassle of changing if they could give me a similar deal. While they didn't match the deal, they did drop the rates significantly over what she had been paying.

They actually came back with a number of different options and I ended up taking the one that offered the exact same service (including the premium channels my mom likes) for $39.95 a month rather than the $79.20, which is good for 6 months—that's nearly a 50 percent savings a month and a total savings of $235.50 over the 6 months of the offer. Certainly not bad for a fifteen-minute phone call.

PACKAGE PROBLEMS

Strain's story hints at the second-biggest problem facing cable consumers—confusion over cable-TV package pricing. Remember
ARPU? Even if you sign up for the lowest level of service, and make
it clear that all you really watch is ESPN and an occasional rerun of
Seinfeld, the cable firm will pitch you on expensive movie channel
packages until the end of time. And many times, they will sign you
up for these packages against your will. Watching the cable bill for
phantom upgrades is a must. Those who move or add a digital service should be particularly on the lookout for surprise additional
channels. Or the addition of digital services that aren't used. Or
monkeying with channel lineups in a way that forces subscribers to
get bundles or HD service that's not really necessary.

Also essential: the "just say no" strategy when the pitches come,
even if they sound like "free" offers. According to Nielsen Media Research, the twenty-most-popular channels account for roughly
three-quarters of all viewing. Do you really need two hundred channels? When you get the occasional hankering to lose an entire
evening to home-improvement television, say, once every couple of
months, check in to an expensive hotel. It'll be cheaper than upgrading. If you do upgrade in a moment of weakness, watch for unmen-
tioned one-time paperwork fees (ask that they be waived).

The long-term solution to the package problem is à la carte programming, something cable firms have been avoiding like the plague
for a decade. Some in Congress, including Senator John McCain,
have long argued that consumers should be able to cherry-pick the
channels they receive—and pay for—when subscribing to cable.
The aforementioned sports couch potato should be able to buy
ESPN, the *Seinfeld* channel and nothing else. A la carte would allow
more consumer choice, the argument holds. Cable firms say it
would actually result in less choice, as no one would pay to see most
of the goofy channels cable offers, and they would quickly disappear.
Never fear: The debate will rage on for another decade or so while

cable firms research ways to make à la carte so expensive and difficult that no one would be able to use it anyway.

If you live in an area where over-the-air reception is impossible,
and you really want to watch only local channels, don't believe your
cable company when it says the cheapest plan is around $50. A very
basic plan with only a few channels must be made available for a
nominal price, which is often regulated by your local government.
It's called a "basic services tier," and it must include local broadcast
channels as well as public television. It shouldn't cost more than
$20. It also won't include ESPN.

INSTALLATION, RETURNS, OUTAGE CREDITS

Waiting for the cable guy is an American rite of passage, like getting
your wisdom teeth pulled or taking the driver's test. Other than the
hidden cost of a vacation day (or two) spent waiting for the cable
guy, installation is generally advertised as a free service. But increasingly, it's not really free. Digital-cable installations and HDTV
hookups can be tricky, and when done incorrectly, the results can
leave you worse off than rabbit ears. Repeat visits by technicians can
be costly. So are awkward installations or extra wall jacks. Sometimes free installation credits mysteriously disappear, while unnecessary digital set-top boxes, at $5 a month, magically appear.

If you cancel the service or return the box, make sure you get
credit for the returned hardware. As is often the case, billing computers are much better at applying charges than granting credits, so
you'll have to make sure you get yours. Returned-but-lost cable-
converter boxes are also common, as there seems to be a black hole
that specifically targets the hardware. Make sure you get a receipt
when you return the cable box. And be forewarned: When you cancel cable and return the box, you may have to surrender another vacation day waiting for the cable guy to come pick it up.

As long as we're discussing credits, keep track of the inevitable days
when your cable service doesn't work. You are entitled to a billing
credit for those days, but you have to request it. Even if it's only $2,
make sure to get what's coming to you. You know the cable firm would.

THE COMPLAINT TREE

However bleak the atmosphere for cable customers may sound, there is good news. Despite the blundering deregulation of the industry in the late 1990s, cable consumers actually have remarkable tools for recourse if (really, *when*) they hit impossible roadblocks. Cable consumers can literally march down to their local city hall with complaints, and actually hold out hope for recourse. In a relic of local governing that is far too scarce in other industries, cable firms really do have to answer to local authorities over issues like billing problems. Local accountability, however clunky, is a blessing for spurned consumers.

Every consumer falls under a local "cable franchising authority" that regulates the cable firm you do business with. The name of your local franchising authority should be on the front of your cable bill. Cities or municipalities are required to oversee local cable companies and enforce federal regulations governing the following areas:

- Rates and fees for equipment, installation, and repairs related to basic service.
- Problems arising from billing disputes, office hours, telephone availability of personnel, installations, signal quality, outages, and service calls. Many cities have a specific "Office of Cable Communications" or staff specifically assigned to deal with cable complaints.

Several large cities have also enacted a Cable Consumer Bill of Rights, which establishes levels and quality of service that local cable companies are required to meet.

Very curious consumers are also entitled to see various public documents that must be maintained and made available to the public. Most of them are make-work paperwork, but for the litigiously inclined, they provide great fodder for formal complaints. These documents include a political programming file, sponsorship identification, employment reports, commercial records for children's programming, leased access requirements, proof-of-performance tests, and signal leakage and repair logs. These are available for public inspection and copying. In addition, firms must make available a current copy of Part 76 of the FCC's rules, which covers cable television.

But not everything is covered by a local governing board. For issues regarding home wiring, equipment compatibility, or a bad picture—or if attempts to resolve other problems fail—consumers must contact the Federal Communications Commission at: Cable Services Bureau/Consumer Protection and Competition Division/ 445 12th Street, S.W., Washington, D.C. 20554/(888) 225-5322.

And if you are inclined to take on those misleading advertisements? As always, advertising complaints can also be brought to the attention of the consumer affairs office of your state attorney general, or to the Federal Trade Commission.

II. Satellite

The true antidote to all this unfair and misleading behavior is competition. If consumers could easily pick from among a half-dozen cable providers, no one firm could get away with misleading pricing structures or advertisements. In the early part of this decade, some urban areas did see limited competition, with a second and even sometimes a third wire-based television service provider entering the market. Of course, giant cable monopolists had no intention of giving up the corner they had on the market, and acted accordingly. There's no need to fight over the wire when it's even more effective to monopolize the programs viewers can watch.

In New York City, for example, Cablevision obtained control of seven of the nine professional sports teams and denied a cable competitor named RCN access to the games—even games Cablevision wasn't broadcasting. Many New Yorkers were left with no option to watch their sports teams. There was an exception, however: RCN could pay for the rights to transmit the games in parts of nearby New Jersey where Cablevision wasn't the dominant cable provider.

In such an anticompetitive atmosphere, regulation is essential, because any firm unchecked by competitors will run amok. So why did the FCC abdicate its ability to regulate cable prices in the late 1990s? In part because of the myth of competition from mini satellite dishes.

Despite all the whining and moaning about direct-broadcast satellite firms, they are cable's best friend when the subject of competition arises. The presence of the dish alternative seems to fend off government regulators every time.

In some areas, there is true competition. Plenty of people do pick the dish over the wire. But it's not a fair fight. For example, about 30 percent of the U.S. population lives in multifamily units, like apartment buildings, where dishes are difficult if not impossible to install. That's one reason that cable customers still outnumber dish customers about two to one, and perhaps a reason why dish competition just isn't quite the same as true wire-based TV competition. Congress's Government Accountability Office found that cable prices are about 17 percent lower in the few areas where consumers can pick from among multiple cable providers than in areas where consumers can only pick between cable and dish.

Making matters worse, the dish hasn't turned out to be quite the competition the FCC envisioned. In addition to the technical hurdles, dish services have misbehaved in ways that made them seem not much different from the cable firms they seek to replace.

The trouble can begin on day one—installation. DIRECTV hookups are trickier than cable. They involve pricey new extra boxes, often a trip to the roof, and perhaps new telephone jacks. Telephone lines are not necessary to use dish services, but technicians who install them are trained to talk consumers into installing phone-line connections anyway. They're told to be as convincing as possible— even if that means lying, according to a former DIRECTV installer.

"Tell the customer whatever you have to tell them," technician Frank Martinez said to a Florida television station in 2006, explaining his training. "Tell them if these phone lines are not connected, the receiver will blow up."

Technicians who aren't convincing enough with their pitch are deducted $5 for every installation that doesn't include a telephone hookup, Martinez said. Why? Consumers can be charged about $50 for each new phone jack, and DIRECTV can use the line to get additional data about its consumers, he said.

Installation surprises are only one element of the DIRECTV story, however. Precisely what programs consumers can watch varies from zip code to zip code. That makes accurate channel lineup advertising a challenge for the firm ("Now! Local news. Well, maybe . . ."). But from 2003 to 2005, inaccuracy didn't seem to bother DIRECTV much.

Do any of these ring a bell?

- Consumers who couldn't get a solid DIRECTV signal couldn't escape long-term contracts. Contract terms were spelled out in unreadable fine print.
- Viewers who signed up believing they would get local channels never received them.
- Sports fans were confused by expensive sports packages and which local games would be blacked out.

Twenty-two states sued DIRECTV for these alleged tactics in 2005. Without admitting any guilt, DIRECTV agreed to refund thousands of consumers who claimed such misbehavior and to pay a $5 million settlement fee to the states in December 2005.

That same week, DIRECTV agreed to pay $5 million to the Federal Trade Commission for violating the Do Not Call list—at the time, the largest Do Not Call penalty ever. The FTC alleged that contractors for DIRECTV repeatedly ignored consumers' wishes that they not be called at home.

So DIRECTV is certainly not the hoped-for angelic savior from cable firms' misleading ways. What about DIRECTV's smaller competitor, the Dish Network, run by EchoStar Communications Corporation?

In 2003, it paid a $5 million penalty to settle charges that it misled customers with advertising in thirteen states. Consumers were surprised by a $240 early-termination penalty they had to pay when they canceled their service. EchoStar also created a cleverly named "free-to-pay" fee, which was charged to consumers who had the audacity to drop services after a free trial period.

When the choice is either pay to keep the service, or pay to cancel the service, it really can't be called a free trial, the states' attorneys general argued.

Third-party contractors—both for sales pitches and for installation services—are a big part of the dish problem. Aggressive resellers will say nearly anything to sign up customers, and can give the satellite providers cover for unethical practices ("We didn't do it, they did."). Fortunately, government agencies don't always buy that excuse: The Federal Trade Commission rejected the reseller defense in the Do Not Call case. But these rulings haven't stopped third-party firms from trying. As satellite-TV services transform into the far more profitable HDTV age, and cable firms dive into the digital-cable age, consumer choices get only more confusing.

DISH ADVICE

To avoid dish-TV traps, your best bet is to avoid long-term contracts. Pay extra for the hardware up front if you have to; maintaining your consumer choice is incredibly important in an age where services are changing so rapidly. What if your favorite sports team disappears from your service? You don't want to be locked in. What if a large building is built next door, ruining your signal? You'll want to be a free agent.

Another thing to watch out for—fees for extra televisions you don't have. Remember the usual rule: Just say no to everything. That was a hard lesson learned by this consumer:

> Under duress, I subscribed to DIRECTV a few months ago. The installer they sent out struck me as shady for several reasons, but the kicker was when he insisted that I keep the "free" additional receiver that his work order said I ordered for my bedroom. My bedroom has no television.

Mostly just wanting the sketchy character out of my house, I let them leave the box there. Sure enough, my first statement listed a $5.99 fee for the second hookup.

Direct-broadcast satellite customers don't have anything like the local cable-franchising authority that hears cable complaints. Dish complaints must go right to the FCC, which often isn't effective. A call to your local attorney general's consumer complaint office is a better bet. For you real fire-in-the-belly types who live in a state that's already sued a dish company, a great strategy is to find the assistant attorney general who worked on the case and attempt to contact him or her directly. Nothing gets a quicker response from a company than a call from a lawyer who's already beaten them.

Pay TV
GOTCHA-STOPPING STRATEGIES

CABLE

1. Play the teaser-rate game, or the "just ask" game; when a low rate expires, threaten to quit and get "retention" treatment.
2. Watch for phantom upgrades.
3. Just say no to upgrades, and upgrade fees.
4. Get to know your mayor, and don't be shy about complaining to the local cable-franchising authority listed on your bill.

SATELLITE

1. Avoid long-term contracts like the plague.
2. Don't pay for extra TVs you don't have.
3. Get the name of someone in the attorney general's office who worked on a prior lawsuit against your dish firm.
4. Stay aware of competitors' deals. Threaten to jump ship if you see a better deal and ask your provider to match it.

5. Thanks to DIRECTV's settlement with state attorneys general in 2005, many consumers have sixty days to return equipment if there's a problem with signal strength or reception—at no cost to the consumer. To exercise this right, you must complain directly to DIRECTV within sixty days.

PAY TV IN GENERAL

1. Before upgrading to HD service, make sure the channels you watch are available in HD broadcasts. Otherwise, your picture can actually be worse than with an old analog television.

2. Make sure the sports events you want to watch are available on your system by asking friends. Availability can vary by neighborhood.

Internet Access

It was supposed to be a small gift from the federal government to Internet users. On August 14, 2006, a $2 to $3 per month government tax on DSL broadband service, known as the Universal Service Fund fee or FUSF, was dropped. The tiny savings was meant to put DSL providers on equal footing with cable-modem service providers, which weren't obligated to collect the FUSF tax. But the consumer victory was short-lived.

Verizon saw an opportunity.

The company's Department of Creative Fees with Obtuse Names went to work and quickly emerged with a doozy. The Universal Service Fund would be dropped from August 2006 bills, but in its place would appear a new line item: "Supplier Surcharge." Verizon's fast DSL users had been paying $2.83 for the universal service tax; now they would pay $2.70 in a Supplier Surcharge. But rather than pass the surcharge on to the government, Verizon would simply pocket it. Given fast DSL's price tag of around $30, the tax-for-fee switcheroo instantly gave Verizon about a 10 percent price hike. What business wouldn't relish a chance to pump up revenue 10 percent cloaked in such a perfect ruse? Consumers, the firm hoped, wouldn't notice the change as their bottom-line price wouldn't change. In fact, they might presume the surcharge was the old tax with a new name.

In a cozy-sounding e-mail, Verizon tried to tell its customers they would hardly notice the sneaky price increase.

"On balance your total bill will remain about the same as it has been or slightly lower," it read.

Naturally, competitors immediately copied the brilliant idea. That same month, BellSouth revealed it would continue to collect its $2.97 a month FUSF fee, and just pocket the money. Its euphemism was perhaps even more misleading: "Regulatory Cost Recovery Fee."

A smaller Internet-service provider named Speakeasy jumped on the fee plan, too. Here's how the managing editor of online journal isp-planet.com described the August 2006 below-the-fee-line part of his bill, sans FUSF.

OLD

Federal Regulatory Fee	$6.00
DSL Reg. Compliance Fee	$5.12
VoIP Reg. Compliance Fee	$4.95

NEW

Federal Regulatory Fee	$0.00 ($6.00 decrease)
DSL Reg. Compliance Fee	$9.52 ($4.40 increase)
VoIP Reg. Compliance Fee	$6.20 ($1.25 increase)
Total	**$0.35 decrease**

A universal service fund fee by any other name smells just as bad. But in this case, none of them got away with it. Careful bill readers jumped all over Verizon, BellSouth, and Speakeasy, and began an Internet call-to-action. Journalists jumped on the story. The FCC threatened to investigate. All the phantom FUSF fees were eliminated.

Competition keeps service providers honest, and keeps prices low. As we've seen in pay television and the world of contract-strapped cell phones, lack of competition hurts consumers. By comparison, the world of Internet access is awash in competition. There are multiple platforms for high-speed access (DSL, cable, wireless, etc.), and often multiple players within each. Many urbanites have the option to pit DSL against cable-modem service. Satellite and wireless broadband options fill out the competitive landscape. And while it's slow, the myriad of dial-up options remaining provide competition of some sort for virtually every Internet user. Who benefits? Consumers and the economy.

There's only one way for sneaky companies to beat back honest competition: sneaky fees. By breaking out items such as "Regulatory Compliance," DSL providers can hike prices without having to raise their advertised prices. Those $19.95-per-month marketing campaigns don't have to be scrapped. Companies wishing to pump up their bottom lines can just raise the fees instead.

In the world of sneaky-fee pricing, consumers never know what they are really paying for a service. It makes an apples-to-apples comparison of DSL and cable-modem service nearly impossible. For example: For most consumers, it's impossible to get DSL without paying for an active phone line, which costs about $20 a month. Phone-line-less DSL, called naked DSL, has been mandated by federal regulators, and will arrive someday, but for most consumers a $19.95 DSL offer really translates into a monthly bill that's closer to $50. That makes it, sadly, essentially the same price as its chief alternative, cable modems.

Who benefits? The sneaky company.

SNEAKIEST FEE OF ALL: BROADBAND THAT'S REALLY DIAL-UP IN DISGUISE

When is broadband not broadband?

Today's Internet is a technological marvel. And yet, a few decades from now, historians will look back on our quaint time the way we look back on Edsels and Model Ts. They'll laugh and say things like, "How did people put up with those slow connections? Why did people watch videos in those tiny boxes?" Despite today's high-speed wizardry, getting fast Internet access is part science and part art. And many people still pay exorbitant amounts of money for very poor, very unreliable service.

We all know that automakers exaggerate—a little—when advertising a car's estimated miles per gallon. That 45 mpg gas-sipper will probably get around 30 to 35 for normal drivers in real life. We all accept this. It's not right, but at least it's not *that* wrong. And everyone pretty much exaggerates by the same factor, so consumers can engage in something like apples-to-apples comparisons.

But imagine if that new car with the 45 mpg sticker really got 2 miles to the gallon? That's how things sometimes work in broadband.

As I type this chapter, I'm connected to a broadband service that promises 400 to 700 kilobytes per second. That's blazing fast—enough to handle full-streaming video with plenty of room to spare for sending e-mail. So why does it sometimes take several seconds for me to load Google, the world's tiniest home page?

The reason: My actual download speed, according to tests freely available on the Internet, is about 29 kilobytes per second. If that sounds eerily like an old modem speed, well, that's because it is.

My story is typical. The broadband marketplace is crazy. DSL users find their bandwidth disappearing. Cable-modem users fight traffic jams on the way home only to get stuck in virtual traffic jams with their neighbors when they log in, since they are all essentially sharing the same Internet pipe. When it rains, satellite broadband users get bogged down. And anyone who's ever asked "Can you hear me now?" can guess how reliable broadband-wireless connections are.

That's not to say consumers can't find happiness with DSL or cable modems. Both are still faster—much faster—than dial-up. In fact, they are generally at least five to ten times faster than dial-up, for only two or three times the cost. That's actually a pretty fair upgrade. But how are consumers supposed to pick the best service when the information is so irregular, and the broadband "mpg" they'll get is so unpredictable? More important, how are people to know if the $50-a-month service they purchased, and committed to with a long-term contract, has been pulled out from under them?

Anyone who pays for broadband should perform regular, independent speed tests on their connection. Numerous websites, like the technology news site CNET.com, lists free bandwidth test sites. Speakeasy.net offers the easiest to use. I like the site TestMyNet .net, which actually stores your test results for reference. A documented archive of poor speed scores might prove useful if you end up in a battle with your provider and must ask for a refund.

But even if you don't find yourself in a fight, taking a speed test is the only way to know if you are getting what you paid for. If the speeds are regularly disappointing, and far below what you've been promised, you should complain.

Broadband providers will cry foul when you run such a test. They'll tell you that you misunderstand. They'll have an explanation. It's not the pipe they're supplying to your home. The fault lies with your computer, your applications, spyware, the phase of the moon, Microsoft Office, or your teenager, they'll say. Each of these explanations are plausible (well, except the one about the moon). Many, many factors can impact your upload and download speeds. Just as many, many factors can impact how fast your toilet flushes. But clogged pipes are often to blame, and for bandwidth providers, too many users and too-narrow pipes often cause the problem.

Since there is no way to know the true size of the Internet pipe into your neighborhood, your safest way to select a service is to find a nearby neighbor you trust, who's happy with their service, and try it out yourself for a few minutes. Then, when you sign up with the service, take the shortest contract commitment you can, and ask what happens if you just can't get the download speeds the service has promised you—now, or in the future.

DSL

When Verizon started the broadband price war with its introductory $14.95 DSL offer in 2003, it changed the broadband Internet-access market forever. Other DSL providers were forced to join in the price war, and so were other broadband providers. Soon after, broadband customers outnumbered dial-up customers. The competitive pricing was a boon to customers, and today, there are many happy DSL users.

But consumers who signed up for the $14.95 deal found there was no way to get broadband access for $14.95, or anything even close to that price. We've already mentioned the tack-on price of the phone line, which more than doubles the price consumers have to pay in order to get DSL—since it's generally not possible to get DSL without a landline. Then there was a sign-up fee/activation charge, which was sometimes waived. There was also an equipment charge, though many versions of the promotion also included a free DSL modem.

Those same tactics continue, even though the price point of Verizon's DSL sign-up offer changes. Consumers shouldn't pay more than a few bucks for a DSL modem. You will have no trouble buying one on Craigslist for a pittance, and a family member almost certainly has one they're not using now. Most important: There is no need to rent a DSL modem or a wireless router from a telco. These things are cheap and identical. Buy them somewhere else.

Many advertised discounts also require consumers to sign up over the Internet. Calling in an order and talking to a human costs extra. That seems OK, until you try to order online and the website craps out, or simply instructs you to finish your order by calling customer service. During one promotion in Washington, D.C., the online price quoted by Verizon was $14.95 a month including a free modem, but the call-in-an-order price was $20 a month with a $30 modem fee. After being forced by the website to call in the order, one consumer who called was told, "What $14.95 price? And there is no free modem . . ."

Even if you call, always ask for the Web price anyway. Like many companies, Verizon has a standing "Don't offer, but honor" policy when it comes to Web discounts. Make them honor it.

The biggest hidden DSL fee of all is the arrival of long-term contracts combined with price escalation. Low-priced DSL requires a twelve-month commitment, and early termination can cost $100. And at the end of your introductory term, the price can double!

That might not sound like such an awful thing, until you browse through thousands of posts on the Internet from frustrated DSL users who suddenly find the service has gone from blazing fast to slower than dial-up overnight. Getting out of a failing DSL service can be maddening and pricey. Of course, frustrated consumers are often given the chance to upgrade to faster DSL for about twice the price—a trap that's easy to fall for. After all, it's easier to just pay more than switch to cable or satellite, wait at home for another installer, and so on.

But notice what's happened: You've been acquired as a customer by that rock-bottom price. You probably picked DSL because it was cheaper than cable. Suddenly, you're paying cable-modem prices after all.

Getting reliable DSL speeds is a tricky affair. There are too many technology factors involved for the company to promise you you'll get a certain speed and certain service. If you must sign a contract, get the shortest term you can, knowing your service may eventually degrade, and a better service is likely to come along.

And if, after calling tech support a couple of times, your DSL is still crawling, ask for the cancellation fee to be waived. The telco shouldn't charge you to get out of a contract it isn't honoring. Why should you have to pay to stop using a service you can't use?

If your DSL firm isn't playing ball, you have the option of calling your local utilities commission, which has regulatory power over the telephone firm that supplies it. A formal complaint may get their attention. The local utility doesn't directly regulate the DSL service, but it does have power over the telco's other local services, so you might get its attention that way. Otherwise, you'll have to complain to the FCC, which regulates DSL.

CABLE-MODEM SERVICE

Little needs to be said about frustrations waiting for the cable guy. The same rules apply to the cable-modem guy. Waiting around all day for installation is a drag, and probably will cost you a day's vacation. It can also cost $100 or so, unless you catch the occasional free-installation deals. But if you do, make sure free really means free. Where are your TV cable boxes? Will they work for your computer setup? Additional wall jacks will likely cost extra and, thanks to wireless routers, often aren't necessary. Don't be talked into installation of wall jacks you don't need.

Cable modems also cost extra. You can rent them from your provider, which is generally a bad idea. Since all cable modems are created equal, buying one from a retail store will put you back in the driver's seat as a consumer and get you what you need for around $50. Used boxes are even cheaper. Buying a modem will allow you to evade a recurring monthly cost ($3 to $10 a month) that will eventually far outpace the up-front cost. Your cable Internet provider may offer you the chance to buy the modem, which isn't a bad idea, as long as you know that's what you're getting and how much you're paying. Even if you do rent, you may be forced to leave a pricey $50 deposit, so you might as well buy one.

And if you rent hardware from the company, you may regret that choice when the time comes to break off the relationship. Many consumers find returning a rented cable modem is actually a barrier to switching services, and others report frustrating episodes where the cable-service provider doesn't credit consumers with returning modems and spends months sending phantom bills. If you do rent the modem, make sure you get a receipt when you give it back. At a bare minimum, you may have to wait another day at home for the cable guy when you return the modem. Bottom line, you're better off keeping this transaction separate from your monthly cable bill.

All that goes double for wireless routers; buy your own. They are easy enough to install.

If you are ordering a package that includes television and broadband cable Internet, the price of the boxes can get very complicated. You'll need a cable TV box for each TV, you may or may not need a digital box or digital video recorder box for each TV, and you'll need a cable modem. Make sure the hardware fees are spelled out in writing.

Outside of the aforementioned bandwidth-sharing problems, which can lead to download slowdowns at busy times, cable Internet is subject to the same kind of frustrating outages as old-fashioned television. Getting refunds for service outages requires dogged determination.

There is a shining light in the world of cable modems. Long-term contracts are much less common than among DSL providers. That's probably because consumers generally report faster speeds than DSL, meaning consumers are less likely to leave, and so perhaps providers feel less compulsion to entrap consumers.

Or perhaps they've just found another way.

In order to simulate the low price-point offers from DSL firms (about $20 a month and a free modem), Comcast and other cable providers have created a contrived rebate system. Consumers must pay for their modems, and pay regular service prices, up front. After a couple of months, they must remember to fill out separate rebate forms for the modem, and for a $100 credit. It takes another three months or so to process those rebates. And often they aren't really rebates; they are credits against future bills.

Gotcha! It's a brilliant entrapment, since obviously consumers can't really quit the service while waiting for the rebate credits.

All that makes Comcast's "almost as cheap as DSL" offer not quite as good as it looks. Let's examine one such offer, listed in early 2007 on Comcastoffers.com, a Comcast affiliate reseller.

There's the big number, $19.95 per month. Then a bit smaller, these enticements: "Plus free modem, and $125 cash back." Now, on to the asterisks.

"After promotional period, regular monthly service charges of $42.95 and equipment charges (if applicable) will apply." (Translation: The price more than doubles, and soon.)

"Free modem . . . $79.95 mail-in rebate offer is a combination of $49.95 mail-in rebate from Broadbandoffers.com and a $30 mail-in product rebate and is only valid with purchase of new Comcast High-Speed Internet residential service and a Motorola® Cable Modem." (Translation: The free modem costs $80 and requires two separate rebates: And, oh, shipping costs $9, fairly close to the real price of the modem.)

"Please allow 10 to 16 weeks after completed qualifying activity to receive $125 rebate check." (Translation: No one knows when your cash will come.)

The standard rebate advice applies here. If the price sans rebate still sounds good to you, go ahead and sign up, and think of the rebate as icing on the cake. Know that you have just acquired exactly the kind of chase-down-the-paperwork headache you've spent a lot of your life trying to avoid. And make sure you really believe that it's a good deal even if the check, or the credit, is perpetually lost in the mail.

WIRELESS BROADBAND

One of the more exciting developments in Internet access is the arrival of genuine wireless, cellular-based broadband access. Put simply, it's like Wi-Fi everywhere. It's pricey, but not much more expensive than a subscription to that Starbucks T-Mobile Wi-Fi service (which, by the way, is exorbitantly expensive unless you agree to a one-year contract with a $200 early-termination fee). And contrary to popular belief, there really isn't a Starbucks everywhere.

Wireless is a fast-moving world, however. As companies like Verizon and Sprint build out their vast high-speed networks, they would like nothing more than to have you pay for the investment. A fairly-enough-priced $80-a-month service from Verizon or Sprint generally requires a two-year commitment. Perhaps $80 sounds like a decent price. But a $2,000 investment? That's another matter. That's what these two companies are asking consumers to pay them—$1,920 over two years. Now there's a number you'll never see in any marketing materials!

Of course, you can cancel early—but for a $200 fee.

Given how quickly this technology is changing, it's hard to imagine there won't be better, faster services soon. In many places, there are already cheaper alternatives: Wi-Fi as a free or cheap public utility may yet become a reality in places like Albuquerque, New Mexico, New Orleans, Louisiana, and even sections of San Francisco and Washington, D.C. That makes a commitment to a $2,000 wireless service sound like a very big hidden fee.

If you sign up for one of these broadband wireless services, ask if there's a way to avoid that two-year contract and pay month-to-month instead. Wireless firms don't advertise this option, but they do offer it. When free Wi-Fi comes to your block, you'll be glad you held out.

SATELLITE

Satellite broadband has always been, and perhaps will always be, the Net of last resort. Only those who can't get DSL or cable-modem service are forced to use dishes to download. So when you price the service, you'll see what happens when a firm knows its consumers are in such dire straits.

Satellite broadband equipment costs—and start-up costs in general—can be ten times the price of signing up with other broadband access services. Monthly dish fees run about double. Worst of all, the expensive equipment customers have purchased in the past from companies like HughesNet (formerly DirecWay) can become obsolete with system upgrades.

Installation can be simple, or it can be complicated. Tricky roofs that require careful climbs result in $200 extra installation surcharges, or more. You can negotiate with the installer who arrives, often an independent contractor. But if you aren't ready to bargain, you may end up with a small ugly dish right above your front door. Aesthetically pleasing installations are rarely included in the price.

Satellite service is worth the high cost for some users. But those who sign up and are disappointed should know getting a refund for the expensive equipment is much more challenging than returning a DSL modem. And, as per usual, standard-use contracts tie up consumers—in 2006, HughesNet's typical contract was an oddly-long fifteen months. Quitting within thirty days cost a $100 service-termination fee and a $400 hardware-termination fee for a total of $500, though $400 will be refunded in most circumstances. After thirty days, the cancellation fee goes up to $700, with no refunds.

Meanwhile, getting the stuff off the side of your house can cost an extra $100. Signing up for satellite broadband is not for the fainthearted. But then, neither is connecting to the Internet.

Net Access
GOTCHA-STOPPING STRATEGIES

1. Check your bill for taxes that aren't really taxes.
2. Check to make sure you are getting the speed you are paying for.
3. Avoid long-term DSL contracts so you can take advantage of new technologies.
4. Beware of cable-modem rebates, which sometimes aren't rebates at all but are instead future-service credits.
5. Make sure free installation is really free.
6. Refuse two-year wireless broadband commitments.
7. Don't rent DSL or cable-modem equipment.
8. Understand the high cost of quitting satellite broadband before you sign up.

Travel

*Hilton surprises guests with the undisclosed resort fee
only when they arrive at the hotel or at checkout when
it is too late for guests to challenge the fee or obtain
alternative accommodations.*

Lawsuit filed in Los Angeles Superior Court, 2002

Kyle Leung thought he'd gotten a great deal on a Caribbean vacation, scoring a four-night stay at a Wyndham Resorts by bidding for it on the discount-travel auction site priceline.com. As is customary, the New York City resident paid up front.

But when Leung arrived, the good deal went south fast. There was a $15 "Resort Fee" tacked on to the bill. Per night. Per person. It paid for all-you-can-putt mini golf and endless use of hotel treadmills. No matter if Leung had sworn off both. He was sworn to pay. His good deal now cost an extra $120, and Leung had no choice. He'd already paid for the room.

Leung was befuddled by the incident and asked for help from *USA Today*'s *Traveler's Aide* columnist Linda Burbank. He told Burbank that he got a few answers by complaining to his credit-card company, American Express (a smart tactic, because the card firm holds leverage over the resort, as it can refuse to pay the bill). Amex got an explanation of the fee from the resort and broke it down for him—it included an $11 energy surcharge and a $4 housekeeping gratuity, per person, per day. Housekeeping gratuity? I'd never spite a Nassau housekeeper a decent tip, but one has to wonder how much of that money Wyndham really forked over to its cleaning staff. I can only imagine a "housekeeping gratuity collection fee" is deducted first.

The end result: Wyndham Resorts held firm that Leung had to pay the $120 in fake greens fees, but American Express ended up granting him a goodwill credit—no doubt inspired, in part, by *USA Today*'s interest.

Nothing ruins a good time quicker than feeling cheated. When a vacation is interrupted by two-page hotel bills or surcharge-laden car-rental agreements, many travelers look the other way rather than sour the mood. Big mistake. Travelers are among the most vulnerable consumers. Remember, you never want to be the tourist in a transaction. When you're traveling, for business or pleasure, there you are, with a huge neon "T" glowing on your forehead.

The fine art of sneaky fees is a specialty in the travel business. As an industry, it could give banks a run for their money—just on the names alone. Check out this remarkable, albeit partial, list of hidden travel fees (a deep breath would be a good idea right about now):

Hotels: Resort fee. Internet access fee. Maid gratuity fee. Energy surcharge. The "You opened the bottle of water in the room" fee. Parking fee. Telephone fee. Safe fee. The "you touched the bottle of water in the room" fee.

Airlines: Paper ticket fee. Heavy baggage fee. Fuel fee. Meal fee. Miles-rewards booking fee. Miles redeposit fee.

Rental cars: Peak season fee. Concession recovery fee. Facility usage fee. Refueling surcharge. Stadium surcharge. Recoup fees. Consolidated facility charges (CFC). Highway use fee. Vehicle license recoupment fee (VLRF). Frequent-flier miles fee. Tire and battery recovery fee.

Travel Gotchas have become a way of life. Hotels have figured out the best way to lure customers is by back-loading prices. During the 1990s, one hotel chain after another followed suit. Hotel fee revenue tripled from 2003 to 2006, jumping from $550 million to $1.6 billion during the stretch, according to Pricewaterhouse-Coopers. And there's no end to the easy money in sight, despite numerous legal actions that led various courts to declare the tactics misleading.

The aforementioned Wyndham Hotels and Resorts (and parent company LXR Luxury Resorts & Hotels), for example, reached a $2.3 million settlement in 2006 for allegedly unfair "automatic surcharges" levied against Florida state employee travelers after that state's attorney general filed a lawsuit. The state also reached a settlement with Starwood Hotels, which agreed to pay $250,000 after it was accused of tacking on unfair "energy fees." As part of the Wyndham settlement, the firm was told it had to declare the charges up front when it quotes prices to customers. The pact also mandated that third-party Internet-based sellers like Expedia or Orbitz also must include fees in the prices it quotes.

Ah, the Internet. Therein lies the problem.

Overall, the Internet has been a boom for bargain-hunting travelers. The cabal of travel agencies that once controlled access to airline tickets and other travel deals collapsed in the face of open pricing promoted by the various Internet sites like Expedia and Orbitz. Consumers could now shop around for the best price to their heart's content. The onslaught of true competition forced airlines and hotels to lower prices to stay competitive.

But as all prices tended to flatten out to the least common denominator, travel firms decided there was only one thing they could do to rescue profit margins. Lie.

With tack-on fees, travel firms could once again take full advantage of lost tourists. That great price you scored online? It doesn't look so great after $25-dollar-a-day parking charges. And there is this added advantage for travel providers—they keep more of their money when they charge a low come-on price and Gotcha fees. Travel agencies get a cut of the travel they book, often a percentage of sales. Well, tack-on fees aren't included in that cut. Hotels don't have to share any of the resort fees they collect with travel agencies. They are pure profit, after the expense of maintaining the greens on the mini-golf course is deducted, of course.

Let's look more closely at the main travel anti-bargains.

HOTELS

Hotel tack-on fees have little connection to reality. Consider this: In Miles City, Montana, along Interstate 94, discount motel chains compete voraciously for customers pulling off the road for a rest before they head on to Seattle or Fargo. The latest differentiator? Internet access. So the sign hanging across on the Motel 6 just off the exit ramp, in letters fifteen feet high, reads "Free Wi-Fi!" Similar signs dot Miles City's main street.

In contrast, the four-star Fairmont hotel in downtown San Francisco charges $14.95 per day for the same Wi-Fi. There is no sign advertising this price on the exit ramp, in the lobby, or even on the leather-padded work desk.

To borrow a bit from Motel 6 pitchman Tom Bodell, the packets all look the same once the hotel room light is turned off. Yet the Fairmont can add its charge because guests there aren't price sensitive. Few and far between are the Fairmont consumers who check the daily price of Wi-Fi before they book a hotel. It shouldn't be true, but it is; the more you pay for a hotel, the more stars it has, the more sneaky fees you'll find.

Resort fees and parking fees are the biggest offenders. Those two alone can add $40 a night to your stay. Never book a hotel without asking what it charges for these two items. Even if you are booking the hotel online, look up the number and call to check. Virtually all hotels have toll-free numbers, and the reservations department will generally tell you the truth if you ask the right questions. Of course, websites like Expedia don't provide you the hotel number until you've booked the room, because they don't want you to cut them out and book directly with the hotel. But a quick Google search should unearth the phone number you need.

Note: You can often still get a better price by booking at the online site, so don't lose your place online; but so long as you have the reservations clerk on the phone, you might as well ask if there's a better deal to be had by booking directly with them.

When Gotcha-hunting, beware the brush-off conversation with a busy hotel reservations desk. Many overwhelmed lobby employees double as phone jockeys, and will say anything just to get you off the phone. If a hotel operator tells you there are no fees, ask where you can see that policy in writing, on the Web, or in an e-mail. If you can't, be sure to note the operator's name, as ammunition in case you find yourself in an argument later on.

"YOU TOUCH IT, YOU BOUGHT IT" MINIBARS

By now, you know that room service offers $7 toast (along with a $4 jam surcharge), and a $10 or $20 tack-on fee because a guy in a white jacket had to carry it up the elevator. So you probably avoid room service. And you know in-room minibars contain the world's most expensive pretzels, so you probably avoid them, as well.

But did you know you can be charged just for looking at that bag of pretzels?

That's what happens at the Wynn Las Vegas hotel, one of the Sin City's newest extraordinary cathedrals to opulence. In Wynn minibars, there are special sensors. Feel free to pick things up, a small notice warns. But if the item is removed for more than sixty seconds—you'll be charged for it. Forget "You break it, you bought it." This is, "You touch it, you bought it."

DON'T TOUCH THE ROOM PHONE, EITHER

One area that has become a pet target for most hotels is telephone fees. I call this a tax on those who forgot their cell-phone chargers. With the advent of free long-distance mobile-phone plans, consumers' need for hotel room telephones has plummeted, causing a revenue shortfall for hotels. The mobile-phone industry trade group CTIA estimates that hotel phone revenue peaked in 2000 and has been declining ever since—from about $5 per room in 2000 all the way down to around $1 in 2005.

What's the obvious answer to this shortfall? Charge everyone for phones, even if lodgers never touch the thing. Watch your next hotel bill for an automatic $1-a-day telephone charge. Also, watch for surprising room-to-room call charges (walking down the hall to make plans with friends is still free). And of course, when your cell phone does run out of juice and you don't have your charger, beware the emergency hotel room long-distance call, which can easily cost you $20 for a couple of minutes. A long-distance calling card tucked in your wallet—one you hardly ever use—is good insurance against that. The latest cell phones accept universal USB cables and can be recharged through nearly any computer; that's an even better Plan B.

ARE TAXIS CHEAPER THAN PARKING FEES?

Some fees are unavoidable, such as parking fees in downtown hotels. Nearly every hotel will have them. But you'll want to know the amount while you book the rest of your trip. Steep parking prices might tip the scales between renting a car and taxiing during that trip to San Francisco, for example. Downtown parking can easily cost $150 for a week in the City by the Bay—add that to the price you'll pay for a rental and perhaps even pricey taxi rides could be cheaper in the end.

For a time, hoteliers would budge when consumers balked at sneaky fees like all-you-can-putt mini golf for $15. But no more. With business booming, hotel chains have instructed managers to hold fast on fees, so for now, we're stuck with them.

Your only defense against these fees is to be annoying—when you are choosing a hotel, call the reservations desk, tick off the list of fees, and make an itemized list before you book. Tear off the first page of this chapter if you have to and ask about every possible fee. Your goal should be a true apples-to-apples comparison, with no surprises at check-in.

All this means a few extra minutes when booking your vacation— not very fun. But certainly less painful than having a much more frustrating conversation at the end of a long plane trip.

Here's a special note about online hotel shopping. With regulators watching, hotels are disclosing more fees when consumers price rooms on the Internet—but there still is the critical question of timing. Some fees don't appear until the very last page at checkout, at the very last moment, after a consumer has committed to several minutes of booking procedures, selecting dates, etc. The hotel's hope, of course, is that buyers won't want to waste their time invested in the process, so they won't abandon the process at the last minute over a $10 or $20 fee. To be a smart consumer, and a smart negotiator, you've got to be willing to virtually walk away at any time.

It is in the realm of hotel fees where we see shrouding play out to perfection. Shrouding, you might recall, is the term used by economists Gabaix and Laibson, for hiding prices with add-on fees. According to Gabaix and Laibson, no company has an economic motivation to educate consumers about hidden fees. Obviously, the hotel industry agrees.

In 2005, the InterContinental Hotels Group, which operates Holiday Inn, Crowne Plaza, and InterContinental hotels, experimented with up-front, Gotcha-free pricing.

The hotel found it repeatedly lost out to its low-balling competitors.

"When we gave people the estimated total price up front, we found that abandonment rates were higher," the company's Director of Global E-Commerce Del Ross told the *New York Times*: "The reason, we believe, is that they weren't getting this kind of information from anyone else."

Should Holiday Inn try to educate consumers about fee-free prices? It could try, but consumers would still head to the hotel with the lower advertised price and attempt to avoid hidden charges there to get the best price. That's straight out of Gabaix and Laibson's paper. It's too bad Holiday Inn—once America's family hotel—just can't afford to be fair. And it's a shame that government regulators don't seem interested in creating a level playing field where honesty is rewarded instead of penalized.

RENTAL CARS

Picking the best rental car by price is probably the most challenging task of all for travelers. The quoted weekly prices often have no relation to the bottom-line price you end up paying. We're all well versed in one-way fees, airport fuel surcharges (why is gas *so* expensive at airports?) and the you're-one-minute-late-and-that's-the-same-as-a-whole-day charge. But how much do you know about "airport concession fees"? They can add 10 percent or more to every bill. What are they? I'll let Alamo tell you.

> At certain airport locations where Alamo is an on-airport concessionaire, Alamo has elected to impose a charge, often referred to as a Concession Recoupment Fee or Concession Recovery Fee, to recover all or a portion of the concession fees which it is obligated to pay to the airport.

Let me translate. Let's say you buy a $3 sandwich from your local grocery store. At checkout, you are charged $3.30 plus tax. When you ask, the clerk says, "Oh, that 30 cents covers—recoups—the rent we pay our landlord."

Car-rental fee disclosures are often a ghastly abuse of the English language. But taken in the right light, they can be entertaining. So let's have a look. On Alamo's website, after describing the concession fee, the description continues:

> Many airports impose a fee on revenue from off-airport rental car transactions at locations where Alamo is an off-airport concessionaire; Alamo elects to impose a charge to recover all or a portion of this fee from customers. The fee, which varies by airport, will appear separately in the charges section of this Agreement as Airport Fee, or the like. Other recovery fees that Alamo elects to impose at some locations include, without limitation: a vehicle licensing and registration recovery fee, often called Vehicle License Recoupment or Recovery Fee or "VLRF", which is the recovery of Alamo's average annual cost to license and register its fleet in the applicable jurisdiction calculated over the estimated annual utilization rate for that locale; certain tax recoveries not mandated to be charged to the customer by a governmental entity; a hotel concession recovery fee, which is the recovery of concession fees Alamo is obligated to pay to some hotel-based

locations; and a tire and battery recovery fee, which is the recovery of certain fees related to tires and batteries which Alamo must remit to certain jurisdictions.

My favorite is the vehicle licensing fee. ("Oh, you wanted a car you could drive on *the street?* That'll be extra.") Meanwhile, I wonder if you can decline the tire fee at Alamo ("No thanks, I brought my own Goodyears.")

Car-rental fees are big business. Travelers to Phoenix's Sky Harbor Airport can expect to pay 52 percent more than the base rental price, according to research published by online travel site Travelocity. That includes a flat $4.50-per-rental fee that's collected to build facilities for . . . you guessed it . . . car-rental companies.

Believe it or not, Phoenix isn't even the worst offender. Travelers to Houston's Bush Intercontinental Airport pay a full two-thirds more than the base price for car rentals, thanks to fees and surcharges. Aftercharges turn a $194 rental car into a $281 rental car. Ouch! And that's not including the $6-a-gallon gas.

Bottom line: Call ahead and get the bottom-line price when renting a car. Otherwise, rental fees may be the nastiest surprise of your trip.

AIRLINES

Airline travelers who shop online know all about good deals that suddenly vanish right from underneath their mouse pointers. Bait-and-switch fares are so common—the price is there when you start clicking, but gone an instant later when you click "purchase"—that most consumers accept this as part of the game now. But there are other tactics to watch for.

Some airlines include airport booking fees and 9/11-security-related fees while consumers are window shopping for tickets. Others don't. At continentalairlines.com, for example, the total ticket price, including taxes and fees, isn't shown until fliers are several steps deep into the purchase process. That's akin to newspaper ads which say "New York to Dublin: $249*" and somewhere lower down the page is mouseprint with the discouraging words: "One-way on round-trip purchase. Fees excluded." So the real price—assuming you'll want to go home—is more like $550. And since you can't buy a one-way ticket at that price anyway, why are airlines allowed to advertise it for $249?

Final question: When is a $199 plane ticket more expensive than a $205 ticket? When you have to pay for an on-board meal. Perhaps you're the type to pack a lunch for travel. Otherwise, that $199 round-trip ticket really costs $209—so a $205 flight that includes a meal is actually cheaper. But airlines that break out the meal price using this trick rank just a touch higher when price-based search results are displayed, which is why they do it. But you don't have to fall for it.

CURRENCY

One other fee that always baffles world travelers is the "Currency-conversion fee" charged by credit cards. Anyone who's traveled overseas knows currency conversion is a complicated affair. We're generally resigned to losing a percentage point here or there when we shop in a foreign country. Overseas travelers are the classic tourist in our local-vs.-tourist model, because generally they have no idea what a fair exchange rate is. For years, travel agents have correctly told consumers that the safest way to manage that information dearth is to use a credit card and rely on your U.S.-based card-issuing bank to be fair.

Guess what? For years, banks were anything but fair. Sure, your bank used a decent currency-conversion rate. But it also took a little something for itself—generally 2 percent—with each purchase. This payola was impossible to spot, however, because that 2 percent skim was *cooked right into the conversion rate published on credit-card bills.* Until 2005, this currency-conversion fee was the ultimate hidden fee, as it was entirely disguised by the card-issuing banks. Only a consumer who doggedly took their credit-card bills and matched them up with published exchange rates, then sat down with a calculator and ran through the complicated formulas to find the real price of things, would have any sense something was wrong.

Years of lawsuits finally forced card companies to change their ways. No, they weren't forced to stop gouging consumers for conversions. But they were forced to break out the fee clearly on credit-card bills.

These charges started appearing on bills in early 2006. Naturally, confused consumers were outraged, thinking a new fee had been cooked up. In reality, disclosure of the fee was an upgrade for consumers, who until then had no idea they were paying extra.

To make matters worse, the Visa and MasterCard associations also pile on, adding another 1 percent fee to overseas transactions. Still, even with a total currency conversion fee of 3 percent, credit cards are still usually the best choice when traveling overseas—just not quite the bargain you once thought.

If you travel overseas often, it really is worth shopping around for a card with a lower currency-conversion surcharge. Bankrate.com is a great source for information on credit-card currency-conversion rates. The extra research is really worth your time, as the fee can vary by a full 2 percent. If you spend $2,500 during your vacation, grabbing the right card instead of the wrong one out of your wallet will save you $50—that's time well spent.

It's also worth taking the time to find your bank's overseas ATM cash-withdrawal-fee schedule. These can vary wildly, too, and can be avoided altogether. For example, Bank of America is part of the Global ATM Alliance, which allows free withdrawals in local currencies, a real boon for travelers smart enough to keep the list of participating banks handy.

A warning note to debit-card users: Only place them in ATMs you trust completely while traveling. Don't use them like credit cards to make purchases. It's far too easy for criminals (even waiters!) to steal the debit-card information off your magnetic strips and drain your checking account while you travel, a headache you don't want to deal with while overseas. Buy things with your credit card, or local cash you've withdrawn from an ATM, and you'll be much safer.

And one more debit-card warning—don't use cash cards when renting cars. It's customary for car-rental agencies to put a "hold" on credit or debit transactions of up to $500 more than the actual cost of the rental, in case a car is returned damaged. This ensures the rental agency that you have enough credit to pay for the damages. The money isn't taken by the rental agency; but the money isn't available to you, either. It's in credit purgatory. With a credit card, you probably won't notice this "hold," but it can wreak havoc with your debit card. The extra funds from your checking account may not be available until you return your car, a $500 gap that might put a dent in your travel plans. If you really want to pay with your debit card, use a credit card when you pick up the car, then switch payment mechanisms and settle the charge with your debit card when you return the car.

Travel
GOTCHA-STOPPING STRATEGIES

HOTELS

1. Call ahead and ask about extra fees: Parking fees, resort fees, housekeeping fees—inquire about as many as you can think of while talking to the reservations desk.
2. Don't touch the minibar. Ever. Not even out of curiosity.
3. Don't touch the room phone, either. And even if you don't, you might still be charged $1 a day or so, so eye your bill carefully.

AIRLINES

1. Make sure the price you are quoted includes airport charges and 911 fees. You may have to click through multiple screens to get that bottom-line price.
2. Don't be surprised if you have to pay for a meal, baggage service, or a premium seat.

RENTAL CARS

1. Use websites that provide full-fee pricing while shopping.
2. Do the math on hotel parking fees before you book your rental car. Even a pricey taxi trip and a few train rides are often cheaper than $20-a-day parking. You can rent a car for that one day you really need it—increasingly, rental-car agencies are even allowing hourly rentals.

TRAVELING ABROAD

1. Check on credit-card currency-conversion fees before you leave.
2. Plan ahead to withdraw from ATMs that are in your bank's network.

Groceries

*[It's] called "padding" by retailers. Basically it's a practice of
upping the price of an item and turning around and
offering it at a discounted price, giving the appearance
of it being on sale when in actuality it is not.*

**Donna L. Montaldo, about.com coupon expert,
describing how supermarket loyalty cards work**

Eighty-nine-year-old Esther Shapiro once ran Detroit's office of consumer protection. Now, she fights for price tags one nickel at a time.

Shapiro does her shopping in Michigan, one of the last states to require price tags on every item in grocery stores. She makes a lot of bonus money doing it. She often finds price-tag mistakes on bread, milk, cereal, and everything else in grocery stores. In Michigan, state law grants consumers a bonus of ten times the difference every time they spot a price-tag error, up to $5. So stores get nervous when Shapiro arrives.

"When I feel like enhancing my income there's always one store I shop at," she says. "They just look at me and pull out the money."

The extra cash is nice, but Shapiro says her be-a-pest grocery trips aren't really about getting her bonus money. She is fighting a one-woman crusade. Consumers need price tags to make sure they're not getting cheated at the checkout, Shapiro says. And so, she shops, and she makes her point.

"It's the nibbling away of those dimes and dollars over a period of time," she says. "It's not pennies. It adds up to a lot of dollars over the years."

WHITHER THE PRICE TAG?

Like drive-in movie theaters and small, neighborhood hardware stores, price tags have become a quaint relic of the past. The basic challenge for every consumer today is simply discovering what things cost. It is a struggle, a constant fight, for shoppers to investigate and determine hidden prices. Consumers must ask, ask, ask, and often find themselves still struggling to answer this most fundamental question: "How much is this?"

Without simple price tags, this can be a losing battle. Nowhere is this more obvious than in a grocery store. In this fight, Esther Shapiro is lucky: Her state requires price tags. In most states, they are now a thing of the past.

During the 1960s and 1970s, many states passed aggressive consumer-protection laws that forced grocery stores to put price stickers on everything. The stickers are important for all kinds of reasons. Without them, how can shoppers be sure they are being charged the right price at the checkout register? Other than Mensa members, there is virtually no one capable of remembering the price of everything in their shopping carts. That means there's no way to compare the price of a bottle of spaghetti sauce picked up from a back aisle with the price of a bottle found near the front of the store. Perhaps the exercise of running up and down store aisles is good for national health, but missing price tags make price comparisons of items in different parts of the store nearly impossible and certainly exhausting.

The stickers have been replaced by machine-readable, human-unreadable Universal Price Code tags, and by shelf price labels. Shelf pricing makes sense, from the store's point of view. Anyone who's ever slapped price tags on 400 cans of dog food will tell you what drudgery such a task is. And when the dog food goes on sale? And then the sale ends? *Oy!*

But the price tag's replacement has become a recipe for confusion and overcharging. Remember, the basic principle of Gotcha Capitalism is to keep things priceless. Retailers fight against price transparency, and they fight to keep consumers in the dark. They wear you down by making price comparisons so difficult that you just give in and buy what you've thrown into your cart. The disappearing price tag is the perfect weapon in this war.

SHELF-TAG ERRORS

Shelf price tags with bar-code readers at cash registers aren't a good compromise. For starters, they often lead to mistakes.

Extensive studies on error rates at checkout counters show that, on balance, supermarket scanner checkout errors balance out in the end—overcharges and undercharges occur at basically even rates. That's fine if you are a statistic, but not so fine if you happen to be in the overcharged group. The most recent government study, conducted by the Federal Trade Commission way back in 1998, found that 1 in 30 items scanned incorrectly. At that rate, there would be a mistake in nearly every major shopping trip you take to the grocery store. With the shelf price tag sometimes a football field away by the time the mistake occurs, you're very unlikely to spot it, or bother to get it fixed.

That sounds frustrating, but there's another price inaccuracy that's even more maddening: the shelf label hunt.

When you are standing in the aisle, comparing bottles of spaghetti sauce, which label goes with which bottle? And which size? We've all been there. This bottle has been moved—where does it belong? How much does it cost?

Again, exhaustion is the enemy here. With a baby in the basket and the parking meter running, who takes the time to find a clerk and ask if the $1.99 price applies to the 16-ounce bottle or the 22-ounce bottle?

Edgar Dworsky is a consumer advocate who worked in the Massachusetts attorney general's office in the early 1990s. He wrote that state's price-tag law in the 1980s while working as the Director of Consumer Education for then-governor Michael Dukakis. He is one of America's last remaining price-tag advocates.

"It's the most basic thing. Tell people the price. Don't make them walk around the store to find it," Dworsky is fond of saying.

In the mid 1980s, he spent six months negotiating with retailers over the sticky details of that price-tag law. Today, the Massachusetts law preserves one of the nation's few remaining price-tag requirements. And yet, even two decades ago, the law granted wide latitude to shopkeepers. It allowed grocery stores to leave price tags off hundreds of products, for example.

Still, from the day the law was signed, it was assaulted. Each session, legislators encouraged by supermarkets introduced bills designed to declaw the state's pricing law.

Fast-forward to 2006, when the *Boston Globe* reported that retailers in Massachusetts were simply ignoring the law because fines were tiny, much smaller than the cost of actually pricing items. One example from the paper: BJ's Wholesale Club had paid $49,000 in fines during the prior year, while the cost to price every item in a typical store would have been between $150,000 and $300,000, according to the Massachusetts Food Association.

The economic equation is fairly obvious. Price tags lose. Consumers have been doomed to wander aisles wondering what their groceries really cost.

There has appeared this concession from grocery stores and other retailers during the assault on price tags—self-service price scanners. These are a familiar tool for shoppers at big-box retailers like Target, where they appear throughout the store.

Dworsky, however, says these machines are insufficient. He points to a 2004 study he supervised in which three out of four scanners failed to comply with state laws. In 2005, the Massachusetts Division of Standards conducted a similar study at 124 stores and found that 10 percent of self-service scanners weren't working at all, and 40 percent didn't allow consumers to print a price label, as required by law.

YOU ARE A LAB RAT

Still, it seems hard to develop outrage over absent price tags, and even Dworsky admits that consumers haven't rebelled much against the end of labeling. Perhaps it just doesn't matter? Perhaps the lack of price tags is just a natural step of human progress?

Perhaps. But consider this: The absence of price tags is elemental to every other way grocery stores try to trick you into paying more than you should for things you buy.

Here's something you should understand: The American grocery shopper is a laboratory rat to the industry—poked and prodded, studied, examined, and ultimately highly manipulated. There is nothing casual about the way stores are laid out, the way items are labeled, or the music that is played. And in fact, you are being played. The milk is in the back of the store so you have to walk by all those sale items in order to get what you want.

The method works. Studies show 81 percent of store purchases are in-store decisions, or impulse buys.

Find any former grocery-store clerk and you'll hear the stories. For example: end-cap item placement (the racks at the end of each aisle). Food displayed on end caps with big shelf price labels may look like it's on sale. Often, it's not. Naturally, people pick these items up anyway. If the spaghetti sauce in your basket had a price tag on it, you'd compare prices before picking up another jar at an end-cap. But how can you make that comparison without price tags?

BIGGER ISN'T ALWAYS CHEAPER: UNIT PRICING AND SHRINKING ITEMS

The Costco/Wal-Mart phenomenon has taught consumers the habit of bulk buying. After all, forty-eight of something must be cheaper than twelve of something, yes? Not anymore. Stores have caught on that consumers often assume bigger is cheaper, and now often charge standard or even premium prices for the bulk goods. Gotcha!

At the heart of that problem is unit pricing, which allows consumers to make apples-to-apples comparisons between items that are sold in different amounts. While most states insist on unit-price labels, stores are given great leeway on what they indicate. That leads to all kinds of trickery. Some stores blend English and metric measurements, for example, making on-the-fly comparisons all but impossible.

And those shenanigans play right along with something manufacturers have done for years—slowly shrink their products, creating a hidden price increase. In 2006, for example, Hellmann's shrunk its standard quart-sized jar of mayonnaise to 30 ounces. Many "gallon" jars of paint are now 124 ounces or less.

LOYALTY CARDS

This silent nickel and diming is maddening, once you discover it. But it doesn't hold a candle to the biggest change that grocery stores have implemented since the introduction of frozen vegetables: the loyalty card.

At most grocery stores in America now, there are two sets of prices: one for those in the club, and one for those outside the club. Loyalty-card programs have largely replaced coupons as the preferred method for pushing customers into buying certain products. But more important, these are the tools grocery stores use to reduce shoppers to perfect lab rats. Consumers who sign up for such programs have no way of knowing the real costs of surrendering to such intimate tracking of their purchases. The costs, however, are quite real.

Already, store loyalty-card purchase records have become a staple source of information for divorce litigators. Purchase histories have been used to prove one spouse or another is a bad parent ("Look at all this junk food, Your Honor!"). They have been used to build criminal cases, as happened in Tukwila, Washington, where a homeowner was charged with arson after police found fireplace firestarters in his supermarket purchase records.

The bargain struck by those who sign up for loyalty cards is impossible to evaluate, says Alessandro Acquisti, who studies loyalty cards at Carnegie Mellon University. Acquisti might be the world's first privacy economist. He spends his time trying to see how easily consumers are lured into giving away their personal information. Many will trade their home address or even their Social Security number for something as simple as a 50-cents-off coupon. But that doesn't mean they're dumb. It means privacy bartering is hard to figure. Acquisti will tell you that in most transactions, people trade something obvious for something obvious, like money for meat. But in a privacy transaction, consumers have no idea what they are giving up for what they are getting. Perhaps data traded for 50 cents off a quart of ice cream will ultimately have no cost to you. Or perhaps it will result in more junk mail from ice cream makers, or solicitations for donations from farmers' rights groups. It may someday be used by your health insurance company to deny you coverage for diabetes treatments. The problem is this: No one can tell you what the future cost will be for the surrender of privacy today. That means the Gotchas connected to grocery shopping now are incalculable, perhaps the most serious hidden fees of all.

Meanwhile, those small few who chose to avoid the loyalty-card system know exactly what the cost of that choice is—50 cents on that quart of ice cream. And the price climbs steadily from there. Customers who refuse to join foot the bill for the millions of Americans who do.

Still, members are saving money, right? Not exactly. Loyalty card savings have repeatedly been shown to be negligible. It is standard for stores that implement such programs to raise prices in anticipation. Later, they keep the standard, nonloyalty-card price above the original retail price. This switcheroo would be obvious if your cupboard was full of items that still had price stickers on them. It isn't, because all those price tags are gone.

In short, there is no loyalty-card discount; there is only a lack-of-participation fee. Gotcha. You pay either way.

LOYALTY-CARD SWAP PARTIES

But there's good news. There are fairly easy ways to foil loyalty-card systems. First off, it's crazy not to join. The economic penalty is just too high. Unless you are lucky enough to live near a store without loyalty cards, you must sign up. You don't have to tell the truth, however. Most stores will allow you to sign up with less-than-accurate personal information. Of course, that's not enough to hide your identity, because you could fairly easily be reconstructed from a small slice of your purchasing habits. ("Shops at this store at this address every Friday at 4:30; always buys this brand of toilet paper. Oh, there he is.")

That's why some privacy advocates host what they call "loyalty-card swap parties." Everyone throws their cards on a table and picks up the same store's cards from a friend. That obscures the trail, while still granting discounted prices.

Fighting other supermarket tactics is much harder. Thinking like a grocery-marketing expert is your best bet. The better deals are always harder to reach. If it's at eye-level, you can bet the store wants you to buy it. Be sure to scan bottom and top shelves for lower prices on generic items.

Other tips: A small calculator that can be used to compare unit prices is very handy. Make lists (PDAs are great for this) so you limit your impulse buys. Don't shop when hungry, and try not to shop with screaming kids. Never throw an item into your basket without knowing the price. Ask, ask, ask.

In the future, technology may yet help consumers with this problem. Radio Frequency Identification Tags (RFID) will someday soon replace bar codes. These tags broadcast pricing information and other data to chip readers that stores will use to keep track of merchandise and to scan prices. RFID chips come with even more ominous privacy implications than loyalty cards. They are far more precise. In extreme visions of the future, your empty milk carton or lipstick will be able to radio ahead to the grocery store, through the Internet, and encourage you to buy the same brand when you are back in the shop. Retailers will know when the jeans you wear are getting old, or when your shoes are out of style, and push you to replace them. They might even alert your health insurance company that you are eating too much ice cream, and increasing your risk of heart disease, leading the insurer to increase your premiums.

But, if state lawmakers do their job, the tags can also offer consumer benefits. RFID readers will not be expensive. They can be made available to consumers for a reasonable price, giving shoppers a fighting chance in the information war. A consumer armed with such a device will be able to immediately discover accurate pricing information. A gadget that is only slightly smarter with wireless Internet connectivity will allow that consumer to compare the price of the can of soup in their hand to average prices around their neighborhood, and to the price they paid last month. Correctly implemented, such a device could actually tip the scales toward price transparency. We'll see.

Groceries
GOTCHA-STOPPING STRATEGIES

1. **Sign up, but don't give it up.** Get a loyalty card, but then attend loyalty-card swap parties and trade cards with friends so your purchase trail is obscured. If you can, shop at stores that don't require them.
2. **Stand tall and squat.** The better deals are always near the floor or above your head. Stores want you to buy items that are at eye level.
3. **Walk around.** Similar advice. The best deals are the farthest from the cash register.
4. **Is more really less?** Use your cell phone, a PDA, or a handheld calculator to do real unit price comparisons. If that's too much trouble, at least be skeptical of supposed bulk-buy bargains.
5. **Write it down.** A small notebook or handheld computer is the best way to keep track of prices for comparison.
6. **Eat first.** You always buy more food when you're hungry. Don't shop on an empty stomach.
7. **Dump the candy.** Candy makers are among the most devious marketers—note the pacifier-shaped candy bottles on the bottom shelf at the checkout counter, right at eye level with your eighteen-month-old. Was there ever a sneakier sales pitch? Patronize stores that offer candy-free checkout lines.

11

Gift Cards

Some . . . bank cards carry fees that become scary. The iCARD Visa Gift Card imposes a $25 maintenance fee after six months and then it expires a month later. It will cost at least $25 to get the balance refunded by check and can cost up to $75 if one waits over two years to request a refund.

Montgomery County (Maryland) Office of Consumer Affairs

Not every story ends badly for consumers. Take gift cards: Common sense, fairness, and protest have combined to give consumers some important victories over sneaky fees. Costly so-called "dormancy" fees, which see gift cards slowly leak their value over time, are becoming a thing of the past. Most retailers have abandoned them. But as we'll see, even when consumers win a few battles, corporations often find a way to win the war anyway.

Gift cards exploded on the retail scene in the late 1990s, and slowly but surely caused the death of old-fashioned paper gift certificates. Giving plastic quickly became cool, and sales doubled year after year, until 2006, when nearly $80 billion was spent on gift cards. But for years, they harbored a dirty little secret, hidden on the back of each card in tiny, tiny type. It was the secret of disappearing money. After a while, if the cards weren't spent, they'd lose a dollar or two of value with each passing month.

Here's how it worked. If you gave someone a $25 gift card to Red Lobster restaurants on January 1, 2004, and the recipient tried to spend it in April 2005, it was only worth $23.50. Each following month, another $1.50 in value disappeared. By summer 2006, the card was worthless. Red Lobster got its $25, your loved one got nothing. How is that fair?

It's fair, retailers said, because they had to do some pretty tricky accounting to keep track of that gift card. If people procrastinate when redeeming their gift, it's not the store's fault, they claimed. Sluggish consumers deserved to pay this so-called dormancy fee, and the terms were clearly spelled out.

Not always. In August of 2006, I went to Red Lobster's website to order a gift card and see how clear the dormancy fee disclosure was. The answer: not at all.

Clicking on "Gift Card" from the site's home page brought me to a page that allowed consumers to pick the number of cards they wanted, their value, and add them to a shopping cart. Nothing about dormancy fees there.

Now, that's not to say there wasn't small print on the order page. But these statements all protected the company. There was this: "Orders placed after 3:00 P.M. Mountain Time or on weekends usually ship the next business day."

Or this, clearly designed to prevent fraud: "There is a $500.00 maximum per order. You may not purchase more than $500.00 per credit card in a thirty-day period. Orders over $200.00 must be shipped to the billing address."

But nowhere on that page was there notice of a $1.50 monthly fee. And it was easy to complete a purchase without ever receiving such notice. Only those consumers savvy (or curious) enough to scroll to the bottom of the order page would have found the link that hinted at the other, potentially damaging, details.

"Important: Gift Card Terms and Conditions," it said, in a lovely blue pastel color. It was easy to miss, as it was overshadowed by the words "Your Shopping Cart Is Currently Empty," which were larger, and displayed in bright red.

Still, an industrious visitor who clicked on "Gift Cards and Conditions" was shown a page that was topped by one word in red: "Legalese." Nothing says "Read me" like "Legalese."

Perhaps use of the word was self-effacing fun. But only underneath the word "legalese" were consumers able to find mention of the $1.50 monthly dormancy fee. This important information, the only fact consumers really needed to know before purchasing their gift card (how much was it really worth?), was hidden in a part of the site the company practically told you to skip because it was too hard to understand.

By the time I conducted my experiment, Red Lobster had postponed the start of the dormancy fee from 15 to 24 months after purchase, but it certainly was still there. Here's what the notice said: "If you don't use your card for a twenty-four-month period, a $1.50 monthly maintenance fee will be deducted from the balance until you use it again." In truth, it was pretty easy to understand. Just hard to find.

By law, disclosure requires clarity and prominence. After all, what good are clear statements if they're virtually invisible?

During the same year I ran my little test, the Federal Trade Commission announced it was investigating Red Lobster and its parent, Darden Restaurants Inc., alleging unclear fee disclosure.

There are those who say no consumer waits two years before spending a gift card. That's not true; plenty of recipients throw cards into a drawer and don't get around to spending them for a while, particularly if they are purchased at a store the recipient doesn't often frequent. Look at this note, sent to the *Red Tape Chronicles* by a frustrated gift-getter:

> I recently had a humiliating experience at an upscale restaurant over a gift card. My Realtor gave me a $50 gift card for brunch at [a local restaurant]. It was just a little over a year before I was able to use it and when I presented the card for the bill, they told me there was only $17 on it. When I said that couldn't be possible—I hadn't used any of it yet, the waitress got the manager and for ten minutes they made a scene in the restaurant trying to come up with excuses and giving me corporate numbers to call.

Fortunately, retail-store gift-card dormancy fees have become a dying breed. You can credit a flood of negative publicity and consumer-friendly government action for that. In addition to the FTC lawsuits, several states have passed laws discouraging them.

The reigning authority on gift-card fees is the Montgomery County, Maryland, Office of Consumer Protection, which releases a comprehensive survey on gift cards every holiday shopping season. When it began the study in 2003, half of the cards surveyed imposed dormancy fees. But after three years of pounding by the media and consumer groups, most retailers had changed their tune. By 2006, only two of the forty gift cards studied by Montgomery County levied dormancy fees, and another four wrote policies that left the door open to such fees. That's a dramatic turnaround on sneaky fees, one that should inspire other causes.

THE PROBLEM OF BANK CARDS

But small-print fighters shouldn't be too quick to pat themselves on the back. Generic bank-issued gift cards are still out there, tricking gift buyers across America. As we've seen before, financial institutions have special abilities to create confusing fees, and Visa/MasterCard/Amex gift cards are no exception. In fact, this might be some of the banks' best work. Here's just one example:

In 2005, someone who bought an All-Access Visa Prepaid card would pay $9.95 just to get the card—in addition to the amount of value loaded on the card. So a $50 card really cost $60. The card can be used at an ATM, but each withdrawal incurs a $2 fee. Buying something with the card cost a $1 "signature-based transaction" fee. Want to find out how much is left on the card? Call in, but it'll cost 50 cents. Throw the card into the drawer for three months? That's a $5.95 per month maintenance fee for the inactive card.

Nearly all bank gift cards follow this pattern. There's no nuance here: Avoid bank cards at all costs. They are a terrible deal. So are bank cards that are issued as rebates, a replacement for old paper rebate checks, an increasingly prevalent practice. Some bank/rebate cards begin to lose their value in as little as four months!

BREAKAGE, OR THE UNSPENT GIFT

You might think that consumers who steer away from bank gift cards and toward store cards have steered clear of sneaky fees.

Not quite. Another dirty little secret of gift cards is the free loan they provide to retailers. You buy a $100 gift card on December 1, and it doesn't become a potential liability until sometime after December 25, when the wrapping paper is opened. When you're talking about an $80 billion industry, that month of interest is real money. But it's only the beginning.

Of course, retailers love gift cards because they bring shoppers into the store, and they usually spend more than the value of the card. Who among us can find items that cost exactly $25 or $50? But even if you don't, the retailers win. That's because there's real money in "breakage," too.

It's simple. Some of the money given in gift cards never gets spent. It's lost, or it's neglected, or the $100 card is used for an $85 purchase and forgotten. The difference is called breakage. And in 2006, retailers sneaked off with $8 billion in breakage, according to the TowerGroup. The TowerGroup estimates up to 10 percent of all gift-card money is never spent. That's a tidy bump to any profit margin. In a rare glimpse into the world of breakage, Home Depot announced in 2005 that it had $43 million in unused gift cards sitting on its balance sheet.

Retailers don't always get to keep the funds. Some state governments swoop in and swipe the ill-gotten gains through clever use of escheat tax laws, which allow governments to gobble up unclaimed property. Still, the firm has use of the money for several years (that's a free $8 billion loan, earning interest for corporate America).

Either way, a gift has turned into a Gotcha.

Gift Cards
GOTCHA-STOPPING STRATEGIES

1. Give money. That's really the only one way to beat the gift-card small-print attack. Retailers and banks have leveraged social etiquette that rejects cash gifts to create the entire gift-card industry. Then, they set rules that slowly devalue that gift. But really, what's less classy than giving a gift that really does stop giving after twenty-four months? Show them you really care—give cash instead!

2. Avoid dormancy fees and bank cards. If you must give cards, make sure you understand fees before you do. Never give bank cards; they're simply a bad deal. Store-specific cards almost always offer better terms. And don't patronize any retailer that has a dormancy fee on its cards.

3. Be thoughtful! Know your gift recipient. If he or she is the type to lose plastic in the sock drawer, then know you are probably wasting your giving spirit on a gift that's really going to Macy's, Circuit City, Crate & Barrel, or some other retailer's bottom line. And don't give cards to recipients for stores where they are unlikely to shop; those are more likely to go to waste.

Rebates

All it took was 29 e-mails, three phone calls, several letters and five months of my time. I had to resend everything two, three times, and still I didn't get all the money. It's clear to me they wanted me to quit, but getting my rebate became a personal quest—one of the most exhausting experiences of my life.

Consumer Sharon Dirlam

"FREE!" The ad screams.

"After rebate," it whispers.

Walk into any electronics store, and the good deals are almost too good to pass up: DVDs, cell phones, even televisions, all at rock-bottom prices. It seems the sellers are giving them all away, to steal a phrase.

But what aren't they giving away? Oftentimes, the rebate checks. The words "after rebate" frequently appear in the smallest of small print, rivaled in font size only by the rebate instructions. To get their money, consumers have to jump through hoops so complex even the architects of the new Medicare prescription-drug program must smile with admiration.

To play the rebate game, you must know the rules. And, for the most part, with a lot of persistence, and some good humor, you can win. But you must understand you won't win all the time. If you are playing the rebate game, you are descending into the dragon's lair of mouseprint and choosing to fight on the enemy's turf. It's not a tussle for the timid. About forty percent of all rebates go unredeemed, according to the educated guesses of experts (companies carefully guard the true figures).

Marie Vento, a fifty-three-year-old Staten Island woman, was on the wrong side of that statistic when she wrote to msnbc.com as a last resort after $600 in cell-phone rebates she expected had gone AWOL for more than a year. Her exasperating story is all too common.

Vento thought she had spotted a cell-phone deal that was too good to pass up, and decided to leap into the rebate game, knowing full well she'd have to exert some effort to stay on top of the paperwork. But she had a chance to get the hottest new phone for free, and she took the bait. A website named wirefly.com was offering free Motorola RAZR phones for anyone who agreed to a long-term contract. At the time, in 2005, RAZRs were all the rage, and they were pricey. Vento was so excited she bought two. There was only one small hitch—she'd have to shell out $600 up front for the RAZRs, but the advertisements said she'd be getting all that money back. So she took the plunge.

At the time, Wirefly was no fly-by-night operation—it was owned by InPhonic Inc., which claimed to be the nation's largest general online cell-phone retailer, selling millions of phones each year.

When the phones arrived, the forms were a bit more complex than Vento expected. She read that she'd have to wait 180 days and gather six months' worth of bills before she could file for the rebates. On the other hand, the paperwork also indicated everything was due within 210 days of her purchase. It sounds crazy, but she had only a small thirty-day window of opportunity—between 180 days and 210 days—to file her refund paperwork. And of course, the heap of required forms had to be perfect.

No matter. Vento was undeterred. She dutifully marked her calendar so she wouldn't forget, then assembled six months' worth of bills, and in October sent them off to the InPhonic rebate processing center in Bear Lake, Minnesota.

A month later, she received a rejection notice, with a note saying the bills she had sent did not include an "invoice bill date." She sent an e-mail complaint and never got a response. She called and said an operator told her to simply send in new copies of the first page of her monthly bills, this time to a different processing center in Arizona. She did so and received another rejection letter in December. She called again, asking for an explanation, and says she never got a straight answer.

"I sent them everything," Vento said. "When I ask them to explain [their decision], they just talk in circles. They answer your questions with a question." A full year passed, and it looked more and more like those free Motorola phones would end up costing her $600. In a scene repeated across America every day at a host of electronics retailers, many websites, and other stores, Vento had lost the rebate game.

Of course, it's much more than a game. Rebate shenanigans prop up entire industries, like home electronics, which operate on such thin margins that without sneaky revenue, they'd never survive. Think DVD players, for example. They are practically free. In order to make any money at all, companies that sell such dirt-cheap products count on breakage (those rebates that are never filed), and "slippage," the term for rebate checks that go uncashed.

"In some low-margin businesses, [unredeemed] rebates could be all the margin you're going to get," says Paula Rosenblum, a rebate expert at Aberdeen Group, Inc.

Still, nothing churns the stomachs of consumers more than this rebate bait, which often leads to rebate wait, and eventually, unknown rebate fate.

Vento was hardly alone in her Wirefly frustration. In 2005, wirefly.com was one of the most complained-about firms at the Better Business Bureau. More than 1,400 people had filed complaints about the company in the prior three years, and in November 2005, InPhonic's BBB membership was revoked.

But the company continued on, as so many companies do, offering great prices obscured by these delayed coupons called rebates. Eventually, the Washington, D.C., attorney general's office sued InPhonic in 2006, saying the company imposed "unusually restrictive conditions" on consumers who tried to get their rebates, effectively making things "difficult or impossible" for them. The firm denied the charges, and then later settled the lawsuit and agreed to pay rebates it had previously denied—without admitting any wrongdoing.

Consumers who had complained to the Better Business Bureau or their state attorney general's office were first in line to receive compensation when the company was forced to pay up. So that's the first tip to keep in mind while engaged in a rebate debate—file a formal complaint. Here's a compilation of other rebate recovery tricks, divided into three categories: What to do *before* you make a rebate purchase, what to do *when* you're filling out the forms, and finally, how to wrangle a wayward rebate from a neglectful or slippery company *after* you don't receive it.

Rebates
GOTCHA-STOPPING STRATEGIES

BEFORE A PURCHASE

1. **Not the deciding factor.** Perhaps the most important suggestion of all: Don't play the game. Remember, by mailing in the form you most certainly are going to end up on some marketer's mailing list. If you can find a sale at a competing store that comes anywhere close to the rebate-reduced price, buy it there and escape the rebate game. But if you must do the rebate thing, don't let the rebate be the deciding factor in the purchase. Know that you may never see the money. If it's a good deal *before* the rebate, then fine. Consider the expected rebate check to be play money. That'll take the pressure off.

2. **Read early and often.** Make sure you understand what's required of you before you make the purchase. Turn the box over, or click around the site, and spend a moment reading the rebate terms.

3. **Do an online credibility check.** By the time Marie Vento purchased her RAZR phones, there were already a series of complaints about Wirefly all across the Internet. Before buying a rebate-laden item from a store you've never heard of, do a little Google background check on the company. That goes double if you have trouble finding rebate specifics before the purchase (some companies make rebate details very hard to find). Your best bet: See if another consumer has posted the rebate terms, or complained about them, online.

4. **Understand the role of third-party fulfillment houses.** Few manufacturers and retailers send out their own rebate checks; most contract with outside companies to do so. When things go sour, your fight will often be with a fulfillment house, which can complicate things. Because they have no direct relationship with consumers, they have less incentive to treat them well. But they do have to abide by the law.

5. **Easy rebates are good.** Some retailers have significantly streamlined their rebate processes, and strong-armed their suppliers into doing the same. Staples was a market leader here, creating the "Easy Rebate" process. Staples shoppers just go to a Web page and type in a number printed on their receipt. Staples spent two years getting suppliers to play along, but it was worth the wait. When you shop, consider supporting Staples and other retailers that use consumer-friendly rebates.

WHEN FILLING OUT THE FORMS

1. **Copy everything.** Think like a lawyer. You are gathering evidence. If you like rebates, invest in a copier for your home office so you don't have to bring the paperwork into the office and risk leaving documents in the mailroom. I recently saw a copier on sale at Staples for $30—after rebate.

2. **Ask for the rebate price—without the rebate.** Appliance stores sometimes honor rebate-reduced prices if you ask—without requiring the rebate process. You won't know until you ask. If the store says no, start walking toward the door. That often produces favorable results.

3. **Strike while the iron is hot.** Fill out the forms as soon as you get home. The longer you wait, the less likely you'll do it. And the more likely Fido might eat the box with the UPC symbol you need.

4. **Include instructions.** Photocopy the rebate instructions, highlighting each completed step, and include that with your rebate application. It'll be harder for the company to argue that you did something wrong.

5. **Get a receipt from the post office.** Again, more evidence gathering. Send the forms return-receipt-requested in the U.S. mail, or use an overnight delivery service that provides evidence of delivery. It'll cost a few bucks, but include that in your rebate price mathematics (Is it still a good deal if you subtract $4 in mailing costs from the rebate bonus?).

6. **Mark your calendar.** To paraphrase a tired question, if a rebate never shows up in your mailbox, but you never notice, did the company really cheat you? Mark your calendar when you expect to get the money, so you'll remember to complain in a timely fashion if it doesn't arrive. Internet sites offer free downloadable rebate-tracking software with names like

"Rebate Rebate," that you might find handy. I find them cumbersome. Your wall calendar or day planner should do.

7. **Track the rebate progress online.** Many rebate forms now provide a Web address where consumers can see if that rebate check is getting any closer to your mailbox. Three or four weeks after mailing the forms, log in to check the rebate status. This will tell you if the company has received the paperwork and begun processing your rebate, and alert you faster if there is a lost-in-the-mail problem or a rejection.

8. **It's not junk mail.** Many rebate checks are discarded because they come in unmarked envelopes that look like a dastardly credit-card application, or on postcards that end up shoved inside magazines. Here's where step No. 6 might help—your calendar should remind you when to scan your snail mail carefully!

9. **Be careful with bank cards.** Increasingly, companies are sending bank cards instead of checks as rebates. These might seem convenient, but they often lose their value over time like gift cards—some as quickly as four months after they're mailed! Some merchant credit-card processing systems don't handle the cards well, either, making them a hassle to use.

IF YOU MUST CONFRONT

1. **Call or e-mail.** I don't mean to imply that companies sometimes cheat consumers, but, well, they do. So you've got to be ready to fight for your rebate. Companies count on people who are quitters or are forgetful. It's up to you to notice the problem and complain. Often, only one telephone call will do the trick. If the rebate goes missing, find the copies of the forms you mailed in and call the toll-free number listed there, and call for an explanation. Ditto if your rebate is rejected.

2. **Write a demand letter.** If calling doesn't work, a sternly worded letter is your next step. A sample rebate-refund letter is located in the Toolkit section. The first letter should go to the fulfillment house where you sent the rebate forms.

3. **Complain to the store.** Even if the rebate was to be issued by the manufacturer, or a third-party fulfillment house, the store itself might still have to pay. The Federal Trade Commission has taken on several rebate cases, but none more important than a CompUSA case settled in March of 2005. In that situation, the FTC argued that the retailer was responsible for rebates that a manufacturer failed to pay. Stores often shoo away frustrated consumers toward the manufacturer, telling them they were just the messenger, passing along the rebate offers at the point of sale. Con-

sumers are then sent to complain to the faraway manufacturer of the DVD player, or the fulfillment house that has so far failed to deliver on a rebate. The "we didn't do it," excuse holds less water in light of the CompUSA settlement, and retailers now know they can be held responsible for wayward rebates.

4. **Write a more demanding letter.** If you're still rebate-less, send a testier note to the retailer, manufacturer, and fulfillment house, threatening to file a formal complaint or to take legal action. Citing your state's consumer protection statute would be a nice touch (easily found on your state's attorney general's website). You can also write to the division of consumer affairs in your state attorney general's office and ask for help.

5. **Complain to your legislator.** Finally, high consumer frustration and political opportunism have elected officials buzzing around the rebate issue. Some states have passed laws requiring firms to include clear rebate rules, and to pay up in a timely manner. Consider supporting a pro-consumer rebate law in your state.

Note: Adapted from msnbc.com's *Red Tape Chronicles*

Student Loans

It's a market in which the protection goes to the lender. And the students get served up like turkeys at the Thanksgiving dinner.

Elizabeth Warren, Harvard Law School professor

One of the biggest hidden fees of all is the cost of education. College expenses continue to spiral up, up, and away, leaving millions of twenty-somethings weighed down with gigantic monthly student loan payments, even while they search for their first job. The average bill for attending a four-year public college (the *cheap* kind) rose 52 percent from 2001 to 2007, far more than the rate of inflation, and now sits at close to $13,000 per year. And with each annual increase, hovering near 7 percent, the financial noose around college graduates' necks—and their parents' necks—gets tighter and tighter. Outstanding student debt was close to $400 billion in 2007—putting it not so far from total credit-card debt, which was about $880 billion during that time. Yet who thinks of student debt as the national crisis that credit-card debt is?

Here's a number to ponder: In 2005, one quarter of all college students graduated with $25,000 in loan debt—not including their parents' debt. One in ten students was saddled with $35,000 or more. That last group joins the working world burdened by a $400-a-month loan payment on a standard ten-year loan. You won't see many young teachers or nonprofit workers surviving that kind of stranglehold. Finaid.org, a website devoted to explaining the thicket that is student loans, says students need to earn $48,000 per year to reasonably afford that $400-a-month payment. That's going to exclude a lot of people. The average college liberal arts grad gets a starting salary of $30,000. Even accountants and engineers barely make $45,000 to start. Something's gotta give. Naturally, it all means these folks will seek some magic way to reduce those onerous payments. And that's where many problems begin. Banks are all too happy to turn a ten-year loan into a twenty- or thirty-year loan, and that alone should make you suspicious.

But decades-long, government-backed loans are only the beginning of the problem. Students have much more to worry about when they are forced to jump into the cesspool that is private student loans. Most college loans are still ultimately funded by the federal government, and governed by rules that fairly well protect young borrowers. But the private student-loan business, which has exploded from nearly zero to 20 percent of the student loan industry in the past ten years, is a lending free-for-all. Interest rates can resemble credit-card rates; surprise late fees and other penalties can ultimately double the balance of the loans. And banks can be absolutely ruthless in collecting their money, thanks to changes in the bankruptcy law. Here's the truth: a young person with no money who borrows $50,000 with credit cards to blow it in Las Vegas is in a better financial position than someone who takes out a $50,000 college loan they can't repay. As a society, we are much more forgiving of one debt than the other.

But before we untie the Gordian knot that is the private lender student-loan business, here's a quick refresher on the kinds of loans available to post-secondary school students.

COLLEGE-LOAN LINGO

There's essentially three kinds of college loans: government-backed student loans, government-backed parent loans, and private lender, for-profit student loans. Within each category are a few additional options.

Most students are familiar with Stafford Loans, once upon a time called Guaranteed Student Loans, or GSLs. They are widely available—even to students who don't qualify for financial aid—but are limited to only a few thousand dollars per year. About 7 million students get Stafford Loans every year. Poorer students get subsidized Stafford loans, meaning the government pays the interest while students are in school. Unsubsidized Stafford Loans accrue interest immediately. In 2006, Stafford-Loan interest rates were fixed at 6.8 percent. Upfront fees were set at 2.5 percent of the loan in 2007, though some lenders will pick up some or all of that upfront fee. The upfront fee will decline by 0.5 percent each year until it is eliminated in 2010. Six months after graduation, students must begin repaying these loans. But already, hidden fees have kicked in. During all four years of college, despite the fact that no payments have been due, interest has been piling up and added to the total loan amount, a process called capitalization. The impact of capitalization can be enormous. Consider a single $10,000 loan taken out at the beginning of a student's freshman year with an interest rate of 6.8 percent. Interest capitalization on the loan adds about $3,100 to the size of the loan. In other words, by the time the student starts paying that $10,000 loan, the balance would be $13,095. And that's just the freshman-year loan.

Owing to the impact of interest capitalization, Perkins Loans are a far better deal, but are available to far fewer students. The interest rate is much lower—5 percent—and repayment doesn't begin until nine months after graduation. Most important, the federal government pays the interest while the student is in school. Interest doesn't begin accruing until repayment begins. Only the neediest students qualify.

Stafford and Perkins loans usually leave big gaps in college costs. Students generally turn to their parents to plug those gaps, and often parents turn to PLUS loans (once called Parent Loan for Undergraduate Students). PLUS loans cost a bit more than Stafford Loans (the rate was fixed at 8.5 percent in 2006—not quite as bad as an unsecured personal loan, but a bit more than a home-equity loan at the time). PLUS loans carry a 4 percent upfront fee. In most cases, graduate and professional students get to act as their own parents, and can apply for special Graduate PLUS loans on their own to cover medical school, law school, and other graduate school expenses.

PRIVATE LOANS 101

As college costs have soared, and federal loan limits haven't kept up, few students can cover their expenses with Stafford or Perkins loans, and some just can't have their parents pick up the rest of the tab. Private lenders have been more than willing to step in and make up the difference. The market for private student loans has skyrocketed, jumping from a modest 4 percent in 1996 to 20 percent in 2006. It's now an $85 billion market annually. Private loans have none of the protections of federally-backed loans. Advertised rates of 7 percent or so often only apply to co-signed loans when the co-signer has near-perfect credit. Most students will find actual rates, after sign-up fees and penalties for thin credit histories, are much, much higher. Students at Lehigh Valley College paid an average of 13 percent for Sallie Mae private loans in 2005, the firm told a hearing of Pennsylvania state legislators. Rates as high as 28 percent are not unheard of.

Because private student loans fall through the cracks of some government lending rules, their rates do not have to be reported in a standard annual-percentage-rate format, making loans incredibly hard to compare. Of course, as we learned in the student-loan scandal of 2007, many colleges actively push students toward specific lenders anyway, in exchange for kickbacks, so most students don't bother to comparison shop.

And unlike government-backed loans, the private loan rates aren't capped, and they are very rarely fixed. Getting a student loan is every bit as risky as getting a variable-rate home mortgage. Penalty fees are incredibly hard to determine, and even harder to comparison shop. Sallie Mae's website in 2007 only revealed late-fee structures to borrowers *after* they've signed up for a loan, for example. And they were steep. Sallie Mae late fees ranged from 4 to 10 percent of the outstanding payment—every month. Late fees can ultimately reach 50 percent of the monthly payment, according to Wells Fargo bank. Yet, more and more students are opting for these risky, private loans.

Why? Confusion, no doubt, plays a role. It's common for banks to offer students both government-backed student loans and private student loans. Most government-backed student loans are actually issued through banks like Sallie Mae or Wells Fargo—only 25 percent of federal loans are issued directly by the government to students. So a student can get a Perkins Loan, a Stafford Loan, and a private loan all from the same bank.

Making matters worse, Sallie Mae—the 800-pound gorilla of the student-loan business—was until recently a government-backed enterprise, like Fannie Mae, the mortgage firm. The Sallie Mae moniker derives from its original, helpful-sounding name, the Student Loan Marketing Association. The name is long gone. So is the government association. The firm is now properly called the SLM Corporation, one of Wall Street's most profitable public, for-profit companies—so profitable that the $1.1 billion in profits it made in 2003 could have paid for 4,600 students to go to UCLA for free. But still, it uses the Sallie Mae nickname. So when it offers a 17-year-old a package of loans including a government-backed discounted loan and a private, incredibly expensive loan, who's to blame the student for being confused? And confused they are: Alan Collinge, who runs an advocacy site named studentloanjustice.org, says that only two out of 10 students know where their loans are coming from.

Some families, who are focused only on pursuing the American dream and getting their child into that Ivy League school at any cost, simply gloss over the distinction at enrollment time. In fact, private student loans can seem like a savior, as the missing piece of paper that gets the kid into the dream school. Instead, they often turn out to be a Devil in a Blue Dress.

In early 2007, the private-loan market finally drew the attention of Congress and regulators after disclosures that college employees were getting perks from financial institutions eager to appear on the schools' lists of preferred lenders. There was a lot of noise about improved disclosures accompanying private loans, and of monitoring the perks lenders give to schools. But there was no discussion of the real problem—the unholy alliance between colleges, which continue to raise tuition and fees toward infinity, and lenders, who have no problem lending infinite amounts of money to teenagers. By working in lockstep, colleges have received countless millions that can ultimately help schools afford pet building projects, and banks have earned countless millions in lending fees. Together, the two created an $85 billion market out of thin air, paid for by American students trying to get an education. What alternative do students have? They're told repeatedly that college is the key to their future. It's Gotcha Capitalism at its most shameful.

The short story here is this: Exhaust all available government-backed loans before entertaining private education loans. The government loans will always be a better deal, no matter what the private lender's brochure says. Government-backed parent PLUS loans are a better deal, even if they don't appear to be on the surface. PLUS interest rates are capped at 8.5 percent while student loans come with toxic variable rates. As we'll see later in this chapter, PLUS loans can be consolidated, and can come with discounts for good behavior, which can drop the interest rate close to 7 percent. No variable-rate, Gotcha-laden private loan can compete with that. Understandably, some parents may be reluctant to borrow on behalf of their children, or they may not want to fill out the necessary financial aid forms to get PLUS loans. But parents should know this: With government-backed loans to first-year students limited to as little as $3,500 per year, the system is set up today to either force parents to borrow, or to force children to the wolves in the private loan market.

The Internet is awash in stories of young consumers so deep in college debt that they simply cannot pursue their dreams of working as a teacher or social worker, and instead must take higher-paying office jobs to pay down their debt. Rather than fulfilling dreams, college bills now dash them. Many, many of these twenty-somethings would advise their little brothers and sisters not to follow their path, to instead attend a community college, a cheaper university, or to live at home instead of in the dorms. It's advice that many, many families would be wise to consider. But if you still must play the student-loan game, you need to know the rules.

AFTER COLLEGE: THE CONSOLIDATION GAME

Few students take the option of repaying their loans during school. That makes them the riskiest kinds of borrowers—the kind that signs papers and face no immediate consequences. With no monthly checks to write, the loans can seem unreal. That makes it tempting to pad such loans with enough money to stay in the nice off-campus apartment, or to pay for that all-important spring break "research" trip along with tuition and books. This is a terrible mistake. There's only one formula for college borrowing—borrow as little as is possible. Borrowing more than your first year's professional salary is tantamount to financial suicide.

Why? Because when the bank wants its money, there really is no way to make these loans more affordable. Student loans are, as we'll see in a moment, rather unforgiving. There is a way to transfer the pain a bit, by spreading out the loan payments over many more years, or graduating payments to coincide with (hoped for) raises. Doing so can represent a sound financial plan of attack. But if you're just focused on monthly payments (this is true for any loan) you are likely to miss the true long-term cost of the loan. Despite all the advertisements and all the brochures, there really is no way to lower your cost of funds—to lower your interest rate—even if there are ways to lower your monthly payment for a while. The mathematics might be confusing for recent graduates who feel their backs are to the wall, who might be willing to do just about anything to lower those payments. And in that confusion and desperation, loan consolidators do their dirty work.

Most students end their schooling with multiple loans, multiple interest rates, and facing the prospect of multiple bills. As school winds down, consolidation offers come fast and furious. They come with two promises: One is real and one is often a bit of a fib.

"Make one monthly payment," consolidation pitches always advertise. That's true, and for most people, that's a good idea. Fewer bills = fewer chances to pay one of them late = lower odds of late fees. Makes sense.

But the offers usually come promising something even better: "Make one lower monthly payment," or even "Save as much as 50 percent on your monthly payment." That's a bit of an overstatement. Consolidation loans usually bring with them the possibility of a longer payout term, which does lower your payments in the short term. And they offer some discounts for good behavior, such as automatic debit or consistent on-time payment. These discounts have hidden Gotchas that we'll get to in a moment. But first, anyone consolidating their loans must understand this important principle: Consolidation does not lower the fundamental cost of the loan. In fact, it generally raises the rate ever so slightly. When you mix the outstanding balances and interest rates on a series of student loans, the firm that grants the big loan crunches them all in a formula that averages out the rates, weighted for the loan balances, and then adds one-eighth of a point to the rate. In the end, the student will pay a few pennies more—not enough to worry about. This you should know: Consolidating loans might be convenient, but it does not save money. Here's one example of how it works, thanks to finaid.org:

On a ten-year term, $10,000 at 6.8 percent has a monthly payment of $115.08 and total interest paid of $3,809.66, and $5,000 at 5 percent has a monthly payment of $53.03 and total interest paid of $1,364.03. If you add these, you obtain a total monthly payment of $168.11 and a total interest paid of $5,173.69. But in a consolidation loan of the two, the bank would arrive at a weighted interest rate of 6.25 percent—it's closer to the 6.8 percent rate because that balance was bigger—so the borrower ends up with a $15,000 loan at 6.25 percent, with monthly payments of $168.42 and total interest of $5,210.42. Equal from a cost standpoint.

One big advantage to consolidation—locking in a lower, fixed interest rate—was largely removed in 2006 when the federal government decided to fix interest rates on Stafford Loans. Prior to that, the rates were variable, and could bring bad news every year on July 1 when the reset hit. Graduates with loans that predate this change might still get some benefit from consolidating and locking in a rate, but as with any loan, that depends on the interest-rate environment.

There are some small exceptions to the general rule that consolidation does not actually save you money. Students with older, variable-rate Stafford Loans issued before July 1, 2006 get a 0.6 percent discount on interest rates while in school, and during their six-month grace period after graduation, before repayment starts. Consolidating during the grace period can save students hundreds of dollars in interest, as the lower interest rate will apply when the consolidation interest rate formula is used. There is a cost: Repayments must start as soon as the consolidation is finalized, so this method can cut the student's grace period short. But clever graduates and lenders can time the application just right, allowing students to take full advantage of the grace period and the interest-rate discount.

And here's one more exception: Parents can also get a small discount on PLUS loans by consolidating, as PLUS loans are now fixed at 8.5 percent interest but consolidation loans are capped at 8.25 percent. So generally, it's a good idea to consolidate PLUS loans and save that 0.25 percent. Of course, there's a caveat. Parents may be getting interest-rate discounts from the original PLUS lender that are worth more than the 0.25 percent savings, so unless those discounts are matched by the consolidating lender, consolidation could leave parents with an interest rate that's effectively higher.

Consolidation brings with it some confusing limitations. Essentially, only similar loans can be consolidated together. Government-backed Perkins and Stafford loans can be consolidated. But parent PLUS loans must be consolidated separately. And private loans must be consolidated on their own, too (students can theoretically use private consolidation loans to pay off Stafford/Perkins, effectively mixing government and private loans, but that's a terrible idea because it always increases the cost of the loans).

SPREAD OUT THE PAYMENTS? NOT ALWAYS A GOOD IDEA

Lumping loans together in a consolidation often serves a second function, a bit like a home refinancing—it gives students more loan payoff options. Many students opt for the chance to spread out the loans over longer terms, trading ten-year loans for twenty- or even twenty-five-year loans. Liberal arts grads making $30,000 and facing a $400 monthly payment probably have no choice, but should do this while holding their nose, and making a promise that when a big raise comes, they'll make extra payments on that loan. Changing a ten-year loan to a twenty-year loan cuts monthly payments by one-third, but the total paid over the life of the loan more than doubles. It's possible to cut monthly payments by up to half, but that will more than triple the price of the loan, notes finaid.org's Mark Kantrowitz. Now you know why banks readily encourage recent graduates to opt for the longest term possible. But you don't want to be paying your college loans when you pay your first tuition bill for your kids' college, do you?

One important note about early payments: Many lenders will tell you to take the longer-term loan and advise you that you can "pretend" it's a shorter-term loan later, and make extra payments when you get the money, as long as there's no penalty for early payment. That's true: You can always choose to make extra payments each month, and treat your monthly payment like a minimum payment. But there are obvious risks to this. First, many adults find the chance to pay the least possible amount just too tempting. But even if you are disciplined enough to make early payments, watch out: Many lenders won't apply the extra funds to the loan principle unless you expressly tell them to. It's a dirty trick, but many disciplined early loan-payers find the extra funds are simply saved by the bank and applied to the next month's standard payment. That means the early payment isn't doing anything for you. If you go this route, make sure to include a note with the extra payment expressly directing the bank to apply the extra funds to your principle. Then, watch your statements to make sure your loan principle was correctly reduced.

The good news about federal consolidation loans is there are no fees attached; it's against federal law to change fees for these consolidation loans. On the other hand, banks can offer discounts to students that sound enticing—but instead they can be traps. The discounts are real, but they can also be tricky, so it's in reviewing these discounts that you've got to pull out your magnifying glass.

Most banks offer a tiny break on interest rate for graduates who have their monthly payment automatically deducted from their checking account. That's a great idea.

Most also offer good-behavior discounts, promising to drop the interest rate a full point or more after thirty-six straight months with on-time payment. That's a good idea, too, except for this: You can lose the discount with just one late payment. Notoriously few former students make it through an entire ten- or twenty-year loan without one slipup—Kantrowitz, of FinAid, thinks only one in ten former students make it. Remember, even those who use automatic payments can have a bad month—if your account overdraws, you might be considered late. In many cases, one late payment and the discount is lost forever. In others, borrowers have to go all the way back to the beginning of the thirty-six-month discount clock to earn it back. So those good behavior discounts aren't always quite the good deal they appear to be.

Some lenders offer discounts that can't be lost, even if you are late with a payment. Even if the discount is smaller, that can be the better deal. Others reduce the principal for good behavior, another gift that can't be rescinded. Even better.

Other kinds of consolidations offer other hidden fees. Sallie Mae's private consolidation loan comes with no disbursement fee— if you bring a co-signer to the table. Without one, a 1 percent fee will be lumped into the loan—capitalized, as they like to say. That means it's easy to miss, unless you read carefully.

MIXING COLLEGE LOANS WITH OTHER LOANS

For many students, when consolidation offers come, it seems obvious to use those big loans, spread out the payments to lower the monthly bill, then use the extra cash to help pay down credit-card debt. After all, student-loan interest rates can be much lower than credit-card interest rates. Sallie Mae says one-third of all college students leave school with $10,000 or more in credit-card debt. Consolidating into a thirty-year loan and using the savings to pay off pricey credit-card debt sounds like sound financial planning. In fact, many experts recommend this.

It could very well be the biggest financial mistake you ever make.

There is no such thing as one-size-fits-all financial advice. There are circumstances where lower student-loan payments can help get credit-card debt under control as part of a very disciplined, life-changing financial plan. Switching credit-card debt into loan debt is a terrible trap, however, because rarely do consumers use this kind of one-shot financial lifesaver to change their buying habits. Getting credit-card spending under control is the first and most important step in any financial plan. Until the spending is under control, a stopgap borrowing measure won't help. And it will hurt.

Why? Because student-loan debt is forever. Really. There is no statute of limitations on student loans. Since changes in federal law governing student loans in 1998, reinforced by the draconian bankruptcy bill passed in 2005, there is effectively no way out of a student loan. It is not a stretch to compare the burden of student loans to the financial burden of having children, since the tools available to student-loan debt collectors bear a striking resemblance to the tools used by those pursuing deadbeat dads. The U.S. Department of Education can garnish wages, seize tax refunds, or even take Social Security checks in pursuit of its pound of flesh! The agency now hires private debt collectors who managed to collect $5 billion in loan debt during 2005. Things went so well the agency even inspired the IRS into imitating its methods.

The worst financial plan of all, and one that's far too common, is for a person headed down a financial spiral—as a last desperate effort before bankruptcy—to spread out their college loan in an effort to pay down credit-card debt. That's feeding the wrong beast, as the loan debt is forever. During the first meeting such a borrower has with a bankruptcy attorney, the lawyer will grimace when told of the student-loan mistake.

TRADING A HOME EQUITY LOAN FOR A STUDENT LOAN

Fast forward a few years, and many young professionals with equity in their condo or home might be tempted to use that equity to pay off the student loan. Their interest-rate savings might be minimal on a government-backed loan—a federal student-loan rate with a good behavior discount isn't far from home-equity loan rates. But there's a critical difference—interest on the home-equity loan is fully deductible, while the deduction for student-loan interest has serious limitations.

Is this a good idea? Maybe. The answer is a bit nuanced, says Liz Pulliam Weston, personal finance guru and author of several books on credit, including *Deal with Your Debt*. While student-loan debt is forever, the payment terms are not. Student-loan lenders offer a lot of flexibility in their repayment plans, including the potential of deferments for those who lose their jobs. Mortgage lenders offer no such flexibility. With mortgages, your monthly payment is your monthly payment. Skip those payments for a year and you'll lose your house. That means by trading student loans for a home-equity loan you will have increased your ultimate risk.

On the other hand, you certainly can save a little money on payments and interest, and a sizable chunk on a tax deduction. Those with onerous private student loans, paying 15 percent interest or more for that money, might be better served to trade that debt for house debt.

For that reason, Weston suggests splitting the difference and hedging your bets. Don't put all the equity in your home on the line to reduce your student loans—Weston recommends not leveraging more than 80 percent. But under that limit, if you have equity to spare and you are confident you can make the payments for the foreseeable future, the student loan–home equity loan swap can be smart.

Student Loans
GOTCHA-STOPPING STRATEGIES

1. If you make an early payment, send a note to make sure it's properly applied.
2. Don't use student loans to feed bad credit-card habits. Thoughtfully consider the risks of paying off student loans with home equity.
3. Consolidate variable-rate loans before the grace period is over so the in-school discounted loan rate is used when your new interest rate is calculated.
4. You cannot consolidate all your loans twice. If you believe you might want to consolidate again in the future—say you opt to stick with a ten-year term but would like the option of switching lenders later on—leave one of your loans out of the consolidation. You'll have to make two payments initially, but with two loans, you are eligible for another consolidation.
5. Exhaust all federally backed loans before trying the private student-loan market. Treat such loans as radioactive; borrow as little as possible and pay them off as quickly as possible.
6. When shopping for private loans, get rates and terms from at least three lenders. Don't be afraid to pick a lender outside your school's preferred-lender list, even if the school advises against that. It's against the law for the school to insist you use their favored lenders.
7. Don't believe the interest rate you are quoted on private student loans; the actual rate may be much higher after the bank considers your credit score.
8. Penalty-fee information on student loans is notoriously difficult to find, but it can be deadly to endure. Every fee ends up on the back end of the loan, "capitalized"—meaning you'll pay interest on each fine. Also, some lenders charge continuous penalty fees, even if you only miss a single payment, declaring that your account is past due on every subsequent month—a practice called "pyramiding." The practice is questionable, but it is done, so when you miss a payment, bring your account current as soon as possible, or else you'll face repeat penalty fees.
9. Also, ask about penalty fees, origination fees, and prepayment fees when shopping. High fees can turn a good loan into a bad loan very quickly.

14

Sneaky Fees Everywhere

America used to be the land of the free.
Now it's the land of the fee.

Emily Thorton, *BusinessWeek*

No book could ever list all the hidden fees consumers encounter in their daily lives. But I've tried to collect the most common, frustrating fees and list them all in one place for you. Some, however, don't fit neatly into any of the categories we've already discussed. So this chapter is a collection of all the rest. We'll begin with car-related fees, then hit the hidden costs of website shopping, sneaky insurance costs, and a few more that might really surprise you.

I. Using a Loan to Buy a Car

Outside of buying a house, a car purchase is the biggest big-ticket item most consumers will ever buy. So it's a natural breeding ground for hidden fees. Endless books and websites are devoted to switcheroo pricing and other car dealership tricks, so I won't deal with those here. Instead, I want to focus on one particularly insidious element of car buying—the auto loan.

The fatal mistake for car buyers is to answer this question, posed by the dealer: "What monthly payment can you afford?" Just don't do it. In fact, don't mention a loan at all. Tell dealers you will pay in cash, in full, for as long as you can during negotiations. Tell them you have a rich uncle, you have an inheritance, you are independently wealthy, I don't care. Go ahead, lie. They will, so you can. Do anything to avoid discussing monthly payments.

Why? Car loans offered by dealers are nearly always a bad deal. In the high-pressure environment of a car dealership, the minute you begin talking about monthly payments, you're almost certain to lose. It's far too easy for dealers to pad these payments with small tack-on services like extended warranties or useless undercoating. Before you know it, a $278-a-month four-year loan is a $274-a-month five-year loan and you still think you have a good deal, but you don't.

If you really do need a car loan, there is one surefire way to avoid the flawed monthly payment conversation: Get a loan from your bank before you shop. That will cut off the monthly conversation before it starts, and keep the focus right where it belongs—the car's bottom-line price. I know some dealers will claim they can get you special financing. A bank loan is often *still* the better deal? Why?

Remember the lender's love triangle, the trilateral dilemma, also called reverse competition? That occurs when three people are involved in a transaction and two stand to gain if the price goes up. It's simple: You think the dealer is negotiating on your behalf, acting as your agent to get you a good loan. Instead, dealers get a cut of the loan from the lender, so both the dealer and the lender benefit when the cost of funds goes up. You didn't really trust the car salesman to be fair with your loan, did you? You want to stay out of this lion's den as best you can.

Note: You never want a person shopping for you who stands to gain when things cost you more.

When you arrive at the dealership with financing already in place, you remove one level of complexity from an already complex transaction. Complexity and confusion are the tools of your enemy here, so shedding the dealership car-loan discussion works in your favor.

And there's another reason to avoid dealer car loans. They create an easy opening for dealer tack-on fees.

By the time you are ready to do the deal, even if you already have a car loan, the dealer will still try to rope you into dealer financing. It is possible the dealer might offer a rate that's fractionally lower than the one you already have. Even so, the dealer loan usually is *still* a bad deal. It's often a misdirection play designed to distract you from other fees that are snuck into the loan.

Getting distracted by 0.25 increments in your loan rate is a big mistake. Don't outsmart yourself with the numbers here: A quarter-percent on a car loan is nothing worth fighting for.

For example: You borrow $15,000 to buy a car and pay it back during four years. At 6.25 percent, you'll pay $1,991 in interest during those four years, and make $354.00 payments each month. What if the dealer talks you into taking their "better deal" loan at 6 percent? How much do you save?

Your new payments would be $352.28. You saved $1.78 cents a month. During all four years, you'll pay $1,909 in interest—a savings of $82 over the "more expensive" loan. Meanwhile, you'll be playing with fire, as we'll soon see.

There are endless examples of hidden costs slimed into auto loans, but my favorite is the extended warranty. Auto dealers love tricking naïve buyers into tack-on insurance policies that turn 36,000-mile warranties into 60,000-mile warranties. The plans typically cost $1,000 to $2,000, snuck into monthly payments for $20 to $40 a month. That doesn't sound like a lot, but it's everything to the dealership. In the age of flat Internet pricing, dealer tack-ons are the lifeblood of profits. That's why dealers will do almost anything—including lying—to get consumers to agree to such sneaky fees. Some dealers even tell consumers that they are obligated to buy the coverage, implying that lenders require it. They don't, and you should never buy it as part of your car deal.

Are extended insurance warranties ever worth it? In an age where cars now don't even require tune-ups for 100,000 miles, these policies are less and less valuable. Some consumers might still enjoy the peace of mind they offer, but can always buy the policies later. And you don't have to buy them from the dealer. A simple principle applies: If you really want an extended warranty, get at least three competitive bids for it. If you let the dealer convince you to roll the cost into the loan, you are bound to overpay.

Fortunately, auto buying is highly regulated, because auto dealers have a well-earned reputation for being manipulative. Many states have enacted "regret periods" that allow consumers to void such unnecessary extended warranties. In Washington State, for example, consumers have seven days after the car purchase to send a letter to dealers saying they want to cancel an extended-warranty purchase. The dealer has to refund the money upon receipt.

Other unnecessary tack-ons are also sprinkled into many car loans, such as undercoating treatment (not needed) or prepaid oil changes (cheaper alternatives abound).

But nothing compares to the tack-on interest rates and one-time fees that dealers often pack into auto loans. Called "dealer reserve" in the industry, consumers pay close to $1 billion each year in auto-loan markups, according to the Consumer Federation of America. A study of loans issued by GM from 1999 to 2003 showed that one in four consumers paid marked-up interest rates when buying a GM car.

Moreover, blacks and Hispanics were most likely to face unfair car-loan markups, the report said. African-Americans paid an average interest rate of 9.01 percent on car loans, compared to 7.38 percent for whites. Hispanics paid an average rate of 8.52 percent.

What about those incredibly enticing zero percent loan offers? They always come with strings attached. One of them is this: You surrender any rebate you receive to the seller. However much you think you are saving in interest expenses, you often lose more by giving up the rebate. The dealer has already done all of this math, so you should, too. Before signing up for any zero percent loan, make sure you run the numbers through an Internet calculator. Many factors impact the math: the size of your down payment, the amount of sales tax, the value of your trade-in, and so on. But to keep it simple, we'll do a straight sale without the tax. And you'll see that unless the loan is huge, and the rebate is small, you're better off taking the cash.

Let's look at the rebate vs. zero percent financing dilemma, using the example above: a $15,000 car with a $3,000 rebate or zero percent financing.

Generally, zero percent loans require fairly fast payment, often limited to three years or less. So if you take the rebate and pay 6.25 percent interest for your $12,000 car loan (price of the car minus the rebate) during three years, you'll pay a total of $13,191. That's $1,809 less than that $15,000 loan at 0 percent. On a similarly structured $25,000 car purchase, taking the rebate still saves $816. Only when the price crosses $33,000 does trading the rebate for the interest rate make sense.

But even if the savings is minimal, remember this: By signing up for the dealer loan, you are opening yourself up to other car-loan Gotchas, like processing fees, tack-on charges, and so on. My formula above also doesn't account for the potential of a lower auto-loan rate, which you might find by shopping around to different banks. Then there's this: Those tempting zero interest loans are only available for people with fantastic credit. What if you apply and are denied? Then you'll be tempted to go with your dealer's Plan B, since you've already filled out the application. One thing you *really* never want is an auto dealer's Plan B. In some circumstances, when the rebate is small and the car loan is large, zero percent financing makes sense. But it's often better not to be tempted into the dragon's lair of dealer financing, unless the savings is truly substantial and you have your magnifying glass buffed and ready.

II. Auto Insurance

While we're on the topic of credit and cars, this is a good time to mention the unholy alliance between auto insurance and credit reports. You might not know this, but your credit score has a direct impact on your car insurance. How much? I can't tell you. No one knows. Trade secret.

But it could be a lot. Birney Birnbaum, an insurance expert for the Center for Economic Justice in Austin, Texas, says some consumers are penalized as much as 50 percent on auto insurance for having low credit scores.

The industry's trade group, the Insurance Information Institute, says it's fair to use credit scores in premium formulas because it claims there's a statistical correlation between low credit scores and the likelihood a driver will have an accident. It uses mathematical models all the time to more fairly distribute costs—that's why young male drivers pay more than middle-aged women, for example.

But here's the problem: Consumers have no way of knowing if their credit scores are raising their insurance rates. And they don't know what they could do to fix that. If a 650 credit score dinged your annual rates by $300, perhaps you'd work harder to raise your score, if you knew it would make a difference. But consumers literally have no information about the credit score insurance penalty. Your only weapon, then, is comparison shopping. Not all insurance companies apply credit scores the same way, so it's important to get multiple quotes, particularly if you have less-than-perfect credit.

III. Homeowners Insurance

And while we're on the topic of secret databases and hidden prices, homeowners should know that a data-gathering company named ChoicePoint likely has a big impact on the price they pay for home insurance. The company, which collects data on virtually every American and sells it to various industries and the government, provides data to insurance underwriters about the claim history of most U.S. homes. The database, called Comprehensive Loss Underwriting Exchange, or C.L.U.E., can be devastating to home buyers. New owners may find they are unable to buy insurance at all if their new property has a history of being expensive to insure. Other buyers pay two or three times the going rate because of past claims dating back many years. Similar to auto insurance firms, some home insurers also use credit scores when writing policies. A low credit score can hurt here, too.

There is only one way for consumers to know how much a house's history—or their own credit history—is impacting the price of their insurance. Insurance firms should provide the price they'd charge if all these factors were ideal, and explain what ideal means. No insurer volunteers this "best price" information. But the Fair Credit Reporting Act requires any company that uses a credit score against consumers in any way to provide what's called a "Notice of Adverse Action." Lawyers are still sorting out whether insurance companies will ever have to come clean about their use of credit scores and the true cost to consumers. For now, shopping around is your only defense.

IV. Health Clubs

There's no better way to know your enemy that to interview a defector. That makes Lala C. a gold mine.

Lala (I've changed her name) was an assistant sales manager for a nationwide chain of health clubs. Eventually, she was so sickened by the sales tactics she was forced to use that she quit. It's not that she was *sometimes* asked to stretch the truth about membership fees. She was *always* asked to stretch the truth about membership fees. She wrote in to the *Red Tape Chronicles* one day as part confession, part cautionary tale.

"I never really felt comfortable about a single promotion they offered," she says. "It seemed they had people sit around dreaming up new ways to 'bait and switch' or otherwise deceive customers."

Like this: The chain she worked for regularly ran promotions offering a $0 enrollment fee. Sounds good, right? You would think $0 means free. Not so.

Signing up at the club always required payment of two fees—an enrollment fee and a separate "processing" fee. Fee No. 2 cost $79 when Lala worked there. So free enrollment actually cost $79. But there's more. New customers were forced to pay their first and last month's health club dues on sign-up day. Add it all up, and customers who walked in the door with the promise of free enrollment found their wallets lightened by $180. And that fee bought consumers a membership that could only be used on certain days each week. Some $0 enrollment.

Another favorite tactic Lala's company employed was to offer two-for-one membership promotions. Seems like a great opportunity. Everyone needs a workout buddy, right?

But watch the math as we start to work through the details Lala provided. For starters, the enrollment fee changed nearly every day of the month. So a sales clerk working on a two-for-one deal would simply raise the price—perhaps by $50—to create an inflated enrollment price. The new price, $129, would be waived for the second member, but the first would be paying enough for both of them. Then, both would have to pay the aforementioned $79 processing fee. And finally, both would have to pay for the first and last month's membership. Add it all up, Lala said, and where a single person would pay perhaps $350 to walk out with a full membership on a given day, a two-for-one pair would pay about $600. Still a savings, but probably not what the newly motivated workout buddies had in mind when they stopped in for the two-for-one deal.

Another typical promotion involved the promise of free months of membership. Lala's club sometimes offered six months free. But those six months were tacked on to the end of a membership—an eighteen-month membership. And only those who prepaid for their entire membership got the free six months.

"For myself and many other salespeople, it was a true struggle to present these sales in a manner that . . . would not get (anyone) upset," Lala said. "It still upsets me to drive by (the club) and see huge signs and banners advertising too-good-to-be-true offers. I'm still in sales. It's people like them that make my profession look bad."

Anyone who's ever tried to join a gym knows Lala's club isn't unique. In fact, such hidden fee tactics are standard in the health-club industry. In New York City, health clubs became so sneaky that the New York City Council's Investigation Division conducted an anonymous survey of health clubs in 2003. The survey studied clubs from eight different chains. As you might guess, there were few gold stars issued.

All across the city, the hard sell was in. Four out of five clubs refused to allow faux consumers sent by the city council to take the health-club contracts off-site for further review. Half the time, there was a perfectly logical reason for this: There was no contract. The clubs had no written materials at all explaining the club's fee structure.

Other club behaviors were neatly uniform. For example, 96 percent failed to explain exactly how club members could cancel their memberships.

The following year, New York officials continued to scrutinize health clubs. New York's attorney general at the time, the fiery Eliot Spitzer, announced that Bally had agreed to change its marketing tactics after hundreds of complaints led to an investigation by his agency. The company repeatedly signed up new members for three-year contracts under dubious circumstances—many of the consumers were young or not proficient in English and did not understand the binding terms of the contract, Spitzer's office said. Bally also advertised deceptively low monthly fees without telling consumers they had to pay thousands of dollars in initiation fees. In a settlement, Bally said it had done nothing wrong but agreed to issue refunds.

Perhaps the best part of the settlement: Going forward, Bally was bound to give members a much more generous "regret" period. New members could cancel with a full refund up to seven days after they'd signed up, no questions asked. For other clubs, New York state law requires only a three-day regret period.

The compulsory puns flowed from Spitzer's office.

"People joining health clubs expect trimmer bodies, not trimmer wallets," Spitzer said in his announcement.

There's nothing funny at all about the jungle that is joining a gym. Because many clubs insist on hooking monthly payments directly into your checking account, and they require long-term contracts, these memberships should be treated with great skepticism. Sales tactics are even more cutthroat than what you'll hear in used-car dealerships. Consumers venturing into a club should keep all these tactics in mind, and start with a few simple rules:

1. Never sign up on the spot. Always take the paperwork home with you to read it over. Most people are confused and overwhelmed by the flurry of numbers that come from a health club sales pitch. Time is your friend here. Whatever you are told, the deal you are being offered does not expire today. The club is going to sign you up using the same terms tomorrow, next week, even next month. Take the contract home.

2. Avoid direct deposit payments, if you can. Canceling health club memberships is notoriously difficult. The trickiest part is to stop paying for them. When a club is hooked into your bank, canceling can take monumental efforts—some consumers find the only true escape is to close their checking account. If possible, write the club a check, use automatic online bill-pay (not automatic draft!) or pay with a credit card. You'll have an easier time cutting off the flow of funds if the relationship goes sour.

3. Know your rights to quit. Many states have "regret" cancellation policies of three days or more. Know what your state's law is before you go shopping for a membership. That way, even if you are talked into signing a contract on the spot, you still have an out. And after you sign, many states grant additional consumer cancellation rights—consumers can often void a contract if they move a certain distance away from the club, for example. In New York, it's 25 miles. You can also cancel the contract if the club no longer offers you the service you signed up for—for example, if the club's pool closes. If you are struck by a physical ailment that prevents you from working out, you may also be entitled to drop your contract.

4. There are perils to long-term contracts. Sign up for the shortest contract you can. As with cell phones, there is value in flexibility. Long-term health club contracts can be a lot of trouble; prepaid contracts can be a disaster. Put simply, how do you know the club will be there for you in three years? Clubs go out of business all the time, and it's very hard to get a refund from an empty building.

V. Website Shipping Charges

The Internet, in some ways, is a consumer's dream. True comparison shopping is always good for consumers. Only ten short years ago, true price comparisons generally required a whole lot of driving and rarely involved more than three stores. Economists call this the "search cost," and it used to be pricey. Search costs limit a consumer's ability to get the best price. That's why search engines are a consumer's best friend. Today, shoppers can literally bargain globally, playing merchants off each other from anywhere on the planet. To stay price competitive, a store must be willing to match a price offered by a company halfway around the world—assuming, for the moment, no added shipping costs. As Thomas Friedman might put it, a world without search costs is nearly flat—an optimal situation for consumers.

Merchants, of course, hate this state of affairs. So there's only one way to fix it. Cheat. Lure consumers with a low, low price (websites call this the "landing price") and then pump up that bottom line with tack-on charges. These almost always involve shipping-and-handling charges.

The phenomenon is easy to see in action on auction site eBay by simply searching for all items that are for sale at 1 cent. Obviously, these sellers only make money by charging high shipping-and-handling fees, but by charging 1 cent for items, they end up at the top of eBay searches, a clear advantage scored by cheating the system.

High shipping charges are so annoying for consumers that many websites have created free-shipping offers as a marketing lure. These almost always come with a catch, however—they are "throttled," or kept intentionally slow. Throttled packages are temporarily lost in the mailroom, if you will. Consumers who respond to free-shipping offers are primed for a website Gotcha—the "Rush Order Upgrade" or similarly named deception. Sure, the shipping is free, but the package will sit in the mailroom for ten days or so. The rush order, however, will be there in a few days. Note that rush order doesn't mean faster shipping. It means faster handling inside the company—or, correctly translated, it means no throttling.

Consumers are often tempted to pay this rush-order fee. When they've gotten that far and are now that close to clicking "Purchase," and now have their heart set on getting that CD/radio/hockey jersey, a moderate tack-on fee to get the stuff five days quicker is awfully tempting. Exploiting this impulse with just the right nuance is critical to the bottom line.

Here's how an e-commerce trade magazine named *Marketing Experiments Journal* puts it:

> The average customer is not so gullible as to be fooled by a merchant with a low "landed price" (total cost) but a high purchase price . . . KEY POINT: Offer free shipping, but keep the total landed price less than your major competitors. Then offer a "rush order upgrade." This would NOT be an upgraded shipping service; it would be an upgraded "handling" service (i.e., from 48-hour order processing to same-day order processing).

It's good to know marketers don't think of consumers as completely gullible—just partially gullible. Your key point: See right through landing prices and only compare websites deals on true, actually get-it-in-your-hands purchase prices.

3
Toolkit

Introduction to the Toolkit

Okay, now that you know the game, and you know the rules, I want to give you the tools. In this section, you'll find a host of essential, specific tools for fighting back against sneaky fees and deceptive practices. They run from simple to complex, starting with how to make a successful complaint phone call, rising through letters to government agencies, and eventually, a primer on your legal options. This section also includes detailed results of the Ponemon Institute Gotcha study, including specific amounts average Americans lose each year on various bills, and most important, the likelihood that you'll get a refund from each industry. We begin with a discussion of customer-service phone calls, including tips from employees who take calls in phone-bank sweatshops and sample scripts you can whip out if you feel you need help breaking through those brick walls.

1

Customer-Service Calls

Of all the fibs uttered to you by corporations, here's the one I bet you are least likely to believe.

"Your call is important to us."

The fib is often followed by a rare moment of precise, but disappointing, honesty. "It will be answered within twenty-two minutes."

When you hear these words, you know you're in for a tough time. Sitting on hold, waiting for the privilege to fight with some company, is the last thing in the world you want to be doing. And yet, you wait. What happens twenty-two minutes later may very well be worth a lot of money to you.

Perhaps nothing evokes consumer frustration in the twenty-first century more than customer-service phone calls. During his 2005 National Customer Rage Study (the fact that such a thing even exists should tell you something), consultant Scott M. Broetzmann found that 70 percent of consumers had experienced rage at a company in the past twelve months. Perhaps that's because 25 percent had one incident that took at least nine hours of complaining to resolve.

And yet, like death and taxes, these blood-boiling phone calls are inevitable for all of us. No matter who you are, your time will come, and the call will cost you. Whether it's your lunch break, work time, or a Saturday afternoon on the rocking chair, a company you do business with is about to rob you of twenty-two minutes of your time. And during that time, your blood pressure will almost certainly rise, leaving you, perhaps, not at your levelheaded best when you finally get your turn.

But if you let your frustration get the better of you, if you start to rage, you'll end up really wasting your twenty-two-minute investment. So the first rule of a successful customer-service call—no matter whose list of recommendations you read—is to keep calm. How do you do that? By feeling confident that you'll get what you want in the end. Rage is what anger becomes when it's fueled by helplessness. But you're not helpless. You know you have rights. You know you can write letters, involve regulators, join lawsuits. With any luck, it won't come to that—because you have a plan to get what you want right away, with one phone call. Here's how to make that call.

BEFORE YOU CALL

There's a lot you can do to increase your chances of success even before you pick up the phone. Make sure you have a decent speakerphone to work with. Nothing makes those twenty-two minutes pass more slowly than a creaky neck. If you can move around while you're waiting—if you can fold laundry, perhaps—the time won't feel wasted, and you'll be calmer.

It's also important to be realistic about your time investment. If you're trying to challenge a hidden fee on your cell phone, don't place the call when you know you'll have to hang up in seven minutes. Set aside at least half an hour for most of these confrontations. That means, generally, you should only pick the battles that are worth thirty minutes of your time.

Don't call before you gather the necessary supporting documents you need, and make sure you have a very clear idea of what you plan to say and what you want. You should be able to say it in one or two sentences: ("I was told the cable installation would be free, but there's a $29 charge on my bill. I want that charge refunded.") And don't touch the phone before you have a pen and a blank piece of paper for note taking. Use the blank forms at the back of this book.

MAKE THE CONNECTION

Of course, negotiations cannot begin until you get someone to talk with. Most U.S. companies will force you through a frustrating automated telephone tree—Lands' End, Dillard's, L.L. Bean, and Hyatt are among notable exceptions. In the business, they're called IVR systems, for Interactive Voice Response. There might be times when these work for you: for example, when you only need to hear an account balance. But most times, you'll want a person. A visit to gethuman.com can help. The site was created by Paul English, a software developer who was once a vice president at Intuit, out of sheer frustration with all the computers he had to talk with when calling customer service. GetHuman.com is the ultimate cheat sheet for reaching human beings. On the site, with the help of thousands of volunteers, English publishes the tips to faking out IVR systems and getting a human (example: To reach a real Telecheck operator, the site says, Press 1, 3, * at prompts).

Another trick that works wonders is to call the sales or advertising office when customer-service lines offer nothing but hold music. Sales calls are always answered during regular business hours because companies are always organized to take money. So you'll no doubt get a human that way, and then can ask to be transferred.

You might just end up in the customer-service queue again, but here's a tip used by NBC producer Mike Fomil, an expert at getting humans on the line: If you do end up back on hold listening to Muzak, call the sales office again, and with any luck, the same person will answer. Say to him or her, politely, "Look, I don't want to ruin your day. But I really do need to speak with a person who can help me. Please help me find the right person. If you transfer me back to the customer-service hold line, I'm just going to keep calling you and neither of us will get anything done all day." It takes a bit of moxie, but it does work.

KNOW YOUR ENEMY—ER, HELPFUL AGENT

After you get a human, you'll want to act like one. You may not feel like it ("This is the tenth time I've had to call to get this overdraft fee refunded!") but you'll want to do it anyway. Timothy Warner runs a website called Mother Tongue Annoyances that's devoted to abuse of the English language. He offers very good advice on using words to your advantage, and to our point here, about how to use language as your ally while talking to customer-service operators. The way to start, he says, is to "Have a Copernican Revolution."

Copernicus, of course, was the astronomer who first asserted that the earth was not the center of the universe. Neither are you. However awful that unfair cell-phone charge may be, it will only help you if you can realize and understand the circumstances of the person you are talking to. He or she probably doesn't work for the company you are calling, so yelling out "You people are thieves!" rarely works. Asking questions like, "How are you?" "What's the weather like where you are?" or "How late do you have to work tonight?" creates a friendly atmosphere. Later, when you're getting into the thick of the discussion, you can ask nonconfrontational questions like, "What options do you see on the screen in front of you?" You'll get further being friendly.

The rest of Warner's column, "The Zen of Placing Customer Service Calls," is worth a read. You can see it on his website at mtannoyances.com.

But before you ask a customer-service agent about the weather, your first question should be "What is your name, operator, and how can I get back in touch with you if we get disconnected?" Since many operators introduce themselves when they pick up the phone, and many consumers usually don't understand what's been said, politely ask the operator to repeat the greeting ("I'm sorry, I didn't catch your name. What is it?"). If he or she won't give you a name, at least ask for a first name, an operator number, or an extension. As a last resort, have the operator write down your number in case your cell-phone battery dies or some other surprise occurs.

YOU GET MORE BEES WITH HONEY

Once you are on a first-name basis, you are well on your way to seeing the operator as a person, which really is to your advantage. Picture this situation: You're a college student earning extra money at night dealing with a steady stream of angry customers upset about cell-phone text-message rates. Customer-service representatives (CSRs) sometimes take fifty calls per shift. To give you an idea of their perspective, here's what one cell-phone CSR wrote in to *Red Tape Chronicles* recently (misspellings included):

> i'm a CSR and i must say one thing, i dont care if your right or wrong. my job sucks . . . so it is my main goal to say no. I say no because its fun . . . if somebody wants to be rude with me, i'll step down to their level because my company allows it as long as i dont use profanity.

If you are really brave, for an even better picture of what *they* think of *us,* visit customerssuck.com. At this site, frustrated agents tell stories of greedy, cheating, and stupid consumers. In fact, to site users, we've been bestowed with the nickname "SCs"—for Sucky Customers.

The classic case of demonizing consumers involved a Comcast customer from Illinois named LaChania Govan, who called the company's customer-service line many times during a four-week stretch while trying to get her digital-cable service to work.

Someone she talked to didn't take kindly to her repeated cries for help. The following month, her bill arrived and the name on her account had been changed slightly. It was addressed to:

"Bitch Dog."

Govan, a twenty-five-year-old working mother, became a national celebrity for fifteen minutes. Her story dripped in delicious irony: Govan worked in customer service at the time. Soon after Govan's tale hit the newspapers, Comcast said it had fired the misbehaving employee. And yet, it's easy to imagine that, in those dark rooms where customer-service folks take our calls, Govan is hardly the first person ever called a bad name. Now, imagine you are the one friendly call this agent receives on a given night. You are warm, you are even-keeled, you are reasonable. You say please and thank you.

You will have a leg up on every other caller that night.

RUN OUT THE CLOCK

An old school of thought holds that if you aren't getting the answer you want from one CSR, just hang up and try another operator. That doesn't work as well as it used to, said Broetzmann, the rage study author, because sophisticated databases track customer calls now. CSRs enter copious notes about calls, so if you try the hang-up-and-call-back method, you are likely to hear, "I see you just called in a minute ago . . ."

In fact, according to one anonymous *Red Tape Chronicles* reader and working CSR, consumers should do just the opposite. He advises running out the clock on call centers, which are sometimes paid per call:

> The strongest tool a customer has is call length . . . They pay these companies a very small amount for each call taken, so the call center wants to have the shortest call length possible, and take as many calls in a given period of time as possible. They want to see 3 to 5 minutes per call . . . If your call goes 10 minutes, you (or the rep you're talking to) have the attention of a supervisor. The supervisors have computerized call monitors that alert them to long calls.

At a certain point, the economics tip in favor of the caller—it becomes more expensive to keep saying no to you on the phone than it is to give you what you want.

Keeping the line open requires smart tactics. You'll ask for a supervisor; you'll be told none are available. The operator will offer to have a supervisor call back. That will never happen. You must do all you can to keep the call clock running. Say you set aside this afternoon to resolve the problem and you really need to do it today. Keep calmly repeating your story, the same strategy CSRs are taught (they keep reading from their script, you do the same). Don't raise your voice or swear, which makes it easier for a CSR to hang up on you. Just keep talking.

WHEN YOU GET TO THE POINT OF NEGOTIATION

The first rule of negotiating is simple: Say exactly what you want, as soon as possible. Example: "I see a $36 fee on my phone bill. I was never told about this fee. I want a refund."

But rule No. 2 follows close by: Never ask for a yes from someone who can only say no. Make sure the person you are talking to is empowered to give you what you want. Frontline operators can only do so much—like cashiers in a grocery store, who sometimes need to get a special manager's key before giving refunds. If you get a sense the person you're talking to has his or her hands tied by corporate policy, ask for a manager. You'll be told the manager can't do anything else for you. Ask anyway.

When you manage to get a manager on the line, think like a manager yourself, and make a business case, not an emotional argument, says Broetzmann.

"I had a problem with a credit-card company recently, and when I called, I said, 'You'll see I've spent $50,000 in travel expenses on this card in recent years. Do you really want to lose me as a customer over this?' "

The business case must be real, however. A vague "I've been with the company for years" statement probably won't work.

MORE ZEN

Another important rule to follow: If you expect companies to be honest, be honest yourself. CSRs tend to very quickly adopt a bunker mentality about their jobs—read customerssuck.com and you'll get the sense they think we're all cheaters. And with calls like this one, that might be understandable.

"When I asked [the caller] to head over to where their modem and router is they would go, 'That's gonna be kinda hard as I'm using someone else's router.' "

Calling customer support to ask for help setting up stolen wire-less Internet service is a bad idea. When you call and lie, you'll get what you deserve.

As for when to know you are nearing the end of a useful customer-service call, customerssuck offers some good advice:

"I have been talking to some friends and we have discovered that we use different phrases or words that should signify to the customer that the call is not going to go any further," one writes. "My all time favorite is 'Sir' or 'Ma'am, is there anything else I may help you with?' "

To really get you into the mind of the enemy, I asked the moderators of customerssuck.com to provide a top ten list of things they wish consumers knew before calling. Here's what they came up with, compiled by the site owner and anonymous customer-service representative who goes by the pseudonym Rapscallion:

Customerssuck.com top-ten list of phone call tips

1. Be civil. We do understand that this is a frustrating problem for you, and your frustration is probably compounded by the wait you had to get through to a real live human being, but the more civil you can be (not abusive, sarcastic, profane, or belligerent), the more likely it is that you will walk away with a satisfying resolution to your problem.

2. Allow the rep to talk. While this seems like an insignificant point, a good many frustrations arise because callers "talk over" a rep trying to explain something crucial. A good rep will let the caller have his or her say, and then explain the problem.

3. Don't ramble. Jot down the salient points of the problem on a piece of paper if you know you have a propensity to ramble. It's very helpful in allowing you to get right to the point, thus helping solve the problem quicker. The rep doesn't need to hear about all the details of your hernia operation when you are calling to dispute charges on your phone bill.

4. Don't blame reps for corporate policies. The nature of call centers, etc., is that the employees within them are relatively low-level in the organization. They cannot change corporate policy no matter how much they are screamed and yelled at. If you are dissatisfied with an aspect of corporate policy, ask the rep (civilly!) for the address of the corporate office and the names of the customer-services manager and head of strategy, and write to those individuals complaining about the policy.

5. Remember that the person you are talking to is just that—a person. They are not a machine, or a mindless computer-generated voice. It could be your neighbor, your son, or your mother working there. They are as frustrated as the caller by poor policies, but each caller has to deal with the problem only once. The rep has to hear the same litany of complaints over and over again. There is no reason to be deliberately unkind or upsetting to the rep; it just makes the caller look like a fool.

6. Demanding a supervisor will not always work. Doing so for a minor matter is insulting to the representative to whom you are talking, but there very well may be no supervisor available. Many twenty-four-hour call centers have no supervisor at night, and there is often one supervisor per several dozen representatives. Supervisors have to follow the same policies as the frontline representatives in most cases, and will often tell you the same thing. Demanding a supervisor for something the initial representative is unable to do for you is tantamount to calling them a liar. A supervisor should only be needed if the representative doesn't have the training or knowledge to help you.

> (Author's Note: Of course a customer-service representative is going to tell you not to ask for a supervisor. But you should, anyway. It's good to understand that you might be insulting the rep, however, so being polite can't hurt.)

7. Be reasonable and retain a sense of perspective. Decide whether or not throwing a fit over a small inconvenience or 20 cents or so is worth losing your dignity, or the risk of verbally assaulting an innocent representative of the company. Threats of legal action go one of two ways—either you're seen as blowing things out of proportion with an empty threat or you will be referred to the company's lawyers as it then becomes a legal matter for which the phone representative cannot help you.

8. Consider seeing a therapist if you find yourself screaming at a powerless representative.

9. Accept that sometimes you cannot be helped. There will be some circumstances when the entire company cannot do anything for you. Sometimes, the only answer the service reps can give is "No."

10. Don't tell us how long you've been on hold. We're sorry that it took us fifteen minutes to get to your call, but you don't need to tell us about it; we know about it—we've been answering calls nonstop during that time. Now, the extra two minutes you're taking to tell us this is an extra two minutes that is spent not helping you and not helping others on hold.

Of course, the best trick of all is to make as few customer service calls as possible. That means buying reliable brands (not always the cheapest brands) and buying from retail stores that will stand behind their products and take complaints. But if you must call, here's some scripts to rip out of this book and place by the phone.

Sample Phone Scripts
CUSTOMER-SERVICE REPRESENTATIVE

GET A REFUND

Dinera DeDonde: Hi, I'm Dinera DeDonde, and there's a fee on my cell-phone bill I don't understand. Can you tell me your name please?

Ima Stuburness: Yes, my name is Ima, operator 1243. How can I help you?

Dinera: Well, there's an entry on my bill that says "handset upgrade fee." Could you explain what it is to me?

Ima: Sure. When you got a new phone two months ago, you agreed to pay this fee for connecting your new phone.

(Note the trigger words "You agreed." Don't take the bait. Don't argue the point; just state yours.)

Dinera: Thank you for taking the time to explain this to me. But there was a miscommunication. No one told me about this fee.

Ima: Oh yes, ma'am, we did. And it's in your contract, so you agreed to it.

Dinera: Thank you for your patience, Ima, but I'm sorry, this certainly wasn't made clear to me, and $36 is a lot. I would remember that. Can you read to me the part of my contract that indicates I'll have to pay a $36 fee?

(Don't allow him or her to offer to mail it to you—that just creates an opportunity to end the call.)

Ima: I can't access your contract right now.

Dinera: Well, since no one explained this fee to me, and you can't produce the paper I supposedly signed to agree to pay the fee, I would like to request a refund or fee waiver.

Ima: I'm sorry, miss, but we can't do that.

Dinera: Well, if it's something that you can't do, can I talk to your supervisor?

Ima: He's busy right now, but if you leave your number, he will call you back.

Dinera: I don't want him to call me back, I want to fix this. You know, I've been a Big Mobile Phone Company customer for three years, and I just added it up, and I've paid almost $4,000 to your company during that time. I'm sure your manager wouldn't want me to leave your company over this fee. I know I'd have to pay a fee to cancel my contract, but Not-So-Big Wireless Phone Company is running a special right now with more minutes each month for $10 less, and if I have to pay you this $36, that will really tip the scales and I'll leave.

Ima: Oh, my manager just got off the phone. Let me see if I can catch him.

(interminable pause)

Ima: Miss, my manager says we can cut the fee in half because you have been a good customer.

Dinera: I'm glad your manager is agreeable to talking about this. Can I talk to him now? Because I don't believe I should pay any of this fee.

Ima: Let me see, miss.

(another interminable pause)

Ima: Good news. My manager said he'd waive the entire fee.

Dinera: Wonderful!

Ima: But as long as I have you on the phone, I see you don't have a text-message plan on your line. Would you like to add one? We have a special going right now.

Dinera: One thing at a time. No thanks, for now. Let's just make sure this fee waiver goes through.

GET A MANAGER ON THE PHONE

John Roadblock: So, miss, I'm sorry, but there isn't anything I can do to help you. Will there be anything else?

Mary Tothetop: I appreciate your time. And it does seem we've hit an impasse. So can I talk to your supervisor?

John: He's busy right now, but if you leave your number, he will call you back.

Mary: No, it's important that I resolve this today—I actually am taking a few hours off of work and left the kids with Grandma so I can deal with this. I must resolve it today.

John: But my supervisor can't tell you anything different from what I've told you.

Mary: That may be true. But I feel the need to express my feelings about your company to someone who's a manager. So please indulge me.

John: But he's on the phone.

Mary: I can wait. As I said, I've set aside time to deal with this right now.

John: Okay, I'll put you on hold.

(interminable wait)

John: He's still with another customer. I strongly recommend you hang up and let him call you back.

Mary: I ask that you transfer me to your supervisor immediately. While I was waiting I looked up a little bit of information about your company. The vice president of customer support is John Tinear. I was able to find his e-mail and his mailing address. If you put me on hold again, I'll write him a letter saying you refused my request to speak to a manager. Maybe that's okay with you—but you could save me some writing, and I bet it saves you a headache, if you just transfer the phone now.

John: Let me see if he's available.

Mary: I also found Scari Topcop's address. She's head of the consumer affairs division in the New Jersey state attorney general's office. Scari will receive a letter, too, if I don't get a manager on the phone.

John: I'll transfer you now.

NEGOTIATE A LOWER INTEREST RATE

Migoal Isalowerate: Hi, I'm Migoal Isalowerate. Can you tell me your name, please?

Likada Intresst: I'm sorry, sir, we're not allowed to give out our names.

Migoal: I understand, for safety reasons, but I really must have some way of identifying you. Can you give me a direct telephone number or extension where I can reach you?

Likada: I can't give you that, either. But I can give you my operator number—4312.

Migoal: Thank you. Well, here's my concern. I just received my bill and I see that my rate on this credit card I have with you just jumped from 8.9 percent to 29.99 percent. Can you explain to me what happened?

Likada: Yes, Mr. Isalowerate. Let me pull up your records here. I see that we received your last payment on May 23. Thank you. But your payment date was May 15. So we added the late fee and as it says in our agreement, you are now being assessed a penalty interest rate.

(What you'd like to say is: "But I was only a week late! And now you've tripled my interest rate? What kind of people are you?" Of course, that won't get you anywhere. Tell it to the moon. Say the following instead.)

Migoal: Thank you for the clarification. I did not know my interest rate would get so high so quickly. This is the first time I've paid late. Is there someone I could talk to about this?

Likada: I'm sorry, ma'am, this is company policy and you agreed to it.

Migoal: I see. But I've looked through my records here and it shows that I've paid my bills on time every month for a year. It all adds up to about $25,000 in charges. We've had a good business relationship. And I know many credit-card companies have policies to make one-time accommodations or goodwill adjustments. Do you have the authority to waive the late fee and reduce the interest charges just this one time?

Likada: I do see that you have paid your bills on time. But I'm sorry, there's nothing I can do for you.

Migoal: Okay, well thank you for listening. I know there is someone there who can do something for me. Can you transfer me to a supervisor?

Likada: Sir, the supervisor will say the same thing. And no one is available right now.

Migoal: Okay then, I'm sorry for that. The best thing for me to do then is take my $25,000 in charges to another company. Please transfer me to someone who can help me close my account as soon as possible.

Likada: Please hold on, sir . . . My supervisor has allowed me to waive the late fee—just this one time—and reduce the interest charge to 27 percent.

Migoal: Thank you! But I'm looking at a competitor's application here and I can get a 9 percent rate from them right now, so it still makes sense for me to close my account with you.

Likada: Okay, sir. We can drop your rate back down to the original rate. But know that I have made notes in your account and we will raise the rate again if you are late again, and you will not be able to get a waiver like this for another two years.

Migoal: You've kept me as a customer. I appreciate your help very much. Thank you.

END A SALES PITCH DURING A CUSTOMER-SERVICE CALL

Edgar Enpuszchy: As long as we're waiting for the computer to check your file, let me tell you about a new service we're offering—debt cancellation. If for any reason you are unable to pay your bills—

Jane Yornoelp: Edgar, can we talk about my interest rate?

Edgar: —then debt cancellation will take care of that for you. If you can't work because you get hurt, or there's a serious illness in the family, or—

Jane: Has the computer given you the results yet?

Edgar: —or, we hope this won't happen, you pass away, your family won't be burdened by your debts. Can I sign you up for this today? We have a special today. There's nothing you have to do, and you can cancel at any time—

Jane: No, thank you.

Edgar: But don't you want to save money and protect your—

Jane: No, thank you.

Edgar: Okay, I am authorized to give it to you for free for three months—

Jane: I appreciate that your job requires you to tell me about this, but I said I'm not interested and I do not want to hear about any promotions and I do not want to purchase anything additional at this time. I want you to solve my problem.

Sample Letters That Work

Authors and personal-finance columnists often live in ivory towers. We dispense grandiose advice like this: Stay calm, write letters, negotiate from positions of strength, and of course, read everything. It all sounds good, but for busy people, it's often wildly unrealistic and terribly simplistic.

All writers know this, deep down, and that's why so many of us shrink when faced with a circumstance that requires us to actually take our own advice—or, as software developers are fond of saying, when we have to eat our own dog food.

Well, smack-dab in the middle of writing this book I faced such an occasion. At the very moment I was pondering the various ways consumers could get the attention of customer-service representatives, I had an infernal run-in with Verizon's Internet service. In short, I had a new place and signed up for allegedly fast DSL, but I often got little more than dial-up speed. And about half the time, my modem lights went dead and all I got was an hourglass taunting me from my computer screen. After two months of outright frustration, and perhaps a dozen customer-service calls, I was faced with a dilemma no writer wants to face.

Do I dare follow my own advice?

I did. I wrote a letter. But not just any letter; it was carefully crafted to get results. I used all the elements I've recommended in this book. I was polite but factual, direct and purposeful, I made a business case, and I addressed it to as many top executives as I could find. I hit send and hoped for the best. After all, what if I failed? Would I have to admit it to my editor? Would I have to return my advance?

I didn't have to worry long.

Within fifteen minutes of sending the e-mail complaint, I was called by three different Verizon managers, including the director for Verizon DSL in my region. The next morning, at exactly 8 A.M., there was literally a traffic jam of Verizon vehicles outside my building. Three technicians crawled all around my home looking for problems, with a supervisor hovering all the while. A new phone line was installed with seamless professionalism. I received several follow-up phone calls in the next week asking if my service was still operating as expected. And I received a refund for all Internet fees during those frustrating two months.

You can do this, too.

First off, you must know I sent this note as an average consumer, not as a reporter seeking a favor. I am fully aware that journalists sometimes receive royal treatment, so I did what I could to avoid that. The e-mail was sent from a private and unremarkable Yahoo account, for example. At no time did I mention I was a reporter for msnbc.com or an author, and no one from Verizon mentioned that to me or said anything to suggest I had been outed as a journalist.

Now, here's the e-mail that got me these results. After you read it, we'll discuss why I think it was so effective. It was sent to the CEO of Verizon, the head of the company's marketing department, and several other company bigwigs.

E-MAIL

SUBJECT: Notice of Complaint with my local utility district
Re: DSL account on DC telephone XXX-XXX-XXXX

Gentlemen:

Today my Verizon DSL stopped working, for the fourteenth time in the two months since I've been a customer. The other thirteen times, I spent perhaps ten hours on the phone with your technical support staff. But today, at noon ET, your telephone line simply played me this message:

"We're sorry we cannot answer your call at this time."

I'm sure you will all agree this is unacceptable service at noon on a business day.

You are all busy and I will not bore you with a recitation of the other thirteen customer-support calls. Suffice to say I am frustrated and have not received the service I've paid for. I have spent at least ten hours trying to make it work, a costly investment for both of us.

I have been a Verizon customer—at home and wireless—for a long time, and a happy one at that . . . and I have been quite loyal . . . I've spent well in excess of $7,000 for cell-phone services, and another $3,000 or so on my home line.

But since . . . November, I have been nothing but disappointed with your DSL service and support. I must say your technical support staff has always been polite. But no one has been able to explain to me why the DSL works well one day, then goes dead the next day.

Last week, a telephone agent said he was sending someone to my house to investigate the next day sometime between 7 in the morning and 7 at night. I do not know if the agent ever came, because I never again heard from anyone.

I will tell you that the only explanation I've received was from one agent who said to me six weeks ago that you were "oversold" in my area, and asked me to call back if I had continued trouble.

I still would like the DSL to work, and I'm happy to pay you $40 a month for it (DSL fee plus home line fee). But I certainly deserve a refund for the days the service has been inoperable.

I'm sad this experience has soiled what has otherwise been a positive experience with Verizon. Without another explanation, I fear that you have knowingly sold me a service that does not work, and I will pursue whatever legal means are available to me to call attention to that, including a dispute with the local utilities board. I do hope that is unnecessary.

Please let me know how your company plans to fix this so I can continue being a happy customer of your company.

Bob
Verizon Wireless cell XXX-XXX-XXXX

I believe my letter was effective for several reasons:

- The letter shows I'm willing to take legal action. By the time I sent this e-mail, I had already found the website for my local utility office and sent an inquiry asking about the best way to file a complaint. Because I referenced the organization in my note, I've demonstrated that I am aware of my rights, and I'm probably capable of being a real pain in the ass.
- The letter is polite and respectful but firm.
- The letter makes a business case. By describing my long affiliation with the company, and citing a dollar amount, I show the company that I am a valuable, profitable customer, which is the only thing that really matters in the end.
- I make specific requests that I receive a refund, and ask what the company will do to resolve the problem.
- I sent it to several high-ranking people at the organization.

I think the most important thing I did was to find e-mail addresses for Verizon's CEO, head of marketing, and several others in the marketing department and customer-service department. This actually was the most time-consuming part of the process. For obvious reasons, CEO e-mail addresses can be hard to find, but there are a few tricks that work. In my case, some of the research had already been done for me. A Google search quickly unearthed several Web pages posted by dissatisfied Verizon customers who published some of the addresses, inviting more complaints.

But I had to use other techniques, too. My favorite is to take a name and plug it into Google along with a search term that looks like this: *@company.com*. So if you were to search for Doug Douglas, CEO of GiantTelco, you'd plug in *"Doug Douglas" @gianttelcom.com*. That's pretty successful at unearthing valid e-mail addresses that might be lingering in any dark corner of the Web. Do a little poking around to make sure you have the right domain name. They usually mirror the company's website, but not always. Sometimes, there are slight variations—if a company's website is company.com, the e-mail domain might be companycorp.com. Also, you might try slight variations on the subject's name. For Mr. Douglas, try ddouglas, doug.douglas or doug_douglas.

Many executives have a special executive office or executive assistant for dispute resolution. If you manage to find that office or that person, you've hit the complaint gold mine. Action there is usually swift, as the employees usually have wide latitude to resolve complaints.

But don't be afraid to write to folks who are lower-down in the food chain. The game is to find the right level, where a person has the time to see your complaint and the power to fix it. Often, that won't be the CEO but a regional marketing manager or similar middle manager. So, don't stop at the senior vice president of marketing. Find other mid-level executives, such as the head of operations for your state, or your county. Your whole goal is to find the one person who is in a position to help you. At nearly every company, such a person does exist. You just have to dig around a bit to find him or her.

Of course, not every e-mail is going to generate a response within fifteen minutes. So it's a good idea to followup with a snail mail that's similar, if not identical, to your e-mail. You can make things easy on yourself. Simply print out the e-mail, print out an envelope, and drop the missive in the mail. Snail mail can be more effective because it shows the company you mean business—that you weren't simply banging out an angry note that you'll quickly forget about.

With your first letter, communicate directly with the company. You can mention your willingness to pursue the matter with government regulators or the Better Business Bureau, but hold your fire for a little while. Government offices generally prefer to help consumers who have made good-faith efforts to settle their disputes on their own.

Another of my favorite, you're-in-it-to-win-it tactics is to include a relevant citation of law in these letters. If you are enterprising, you can hunt around for something very specific to your case—for example, state law governing refunds of extended automobile warranty fees. But often, it's as simple as citing your state's unfair-and-deceptive-trade-practices law. That will probably be enough to get the attention of the legal department, particularly if you live in a state where consumer protection law allows plaintiffs to recover triple damages. Many states provide for such punitive damages as an incentive to pull wayward companies back in line. An Internet search for your state and "unfair and deceptive trade practices" should unearth the law you need. In most states, the attorney general's website also links to the consumer protection statutes.

If you don't get satisfaction, then ready that second round of letters, and send a copy to the company you're complaining about.

There are endless situations where you might have to write a complaint letter, but they all follow similar patterns. You'll just have to plug in your own facts. But before we get to a few sample letters you can copy and adjust to your own needs, here's a quick list of things that should be in any letter:

Techniques of effective complaint letters

- Be factual, not personal.
- Include specific dates and times, and, if possible, names of employees you've spoken to.
- Include a one-paragraph summary at the beginning of your complaint and the relief you seek ("I was charged a $36 fee by Nextel that was not previously disclosed to me, and I want a refund.").
- To help organize your thoughts, and keep your letter brief, break the story into obvious chunks—first problem, first attempt to resolve, current status, etc. You'll see one example below.
- Limit the letter to one page. No doubt your story is frustrating, and has dramatic twists and turns, but save the venting for your friends. Your only goal is to get your money back.

Remember, the people you are writing to are busy, and the more succinct you are, the quicker they can help you. If your story genuinely requires more detail than can fit on one page, include a one-page summary as a cover letter and then include additional documentation as needed.

- Write to the company privately first, and give it a chance to respond. Regulators generally won't step in if you don't show a good-faith attempt to solve the problem on your own first. But if you get no satisfaction, rope in government regulators and tell the company about it. Raising the stakes a level often gets the attention of a neglectful customer-service department. Complaining to the government is often easy. The Federal Trade Commission accepts complaints at its website at consumer.gov/econsumer/english/contentfiles/report.html. So does the FCC at fcc.gov/cgb/complaints.html. Your state consumer-affairs department may also accept e-complaints.

- Generally, complain to the attorney general in your state and the Better Business Bureau in the state where the offending company's headquarters is located. If your state AG isn't responding, there may be very few victims in your state, so it may be worth your while to take the extra step and complain to the AG's office in the company's state.

- Do take the time to complain. Your letter might not get individual attention immediately, but you'd be surprised how few letters it takes to get the attention of regulators. Former Massachusetts assistant attorney general Edgar Dworsky said his office regularly circulated something called the "five or more list." Every company that had been targeted by five or more consumer complaint letters got on the list. That's all it took to get the attention of Massachusetts's top cop.

Sample Complaint Letter
CABLE FEES

(Step 1: Write to the company, return receipt requested.)

Your Address
Yourtown, Yourstate 12345

July 15, XXXX

MyCable Company Inc.
Address
Anytown, Anystate 67890

Re: Surprise installation fees

To Whom It May Concern:

I have been charged a $29 fee for installation when I was told installation was free, and I insist that this fee be refunded.

On Monday, April 1, I signed up with MyCable in response to an advertisement I received promising free installation. I was assured installation would be free by the telephone operator I spoke to, Mary. When I received my second bill on May 12, I noticed this line on the bill "Installation: $29."

On May 12, I called customer service and waited on hold for thirty minutes. The operator who answered said the $29 fee was standard, and said the firm never offers free installation. I asked to speak to a supervisor and was told no one was available, but someone would call me back. No one did.

One week later, I called again and insisted on speaking with a supervisor. The supervisor, Charles E., gave me the same answer, but then I faxed him a copy of the flyer that was put in my mailbox offering free installation. I was told a refund would appear in my next bill. When the June bill arrived, no refund had been issued.

Please contact me and tell me when I can expect to receive my refund. If this matter is not resolved within the next billing period, I will be escalating my concerns to my local cable franchising authority and will ask my state's attorney general to investigate your advertising practices.

If you have any questions surrounding this issue, feel free to contact me at XXX-XXX-XXXX.

Sincerely,
Jane Consumer

Sample Complaint Letter
CABLE FEES, PART II

(Step 2: After a month has passed and you've gotten no satisfaction.)

Your Address
Yourtown, Yourstate 12345

August 15, XXXX

Local Cable Franchising Authority
Address
Yourtown, Yourstate 12345

Attorney General's Consumer Affairs Division
Address Capital, Yourstate 12345

Re: Unfair cable installation charges, promised refund never received

To Whom It May Concern:

    I would like to register a formal complaint with your office against MyCable Company, Inc. I signed up for service after receiving a flyer indicating installation would be free, but instead I was charged $29. Promised refunds have not been honored. Here is a quick summary of events:

- **FIRST TRANSACTION:**
  On Monday, April 1, I signed up with MyCable and was told installation would be free.
- **FIRST PROBLEM:**
  When I received my second bill on May 12, I noticed this line on the bill "Installation: $29."
- **FIRST RESOLUTION ATTEMPT:**
  On May 12, I called MyCable customer service and waited on hold for thirty minutes. The operator who answered said the $29 fee was standard, and said the firm never offers free installation. I asked to speak to a supervisor and was told no one was available, but someone would call me back.
- **SECOND RESOLUTION ATTEMPT:**
  No one called me, so I called again on May 19. This time, I insisted on speaking with a supervisor. The supervisor gave me the same answer, but then I faxed a copy of the flyer that was put in my mailbox offering free installation. I was told a refund would appear in my next bill.

- **THIRD RESOLUTION ATTEMPT:**
  When my next bill arrived, on June 12, there was no refund. I wrote to MyCable with a detailed description of my complaint. A copy of this letter is included, along with my return receipt showing the letter was received by MyCable. I received no response.

  I believe I have done everything a consumer should do to resolve the situation. If there is some other step I can take, please let me know. But I hereby request that your office intervene on my behalf and help me obtain a refund, and also request that your office open an investigation into MyCable's free-installation advertising practices. I've enclosed copies of the relevant advertisement and my bills. I would be happy to provide your office with any assistance in such an investigation. Feel free to contact me at the phone number I've included.

  Thank you for your time. I look forward to hearing from your office.

Sincerely,
Jane Consumer
Home: (212) 555-1212
cc: MyCable Company

Sample Complaint Letter
BANK FEES

(Step 1: Write to the bank, return receipt requested.)

Your Address
Yourtown, Yourstate 12345

July 1, XXXX

Great Big Bank
Address
Anytown, Anystate 12345

Re: Overdraft fees

To Whom It May Concern:

I was recently hit with seven overdraft charges during a single weekend, totaling $217, and I believe this is unfair. I request these fees be refunded, considering I had every reason to believe my account was positive by more than $1,000 when these fees were levied.

On Thursday, March 15, my account balance was $45.05. I deposited a payroll check for $1,200 at your Yourtown branch. I asked the teller if I would be able to withdraw money from my account by the weekend, and she said more than likely, I would. I asked for a more definitive answer and she refused, but told me I should attempt to withdraw money from an ATM and if the transaction was approved, I was "good to go."

On Saturday morning, I attempted to withdraw $50 from an ATM in Yourtown and my withdrawal was approved. Assuming my check had cleared, I proceeded to use my debit card to make purchases six times during the rest of the weekend. The purchases were small—one was for $3.89. I thought nothing of it. In total, the purchases added up to less than $50. My total transactions for the weekend were less than $100.

Two weeks later, when my statement arrived, I discovered fees of $217 on my $100 in transactions. It appears from the statement that my payroll check didn't clear until Monday, putting me well into the black. But by then, the damage had been done.

I was unaware that I could repeatedly overdraw my account without being warned. Furthermore, I believe your teller encouraged me to overdraw my account with her advice. I don't understand how your bank could charge me overdraft fees while holding on to a check for well over $1,000. And finally, I don't understand how the overdraft fees—$217—could be twice the amount of the transactions—$100.

Please refund these fees, and also send me a copy of the bank's policies for overdraft fees and for clearing checks.

Sincerely,
Jane Consumer

Sample Complaint Letter
BANK FEES, PART II

(Step 2: Complain to regulators. National banks—identified by the words "National" or "National association" in their titles or the letters N.A. or NT&SA—are regulated by the Office of the Comptroller of the Currency, part of the Treasury Department. The agency offers a complaint form at occ.treas.gov/ConsumerComplaintform.pdf. You can also complain to your state attorney general's office.)

Your Address
Yourtown, Yourstate 12345

August 1, XXXX

Office of the Comptroller of the Currency
Customer Assistance Group
1301 McKinney Street, Suite 3450
Houston, TX 77010-9050

To Whom It May Concern:

I was recently hit with seven overdraft charges by Great Big Bank during a single weekend, totaling $217, and I believe this is unfair. I had every reason to believe my account was positive by more than $1,000 when these fees were levied. I request your office intervene in my attempts to get these fees refunded.

On Thursday, March 15, my account balance was $45.05, and I deposited a payroll check for $1,200 at the Great Big Bank Yourtown branch. I asked the teller if I would be able to withdraw money from my account by the weekend, and she said more than likely, I would. I asked for a more definitive answer and she refused, but told me I should attempt to withdraw money from an ATM and if the transaction was approved, I was "good to go."

On Saturday morning, I attempted to withdraw $50 from an ATM in Yourtown and my withdrawal was approved. Assuming my check had cleared, I proceeded to use my debit card six times during the rest of the weekend. The purchases were small—one was for $3.89. In total, the purchases added up to less than $50. My total transactions for the weekend were less than $100.

Two weeks later, when my statement arrived, I discovered fees of $217 on my $100 in transactions. It appears from the statement that my payroll check didn't clear until Monday, putting me well into the black. But by then, the damage had been done.

I was unaware that I could repeatedly overdraw my account without being told. Furthermore, I believe the bank's teller encouraged me to overdraw my account with her advice. I don't understand how a bank can charge me overdraft fees while holding on to a check for well over $1,000. And finally, I don't understand how the overdraft fees—$217—could be twice the amount of the transactions—$100.

I have asked the bank to refund the fees and have received no response. I request that you intervene on my behalf, help me obtain a refund, and investigate this company's overdraft and check-clearing policies.

Sincerely.
Jane Consumer
cc: Great Big Bank

Sample Complaint Letter
CELL-PHONE FEES

(Step 1: Complain to the cell-phone company, return receipt requested.)

Your Address
Yourtown, Yourstate 12345

August 15, XXXX

Talk-A-Lot Wireless
Address
Anytown, Anystate 67890

To Whom It May Concern:

I recently purchased a new Talk-A-Lot cell phone and renewed my contract for two years. Two months later a $36 "upgrade fee" was inserted onto my monthly bill; I was not told about any fee for an upgrade when I purchased the phone, and I respectfully request that you refund the amount.

I've been a happy Talk-A-Lot customer for a long time—five years. I've probably spent $6,000 on Talk-A-Lot service during that time. When it was time for a new phone, I went to your company's store first. I selected a phone on June 1, and signed a new long-term contract. I was told the phone would be free.

I was disappointed when my July bill arrived and I found a charge for upgrading my phone. Because this fee was not disclosed, I believe I shouldn't have to pay it.

Your firm has always been fair in the past. I trust you do not want to jeopardize my loyalty to your company through this situation, and that you will clear it up quickly.

Please contact me on my Talk-A-Lot cell at XXX-XXX-XXXX to let me know when the upgrade fee will be refunded.

Sincerely,
Jane Consumer

Sample Complaint Letter
CELL-PHONE FEES, PART II

(Step 2: Complain to the Federal Communications Commission, return receipt requested. A blank form is available from the FCC's website at fcc.gov/cgb/consumer-facts/FORM475.PDF.)

Your Address
Yourtown, Yourstate 12345

September 15, XXXX

Federal Communications Commission
Consumer & Governmental Affairs Bureau
Consumer Complaints
445 12th Street, SW
Washington, D.C. 20554

To Whom It May Concern:

I recently purchased a new Talk-A-Lot cell phone and renewed my contract for two years. Two months later a $36 "upgrade fee" was inserted onto my monthly bill; I was not told about any fee for an upgrade, and the company has not acted on my request for a refund. I respectfully request that your agency intervene on my behalf.

On June 1, I purchased a new phone at the Talk-A-Lot store in Yourtown, and signed a new long-term contract. I was told the phone would be free.

I was disappointed when my July bill arrived and I found a charge for upgrading my phone. Because this fee was not disclosed, I believe I shouldn't have to pay it. I wrote to Talk-A-Lot in August and the firm has not honored my request for a refund.

Please contact me during regular business hours at XXX-XXX-XXXX should you have any questions regarding this matter.

Sincerely,
Jane Consumer
cc: Talk-A-Lot

Sample Complaint Letter
HOTEL FEES

(Step 1: Complain to the hotel headquarters, return receipt requested.)

Your Address
Yourtown, Yourstate 12345

November 1, XXXX

Pillow Mint Lodging Inc.
Address
Anytown, Anystate 67890

To Whom It May Concern:

I stayed in the Pillow Mint Hotel in Baltimore, Maryland, for four nights last month. I booked the hotel online and thought I had secured a great price of $109 per night, plus tax. But when I checked out, my bill was $60 higher than I expected. When I looked at it closely, I found there was a $15-per-night resort fee. I said I would refuse to pay it, but my credit card was charged anyway. I was never told about this fee and I demand that it be refunded immediately.

I've stayed at Pillow Mint hotels around the country for years, and probably have spent $3,000 there in the past year alone. I've never seen this fee before.

If it is not refunded promptly I will dispute the charge with my credit-card company and complain to my state attorney general and the Better Business Bureau.

Please contact me at XXX-XXX-XXXX to let me know when the resort fee will be refunded.

Sincerely,
Jane Consumer

Sample Complaint Letter
HOTEL FEES PART II

(Step 2: You can attempt to dispute the charge with your credit-card company by phone call, which is often effective. The card company will ask you to resolve the complaint with the hotel first; by producing a letter you've already sent to the hotel, you will bolster your argument. Also, complain to your state's attorney general, and the AG in the hotel's headquarters state, if need be.)

Your Address
Yourtown, Yourstate 12345

December 1, XXXX

Attorney General's Consumer Affairs Division
Address
Capital, Yourstate 12345

Better Business Bureau
Address of BBB in the state where you stayed in the hotel
Anywhere, Anystate 67890

To Whom It May Concern:

I stayed in the Pillow Mint Hotel in Baltimore, Maryland, for four nights last month. I booked the hotel online and thought I had secured a great price of $109 per night, plus tax. But when I checked out, my bill was $60 higher than I expected. When I looked at it closely, I found there was a $15-per-night resort fee. I said I would refuse to pay it but my credit card was charged anyway. I was never told about this fee and I would like your assistance in obtaining a refund.

I've stayed at Pillow Mint hotels around the country for years, and I've never seen this fee before.

I ask that your office intervene on my behalf to help me obtain a refund. I also ask that you investigate Pillow Mint's fee disclosure practices.

Please contact me at XXX-XXX-XXXX and I would be glad to discuss the matter with someone from your office.

Sincerely,
Jane Consumer
cc: Pillow Mint Hotels

Sample Complaint Letter
A WAYWARD REBATE

(Note: As mentioned in the rebate chapter, be sure to pester both the retailer where you bought the item and the rebate fulfillment house with this letter. They may not be the same entity.)

Your Address
Yourtown, Yourstate 12345

February 1, XXXX

Big Box Electronics Store
ATTN: Rebates
Address
Anywhere, Anystate 67890

Rebate Fulfillment House
Address where you mailed the original rebate forms
Anywhere, Anystate 98765

RE: Failure to Receive Rebate

To Whom It May Concern:

On Dec. X, XXXX, I purchased a personal computer at the Big Box Electronics store on Main Street in Yourtown, in large part because I was promised a $50 rebate. The following day, I fulfilled the rebate requirements and sent copies of the receipt and proof of purchase to the required address. Enclosed you will find copies of these documents, which indicate the rebate will arrive in six to eight weeks.

I have not yet received my refund, and well more than eight weeks have passed. I respectfully request that you send me the rebate check within thirty days. If I do not receive it by that time, I will initiate complaint proceedings with my state attorney general's consumer affairs office.

If you have any questions about my rebate, you may contact me at: XXX-XXX-XXXX.

Sincerely,
Joe Consumer

Sample Complaint Letter
A WAYWARD REBATE, PART II

(Having received nothing, it's time to raise the stakes. Here's a complaint letter to your state's attorney general's office, or the BBB, or the FTC. Send each letter separately, return receipt requested, cc'd to Big Box Electronics and its rebate fulfillment house.)

Your Address
Yourtown, Yourstate 12345

March 1, XXXX

Federal Trade Commission
600 Pennsylvania Avenue, NW
Washington, D.C. 20580

Better Business Bureau
Address of the BBB in the state where you mailed
the original complaint letter
Anywhere, Anystate 67890

Attorney General's Consumer Affairs Division
Address
Capital, Yourstate 12345

RE: Failure to Receive Rebate

To Whom It May Concern:

On Dec. X, XXXX, I purchased a personal computer at the Big Box Electronics Store in Main Street, Yourtown, in large part because I was promised a $50 rebate. The following day, I fulfilled my legal obligations and sent copies of the receipt and proof of purchase to the required address.

I have not yet received my refund, and well over eight weeks have passed. Last month, I sent a letter of complaint to Big Box Electronics Store and the firm has failed to act and resolve my complaint. I respectfully request that you intervene on my behalf.

Enclosed you will find copies of relevant documents, including the rebate forms and my letter of complaint to the company.

If you have any questions about my complaint, you may contact me at: XXX-XXX-XXXX.

Sincerely,
Joe Consumer
cc: Big Box Electronics Store
    Rebate Fulfillment House

3 The Legal Options

This book is about freeing yourself from a world of sneaky fees, and about the art of complaining well. It's about finding the right person to talk with, about writing just the right letter, about bargaining the right way with customer-service agents. It's about asking the right questions and using the right terminology.

But we all know even the most informed consumers complaining in the most appropriate ways don't always get justice. Many times, companies will still find a way to tell you no. You'll ask again. You'll get another no. You'll send a threatening letter to the appropriate consumer protection agency. You get yet another no. You're stalled, but you're not stuck. This chapter will tell you what to do when you hit that brick wall.

One of three things will happen:

1. The company will eventually give up and forget about the money it says you owe, or it will send you what you want. Not likely.
2. You'll end up in a lawsuit. More likely.
3. You'll end up in a dispute over your credit report. Highly likely.

So let's go over these one at a time. We'll breeze past alternative No. 1, which requires little more action on your part than doing a happy dance and drinking a victory iced tea.

THE LEGAL SYSTEM

On to No. 2: the lawsuit. It sounds intimidating and expensive, but it doesn't have to be. Believe it or not, for as little as $50, you can file a lawsuit and take on the company you're fighting. That's what computer programmer André-Tascha Lammé does, and he's managed to win judgments of $6,000 against three companies that were pestering him. And he's become something of a folk hero doing it. In 2006, Lammé sued a set of telemarketers and won each time. When he was granted a judgment of $3,500 by a Sacramento, California, administrative court judge, he says he heard audible gasps.

"You could hear people in the courtroom saying, 'You can sue telemarketers?'" he told me.

In fact, you can. And you can make some decent cash for your trouble.

Lammé wanted to share his strategy, so he set up a website named killthecalls.com, and he contacted the *Red Tape Chronicles* to talk about it. He became interested in small-claims court in 2005 after he started getting pelted with calls from mortgage brokers, just as his adjustable-rate mortgage was about to reset—even though he had registered with the Do Not Call list and told the companies to stop calling. Like many consumers, he quickly reached the boiling point over the frequent interruptions. But unlike many consumers, he discovered the Telephone Consumer Protection Act.

"It specifically deals with unwanted calls," Lammé says. "For each violation, there is a $500 penalty."

Wow, $500! That's a lot of money. Who gets it? The consumer. In this area of law, regarding unwanted phone calls, consumers actually have remarkable tools to win justice. Lammé read more about the law and found he didn't have to hire a high-priced attorney to pursue the penalty fees—he could file the case himself. So he made something of a part-time job of it.

Suing a company might sound like a paperwork headache beyond the means of most people, but it's not. Small-claims court papers are easy to file. In Sacramento County, for example, Lammé didn't even have to walk down to the courthouse. He was able to file online.

E-filing has slowly become the standard at small-claims courts across the country. Consumers who are even vaguely considering legal action against a company should see if their county allows electronic filing. If it does, you might find yourself almost enjoying the process, which can take as little as five minutes.

Even with that, going to court for an actual hearing might still seem like a hassle, but it's often not necessary. Two of Lammé's targets settled out of court with him for about $2,500 after seeing he was serious about the case.

Small-claims courts can hear any kind of case. Consumers who believe they've been unfairly hit by a Gotcha can file a case under their state's consumer-protection statute, asserting unfair or deceptive trade practices. These laws are easily found through an Internet search, or through your state attorney general's website. The trials are informal, and administrative law judges who preside over the cases are sometimes sympathetic to complainers who drag big companies into their courts. After all, the judges have cell phones, too.

These casual trials have limitations, however, including a fairly modest cap on damages that can be awarded, ranging from $2,000 to $10,000. There's also the risk of losing, which does have serious consequences. If you lose, and a judge determines you owe the company money, you will have a legal judgment entered against you. Essentially, that's a bill that has the force of law behind it. If the firm had already begun debt collection efforts, a small-claims judgment gives it additional rights to get its pound of flesh from you. In some states, like Maryland, the judgment will extend the length of time an indebted firm can hound you for the money for up to twenty years. The firm can even gain the right to garnish your wages and engage in other unsavory debt collection practices.

Be warned that while there are sympathetic judges in many small-claims courts, others have become jaded by a steady stream of debt collection cases filed by credit-card companies and other creditors. If you're considering filing a case in small-claims court, it's a very good idea to take a morning off of work and sit in on a few trials to get a sense of how things work, and how friendly the court is to consumers. Based on your experience there, your county's small-claims court may be the best place for you to get swift justice, and it can often be your first option for smaller Gotcha disputes. On the other hand, you may quickly learn that you don't want to risk a trial before that administrative law judge, or in that venue. Or you may find there's some other legal reason you can't file your case in small-claims court—a contract forbids it, or the company in your sites requests that the case be moved out of small-claims. Then you've got to consider your other options.

ARBITRATION

Now, for the bad news. Filing in small claims may be easy, but filing a traditional lawsuit can be nearly impossible. The "tort reform movement," as we mentioned in the first chapter of this book, has helped eliminate your right to many kinds of trials using America's public court system. Here's how.

Many large firms you do business with don't want to see you in court. They certainly don't want to see you with a lawyer, asserting a larger claim than small-claims courts allow. So they've found a way to severely limit your rights to file formal lawsuits. Consumers who intend to pursue claims against their cable provider, cell-phone company, or retail electronics store are often in for a rude awakening. In many of these situations, consumers long ago waived their right to sue by agreeing to mandatory binding arbitration for disputes.

Don't remember doing that? Well, you did, virtually every time you signed a contract with a service provider, used your credit card, or even opened a shrink-wrapped piece of software you purchased at an electronics store. Binding arbitration agreements are everywhere, and they generally cripple a consumer's ability to bring lawsuits. They make consumers submit to an alternative dispute resolution system that basically has been designed by the industries they are fighting.

The legal basis for mandatory arbitration dates all the way back to the Federal Arbitration Act of 1925, which was designed to allow corporations access to streamlined court proceedings during disputes. But arbitration has been turned into a one-sided venue that corporations drag consumers into, often kicking and screaming. They do this by forcing consumers to unknowingly surrender their rights to use the traditional court system through mouseprint arrangements on bills of sale, websites, and other purchase agreements. Binding mandatory arbitration agreements are part of almost every consumer interaction now.

Still, this is America, and access to a fair court of law is a fundamental right, isn't it? Wouldn't consumers have to somehow actively agree to surrender their right to a traditional courtroom?

Not in the land of the asterisk, in the land where small print and mouseprint equal rule of law. Believe it or not, you can thank the Supreme Court for making other courts so irrelevant.

Back in 1991, the high court heard a case involving a Washington state resident named Eulala Shute, who was hurt while sailing on a Carnival cruise to Mexico. Shute sued in a Washington federal court, while Carnival wanted the trial held in its home turf of Florida, where courts were certain to be friendlier to cruise lines. Shute objected, saying the cost of travel to Florida for the case made suing there impossible. Requiring such travel would be the equivalent of denying Shute justice, her attorneys argued.

Shute didn't stand a chance. She had already waived her right to sue in Washington.

When Shute purchased her trip from a travel agent in Washington, Carnival mailed her the cruise tickets and a packet that included terms and conditions. In these terms, this phrase was included:

> It is agreed by and between the passenger and the Carrier that all disputes and matters whatsoever arising under, in connection with or incident to this Contract . . . shall be litigated, if at all, in and before a Court located in the State of Florida, U.S.A. to the exclusion of the Courts of any other state or country.

Shute hadn't signed anything indicating she agreed to limit her legal remedies to the Sunshine State. No matter. The Supreme Court found that simply mailing that kind of mouseprint to her was enough. Shute was not allowed to sue in her home state. And companies got the green light to limit consumers' legal venues with asterisks, and were now assured they could fight all their legal battles on their home court.

The ruling opened the door for companies to pick which judges would hear all their disputes. Designing a new kind of home court—arbitration boards—and forcing consumer disputes into that venue with small print became the next logical step.

Unlike the civil court system, cases heard before arbitration boards are not public. The results aren't public, either. So it's virtually impossible to engage in normal legal preparations, such as studying the court's tendencies, understanding which arguments are persuasive, or even researching precedents. Unlike civil courts—where society bears the cost of the proceedings—litigants pay for arbitration cases. Costs for filing can be hefty enough to stop consumers in their tracks. And when consumers lose, there is no right to appeal. All decisions are final, whether or not they are fair.

Arbitration panels are generally composed of corporate lawyers and retired judges selected from lists maintained by the American Arbitration Association or the National Arbitration Forum. Little is known about how the boards are screened for obvious conflicts of interest, but since companies that use them are repeat "customers," and consumers are nearly always newbies, biases are bound to develop.

As a result, many call these "show trials" or "kangaroo courts," with professional litigants like credit-card companies bringing case after case before the same arbitrators, a situation that's just too cozy for many observers—and even some arbitrators.

A former arbitrator named Richard Neely wrote an article in 2006 called "Miserable Godless Bloodsucking Banks and Other Professional Litigants," in which he says corporate litigants in arbitration cases sent him simple forms with most fields already completed, designed to make ruling against consumers as easy as checking a few boxes and signing his name. For each form he returned, he was paid $150. The experience jaded him toward arbitration:

> If I'm a retired lawyer turning out four $150 credit-card arbitrations for a small group of banks, that's a fact that should be disclosed to consumers. In arbitration the professional litigants have an enormous advantage not only because they write the contract designed to stick it to the consumers, but also because they know the arbitrators who will enforce all illegal and/or unconscionable provisions in their contracts . . . It looks like a collection agency to me!

Neely is no crackpot lawyer. He is the retired Chief Justice of the West Virginia Supreme Court of Appeals.

Perhaps the only true glimpse we've ever seen into arbitration's one-sided tendencies was provided by a lawsuit brought against FirstUSA that raised questions about its arbitration clause. Documents filed in the case show that FirstUSA participated in 51,622 cases soon after initiating its arbitration policy in 1998. Consumers won only 87 of those cases. While thousands of hearings were still pending, the company's success rate was still well over 99 percent.

There's a court of law you probably don't want to land in.

How did America's right to access courtrooms become so mercilessly violated? You can credit "tort reform," a popular buzzword from conservative politicians hoping to free corporations from financial responsibility for their actions. Tort reform has brought you long-standing urban legends like the woman who won millions of dollars when she burned herself by spilling McDonald's coffee while driving. (In reality, 79-year-old Stella Liebeck sued only after McDonald's refused to pay for her medical expenses, about $20,000. Liebeck was a passenger in a car that had pulled over when she struggled to open the coffee cup and spilled its contents. She suffered third-degree burns over much of her thighs and was hospitalized for more than a week. McDonald's had been warned numerous times about its scalding hot coffee, which was served at around 190 degrees, hot enough to burn skin to the bone in less than ten seconds, and much hotter than most café coffee.)

The good news is, many binding arbitration clauses—while severely limiting your access to traditional courts—don't rule out small-claims court, says Paul Bland, perhaps the nation's leading authority on mandatory arbitration. Much of this small print is written specifically for one purpose: To ward off class-action lawsuits. We'll talk more about those later. But if your dispute is with a company whose arbitration clause leaves the door open for a small-claims case, at least you have that option.

Arbitration, despite all the hurdles placed in consumers' way, isn't a total lost cause—particularly if the arbitration agreement indicates your company will pick up the cost of the proceedings under some circumstances.

Consumer Steve Taplits had a problem with AT&T Wireless several years ago and reread his binding arbitration contract carefully. It said that AT&T would pay all arbitration costs for cases filed claiming under $250 in damages. So he filed a $249 claim. AT&T tried to settle with him, but Taplits—an attorney—refused. He ultimately got his $249 and a hearty supply of satisfaction.

There are important exceptions to this strategy, however, Bland warns. Chief among them: "loser pays" provisions. If you will be required to pay attorneys' fees in the event you lose the case, stay away, Bland advises. It's easy for a company to cook up $5,000 to $10,000 in attorneys' fees. With a potential bill like that on the table, your pre-hearing bargaining position is severely hampered.

Also, even if you won't have to pay attorneys' fees, don't outsmart yourself. When firms gets a sense that a lawyer is behind your arbitration case, and that lawyer is readying twenty more cases on the same principle, you won't get a settlement offer. The credit-card firm or phone company will gladly spend thousands of dollars fighting you to ward off all those other cases waiting in the wings. Likewise, if there's anything else special about your case, the company might choose to fight it to avoid setting some kind of precedent.

How do you pick between filing a small-claims case and filing for arbitration? The dollar amount will make the choice obvious in some cases—sometimes, small-claims is out of the question—as will the atmosphere of the small-claims court. Generally, however, you'll find small-claims to be less of a dragon's lair than arbitration. Because the results and the proceedings are public, you will often find your rights are handled with more care.

CLASS-ACTION LAWSUIT

The ultimate deterrent for bad corporate behavior is the prospect of an enormous class-action lawsuit. In fact, the kinds of nickel-and-dime transgressions we're talking about in *Gotcha Capitalism* are precisely the kinds of transgressions class-action cases were created for. No lawyer will take on your dispute for $100 on a contingency basis, which generally nets the lawyer 30 percent of the settlement. But put together 50,000 clients and their $100 disputes into a single case and now you've gotten the attention of the legal profession. In one example, victims sued Cingular after the firm purchased AT&T Wireless. Old AT&T customers alleged they were given a Hobson's choice of either paying $18 upgrade fees to join Cingular's service or paying hefty cancellation fees to get out of their old cell-phone contracts. No individual victim could have sued the firm over an $18 fee—but the class action involved potentially millions of customers, making the case quite worthwhile for the lawyers involved.

Becoming part of a class-action lawsuit can be the ultimate form of revenge. Big-ticket cases garner lots of publicity and can genuinely change the behaviors and tactics of big corporations.

Unfortunately, being a plaintiff in a class-action suit is much less glamorous than it sounds. Justice comes slowly, if at all. Often, victims get an infinitesimal fraction of the settlement, while the lawyers get millions of dollars. Sometimes, victims get nothing more than a coupon worth a small discount on the company's product. Outrageous settlements even force consumers to keep getting the product they no longer want just to receive the discount they've been awarded by a settlement!

Fortunately, many consumers no longer have to worry about the disappointment of being part of a class-action lawsuit. Those mandatory binding arbitration agreements? They usually include provisions that force consumers to repudiate their right to participate in class-action cases.

However, lawsuits filed around the country have slowly chipped away at the legality of class-action-repudiation small print. Several courts have deigned them "unconscionable," because consumers who buy cell phones or open software are not really in a position to negotiate over class-action rights.

Still, your ability to be an active participant in a class-action case is generally a function of pure luck: You must be an ideal victim of egregious corporate behavior and bump into a lawyer who's interested in taking on such a case. The vast majority of class-action participants are swept up in the case later, when a judge declares an entire class of people as plaintiffs in the case—a process called "certification."

But if you are so irritated with what's happened to you that you really want to pursue this larger kind of case, search the Web for your firm and the words "class action." There may be a lawyer looking for plaintiffs in just such a case. You will almost certainly happen upon class-action firms that litigate in the general field you are complaining about and you can pitch them your case.

Of course, you can also sue the company you oppose as an individual—a costly, time-consuming step that brings with it uncertain outcomes. Binding mandatory-arbitration cases often make such lawsuits extremely challenging. The first element in the case is always a protracted battle to convince a court to set aside that arbitration clause. Finding a consumer lawyer who will take such a case is the hardest part of this uphill battle, but there are some organizations that can help. The National Association of Consumer Advocates (www.naca.net) has a "Find a Lawyer" tool that will help you fashion a list of litigators who might have just the expertise you need. All its lawyers argue consumer cases; some are inexperienced but many are willing to listen and help. The National Consumer

Law Center (www.nclc.org) offers plain-language books and pamphlets that consumers can use to educate themselves on points of law and on picking lawyers. And the U.S. Public Interest Research Group offers a host of topic-specific papers on many hot consumer issues, as well as links to state Public Interest Research Groups, which can help you find the legal help you need.

FIGHTING IN THE "COURT" OF THE CREDIT REPORT

While a lawsuit might seem like the scariest possibility stemming from a dispute with a company over a hidden fee, it's really an unlikely venue for your fight. Corporate America actually has a much more powerful tool at its disposal—the power to ruin your credit report and credit score. If a company says you owe it money, and you refuse to pay, it can report you as delinquent to the nation's credit bureaus. By doing so, the company can saddle you with a black mark that can follow you around for seven years or more. And "telling on you" to a credit-reporting agency has an instant impact, unlike the looming threat of a lawsuit. In any dispute with a company, the most likely end game is a fight over your credit report.

This threat is not to be taken lightly. One delinquent account on your credit report can be enough to lower your credit score significantly—enough to cost you big money on your next car loan or home loan. Having an unpaid $150 debt is no big deal. Losing a new house because of a damaged credit report is a big deal. Ruining your credit is the hammer your nemesis company has in any dispute with you. And it's a big hammer.

It isn't fair. It isn't right. But it is reality, so we've got to deal with this, too. First, we'll explain the system. Then, we'll show you how to use it to your advantage.

CREDIT-HISTORY SYSTEM EXPLAINED

Nearly all companies you deal with participate in the credit-reporting systems operated principally by Experian, Equifax, and TransUnion. These three companies maintain detailed financial histories on nearly every American adult. Where do they get this information? Remarkably, they get it for free, from nearly every company that sends you a bill. These companies are known as "furnishers," because they furnish the credit-reporting agencies (CRAs) with detailed lists of who's paying their bills and who's not. The CRAs assemble these into credit reports, with special attention to those unpaid bills. Various companies then boil down the entries in these credit reports to a single three-digit number called a credit score, using a formula that's more secret than Colonel Sanders's fried-chicken recipe. Your credit score impacts nearly every aspect of your life: your ability to get loans and credit cards, auto insurance, home insurance, even employment.

There are many reasons people may find themselves suffering from a low credit score. People who don't pay their bills on time, who declare bankruptcy, who borrow too much money, who are victims of identity theft—all can find themselves with scores so low they can't get a mortgage and must pay outrageous interest rates for car loans and credit cards.

But there is another reason you can end up in these dire straits—because of a billing dispute with a vindictive company.

If you find yourself in a game of chicken with a company over an unpaid bill, and you hold firm, the company can "furnish" a report of your unpaid bill to a credit-reporting agency. This can immediately cost you critical points on your credit score and thrust you into an entirely new judicial system.

Once there, you are in for a serious battle. If you decide to take on this company in the realm of credit-reporting agencies, an entirely new and unfamiliar set of rules apply. Here are the simple steps to follow if you take on this fight.

1. Did they really report you?

The first thing you must determine is this: Is your company engaging in idle threats or has it really reported you as delinquent to a credit-reporting agency? Getting the answer is as simple as getting your credit report. That means after you have that final shouting match ("I'm not paying the bill." "We're reporting you to the credit bureaus." "Go ahead, make my day!"), you'll have to get your report. Unfortunately, not all companies work with all credit-reporting agencies, so you will have to get one report from each of the big three: Equifax, Experian, and TransUnion. Remember, you are entitled to one free report from each company every year, which you can obtain at annualcreditreport.com. You are also entitled to an additional free report if you believe you have been a victim of fraud. If you feel you have been fraudulently hit with a negative entry in your credit report, and you've already used up your free report for the year, send a letter to the credit agencies indicating you have reason to believe you are a victim of fraud and wish a free copy of your report. Their addresses are in the notes section for this chapter.

Unfortunately, your credit demerit likely won't show up immediately on your report. So unless you plan to run right out and get a car loan, you might as well wait two months or so to get your free reports. In fact, the demerit can actually appear on your report up to a year or more after the dispute, so you will have to keep up with your credit report for quite a while.

It may be that your nemesis company doesn't really want to bother filing against you. If no delinquent account appears on any of your credit reports, you're in the clear. But don't count on it. Companies treat consumers who they think owe them money like criminals, and often feel a "moral" obligation to place a digital scarlet letter on consumers' credit reports. Then you'll have to go to step two.

2. *Dispute the entry by asking for a reinvestigation*

This step might sound scary, but in fact, it's easy. And this is the stage where many consumers win. All it takes is a couple of carefully worded letters called "reinvestigation" letters. Your objective, mind you, is not necessarily to obtain justice. Your objective is to be enough of a pain in the butt that your company will decide to let it go and pick on someone else.

The reinvestigation letters should go to the credit-reporting agencies where the delinquency report was filed. They are sometimes called "dispute" letters. Send them immediately, return receipt requested. You will be invoking your rights under the Fair Credit Reporting Act by asking for a reinvestigation of an entry in your credit report. The credit bureaus must do this for you within thirty to forty-five days. If they don't complete the reinvestigation within that time period, the delinquent entry must be removed, and you win.

On the next page, you'll see what a reinvestigation letter could look like.

Sample Reinvestigation Letter
TO A CREDIT BUREAU

Neverorderd Achbeeo
Your Address
Yourtown, Yourstate 12345
January 1, 2008

Supervisor, Legal Department
TransUnion LLC
555 West Adams
Chicago, Illinois 60661

(Or similar dispute correspondence address listed on your credit report)

Re: Neverorderd Achbeeo
DOB: November 3, 1967
SSN: 123-45-6789
Credit report number: 1981-111
Account: ABC Cable Company
Account Number: 12345
Amount: $123.45

To Whom It May Concern:

    I am writing to dispute the following information in my credit report. I have circled the item I dispute on the attached copy of the report I received.

    From January to July 2007, ABC Cable Company erroneously billed me $123.45 for premium movie services I never received. The firm has now erroneously reported this amount as delinquent to your company. Under the rights granted to me by the Fair Credit Reporting Act, I dispute this entry. Please reinvestigate, delete, and suppress this erroneous information.

Sincerely,
Neverorderd Achbeeo

You can also initiate a dispute through online forms available at each credit bureau's website. There does not appear to be any advantage to using one format over the other, but if you file online, you won't have the paper trail provided by postal service returned receipts.

Upon receiving this dispute notice, the credit-reporting agency will immediately send notice to the "furnisher" that it must acknowledge it reported the negative entry about you. It would be nice if the firm were required to produce evidence in the reinvestigation, and there were some kind of hearing where your side of the story could be told. That is not how it works, however. The reinvestigation is generally an instantaneous electronic process conducted using a piece of software named E-OSCAR. And as long as the furnisher "verifies" the debt and confirms its accusation (generally by sending a single electronic blip back to the credit-reporting agency), E-OSCAR will be grouchy and rule against you. The account delinquency will remain on your report. Your hope at this stage is that the nemesis company fails to complete the task within thirty to forty-five days out of neglect or confusion. Then, you are off the hook.

One important note: Do not spend any serious time or effort compiling evidence or writing lengthy missives at this stage. You'll be tempted to bolster your case with copies of bills, letters, etc. That's a waste of your time, because no one will read the documentation.

If forty-five days pass, and you haven't heard a thing, you win. Send a follow-up letter to the credit-reporting agency dispute-resolution office requesting that the item be removed, and that it send you an updated copy of your credit report reflecting the change. And you're done.

One word of caution: Louisiana attorney David Szwak, who frequently represents consumers in these kinds of disputes, says it's not uncommon for deleted entries to reappear later—often resubmitted by the nemesis company. That's why he recommends demanding both removal and suppression of disputed entries. When a consumer wins a reinvestigation, the credit-reporting agencies are required to take active steps to prevent reappearances of those entries. If they don't, consumers with a solid paper trail have a fairly strong case for a lawsuit, Szwak says. But to do that, you've got to notice the mistake first. That means you've got to peek at your credit report on a regular basis.

3. Demand the furnisher reinvestigate

Unfortunately, many furnishers know this game well, and they will quickly verify the debt to the credit-reporting agency. That means you'll have to take things at least one step further. Fortunately, the Fair and Accurate Credit Transaction Act (FACTA) of 2003 made this much easier.

Your next step is to file a dispute directly with the original creditor. There can be quite a bit more action at this stage. Essentially, you are going to ask ABC Cable Company for proof that you really do owe the money it says you owe. Once again, it has only thirty to forty-five days to comply with such an investigation. This request can be a major headache for the cable company. It can be forced to find signed forms, taped customer-service phone calls, and other documents proving you truly owe the money it says you owe. In fact, you should ask directly for bills, application forms, and any other document you know exists, complicating your request even more. You might be surprised to find that many creditors will have trouble assembling this documentation. Doing so can easily cost a company more than the $100 it says you owe. It might cry uncle.

And better yet, if the company fails to respond to your request, it is automatically in violation of FACTA and subject to penalties. Failure to provide adequate evidence also opens the company up to a $1,000 fine for each inaccuracy it reported about you. Feel free to dangle that threat, but remember what you really want—removal of the delinquent account from your credit report.

On the next page is a sample letter to a furnisher.

Sample Reinvestigation Letter
TO A FURNISHER

Neverorderd Achbeeo
Your Address
Yourtown, Yourstate 12345

January 1 XXXX

ABC Cable Company
Attn: Legal Department
123 TV Street
Anytown, Anystate 67890

Re: Neverorderd Achbeeo
Account Number: 12345
Disputed Amount: $123.45

To Whom It May Concern:

My TransUnion credit report indicates you have reported me thirty days late on this account in January XXXX. I immediately disputed this information with Experian and was told the account was "verified."

The $123.45 bill in question was generated by your company in error. It represents the price of premium channels I never ordered. I demand that you immediately reinvestigate this account, a right afforded me under the Fair and Accurate Credit Transaction Act. Please furnish me with billing statements, telephone recordings, and application forms that you believe show that I in fact ordered these premium television channels from your service.

Please note: Failure to respond to this request within forty-five days will incur further legal action from me, as provided for by the FACTA and FCRA.

Please correct this entry on my credit report by reporting me as "paid as agreed—never late" to any credit bureau you supply with data, and remove any reference to late payments, or I will be forced to take additional legal actions.

Sincerely,
Neverorderd Achbeeo
cc: TransUnion

Letters like these obtain mixed results, of course. A company with solid record keeping will be able to produce enough documentation to satisfy its legal obligations easily. You're hoping the company is a bit more disorganized, so it will see you as more trouble than you're worth.

Remember, at any step of the process, you can also cry uncle and pay the bill. But before you do so, get a letter in writing from the company promising it will remove the negative entry as soon as it receives payment.

And most important: Do not skip Step 2 and begin with Step 3, advises attorney Szwak. Dispute the item first with the credit bureau, then with the furnisher. That's the best way to trigger your legal rights to reinvestigations and compensation for willful neglect by a furnisher or credit bureau.

4. Your hundred-word statement

If your nemesis company is still matching you chess move for chess move, and the entry remains on your credit report, you have additional rights. The credit-reporting agency may advise you that you are entitled to place an explanation on your credit report detailing your side of the story. It's called a "Statement of Dispute," and it's also known as a "hundred-word statement." The law that grants the right, the Fair Credit Reporting Act, allows CRAs to limit consumers to hundred-word explanations.

Sadly, these are useless when consumers apply for credit from a company that relies solely on credit scores to grant loans. Companies that pull entire credit reports—mortgage lenders, for example—might see the statements.

But note: Many professional credit counselors think these hundred-word statements are worse than worthless; they do more harm than good. The statements form a backward-logic kind of verification that the debt exists. Because of that, many recommend that consumers never file them.

5. If creditors start calling

Of course, part of the charm of this dispute kabuki dance with the credit-reporting companies is the debt-collection process, which may run in parallel. That means debt collectors might start calling. For many people, these calls are the ultimate nightmare. Debt collectors are notoriously rude, threatening, and manipulative. But you don't have to put up with that. The Fair Debt Collection Practices Act has very clear rules about what debt collectors can and can't do. Naturally, collectors often don't follow the rules, so it's important that you know what they are. For example, debt collectors may not contact you "at inconvenient times and places, such as before 8 A.M. or after 9 P.M." If a collector harasses you by calling you late at night, you can sue for damages. Most will stop when they hear you invoke the Fair Debt Collection Practices Act.

Other things debt collectors can't do, according to the Federal Trade Commission's interpretation of the Fair Debt Collection Practices Act:

- Use threats of violence or harm.
- Publish a list of consumers who refuse to pay their debts (except to a credit bureau).
- Use obscene or profane language, or repeatedly use the telephone to annoy.
- Use any false or misleading statements, such as imply that they are attorneys or government representatives, imply that you have committed a crime, hint that they work for a credit bureau, say you will be arrested if you don't pay the debt, or use a false name.

If a debt collector does any of these things, you can sue in state or federal court and win $1,000 plus recover the cost of any damages you suffered, along with attorneys' fees.

In fact, debt collectors must cease contact with you altogether if you send them a letter telling them to stop.

To get a debt collector off your back, write a letter indicating you believe the debt is in error, and specifically invoke the Fair Debt Collection Practices Act's requirement that it stop contacting you. After that, the collector can only call you or write to you if it is communicating an intent to file a lawsuit or other specific legal action.

Remember, sending such a letter may stop the phone calls, but it does not erase the debt or in any way mean the end of the problem. A sample "get off my back" letter is below.

Sample Complaint Letter
TO DEBT COLLECTORS

Neverorderd Achbeeo
Your Address
Yourtown, Yourstate 12345

January 1, XXXX

DEF Debt Collectors
100 Loss Lane
Anytown, Anystate 67890

Re: ABC Cable Company
Account Number: 12345
Disputed Amount: $123.45

To Whom It May Concern:

    I am writing you concerning a debt-collection proceeding initiated by your company against me concerning a claim made by ABC Cable Company. The firm says I owe $123.45; it is in error. Under the rights granted me by the Fair Debt Collection Practices Act, I hereby request that you:

- Explain in writing the nature of the debt and how much I allegedly owe, along with the rationale for the amount listed;
- Provide copies of any documentation furnished to you about my case by ABC Cable Company;
- Inform any credit agencies you are in contact with, and the original creditor, that I am disputing this debt; and

> • Cease all contact with me, other than to respond to the requests in this letter, or to inform me that you are taking specific action in connection with this debt, as provided by the Fair Debt Collection Practices Act.
>
> Sincerely,
> Neverorderd Achbeeo

6. More legal help

Because consumers only recently won the right to demand re-investigations directly from furnishers, it is too early to know how often furnishers surrender and how often they enjoin the paper battle. Of course, some companies will fight to the death on this one, and you should be prepared for that. If a company insists your dispute is really a bad debt, and you've gone through the FCRA dispute process, and you've written your attorney general's office and the Federal Trade Commission, it might be the time to call for professional help. There's an army of lawyers who litigate Fair Credit Reporting Act cases. Now might be the time to enlist one of those.

One place to look for help is from other consumers fighting the same battles. You can find them in consumer-dispute forums at myfairdebt.com and myfaircredit.com, which are both operated by Szwak. The sites can be a good place to begin a search for professional legal help. You can also turn to the National Association of Consumer Advocates (www.naca.net), which has a "Find a Lawyer" tool that will help you narrow a list of litigators who have expertise in the area where you need help.

Sneaky-Fee Survey

During November 2006, independent researcher Larry Ponemon of the Ponemon Institute conducted an extensive survey on Gotcha Capitalism in action at my request. The goal was to arrive at a dollar figure that accurately reflects the true impact of hidden, sneaky fees on the average consumer. We asked consumers around the country how much they believed they've lost to sneaky fees in ten important industries during the past twelve months. While preparing the study, we spent a lot of time discussing the fundamental problems of conducting such a survey. After all, we were looking for things that were designed to be hard to find. And by surveying consumers, we were dealing with people's recollections of things designed to elude them.

Nevertheless, consumers do catch such fees. Often sneaky fees are a matter of timing. People notice a bogus hotel charge when they see the bill, for example, but not when they make the reservation weeks earlier. By then, it's usually too late to avoid the charge, but the sting makes the fee memorable, and it makes that consumer a useful survey subject.

Companies might also have a different opinion about what we defined as sneaky fees. You can imagine a cell-phone company arguing, "That's not sneaky . . . If you'll look on page twenty-four of the user agreement, that fee is disclosed . . ."

But sneaky fees are like pornography. You know them when you see them. It's the burden of companies who sell things to make sure consumers know what the true price is before they leave the store or the website. Burying the price on page twenty-four might make the fee, strictly speaking, legal, but it's certainly still sneaky. So these legal-but-still-sneaky-fees are included in our survey. That's why we used the phrase "sneaky fees" rather than "hidden fees." It's a bit more inclusive, and gets much more to the heart of the matter—the tools of Gotcha Capitalism.

There are other pitfalls to such research, and we had to make several assumptions in order to arrive at our research conclusions, which you can read about in this book's endnotes if you like.

Still, Ponemon went to great pains to account for these factors and I think you'll agree the results ring true. Roughly speaking, people think they end up paying about $100 to $125 a year more than they should for cable or satellite television each year, and they're overcharged about the same amount by cell-phone and credit-card companies. They pay about $220 extra for groceries. They think they lose a little less on Internet access, retirement, and insurance fees (or at least those fees are more deftly disguised).

First, here's an industry-by-industry analysis of our nationwide sneaky-fee survey. Then, you'll find important overall conclusions at the end of the chapter, including an explanation of where you should best spend your precious complaining time—and what industries are the worst sneaky-fee offenders.

1. Cell phones

Consumer frustration with cell-phone firms consistently ranks very high, and that sentiment carried through in our survey. In fact, cell-phone bills got the largest reaction from consumers in the study. Nearly 90 percent of respondents who had anything to complain about said they'd been nicked for fees by their cell-phone company.

About half of those who complained about cell phones said the hidden fee was between 5 and 10 percent of their monthly bill— that's a number we'll see again and again in our study. It all averages out to slightly less than $10 a month. Clearly, companies have figured out that $10 or 10 percent is a magic number for sneaky fees; that seems to be the breaking point for consumers. Apparently, many people who would call to complain over a double-digit fee will let a $9 fee go by.

Cell-phone companies turn out to be particularly relentless about such fees. Most consumers (85 percent) told us these fees appear on their bill either every month, or at least two to six months out of the year.

The total amount, $5.97 billion, was among the largest amounts in our survey. The average loss per cell-phone consumer was about $116 each year.

As for a description of those sneaky fees, about four in five consumers said the charges were made without their consent, seven out of ten said they were not clearly described in their statement, and half said they were charged for services not received.

While frustration with cell phones is high, consumers aren't acting out of their frustration. Only 17 percent said sneaky fees led them to dump their cell-phone company. Another 65 percent, however, said they plan to change cell-phone firms at some point in the future.

That's not surprising—in Chapter 5 of the second section, we described cell-phone "jail" in detail. Suffice to say that consumers in long-term contracts cannot quit their services out of fee frustration because, naturally, they would have to pay a large contract-termination fee.

Refund outlook:

One in five consumers told us they'd called customer service and managed to get a refund. That puts the cell-phone industry in about the middle of the pack. However, 52 percent said they'd called to get a refund and been denied, a high rejection number in the study. That means cell-phone customer-service representatives can be fairly stubborn, so expect a fight when you call.

2. Credit cards

Credit cards also frequently raise the ire of consumers, and our study bears that out. Four out of five consumers who said they'd been hit by sneaky fees complained about credit cards. Only cell phones ranked higher.

The complaints were across the board. Eighty percent said fees were assessed without their consent; 54 percent said charges weren't clearly described. The fees were a bit smaller than cell-phone fees (average fee: about $8) but appeared with greater frequency, often several times on each monthly bill. And about half of consumers who complained about credit-card fees said they'd been hit by multiple fees on multiple cards.

It all added up to $11 billion in hidden credit-card fees reported by consumers, an average of $93 per cardholder.

Frustrated credit-card users are more likely than cell-phone users to do something about those sneaky fees—46 percent said they'd changed credit-card companies, and another 28 percent said they were likely to do so in the future. Most of the rest said they hadn't quit their cards because "all credit cards are the same." Those consumers are on to something. Thanks to rapid consolidation in the industry (like Bank of America's 2005 acquisition of MBNA), consumers are finding out it's harder and harder to switch credit-card companies. Robert Manning, author of *Credit Card Nation*, said in 2007 the top three card issuers—J.P. Morgan Chase, Citibank, and Bank of America—owned 62 percent of all U.S. credit cards, and the top ten issuers controlled 90 percent of the market.

Refund outlook:

Here's good news for consumers. While credit cards are clearly among the most cutthroat fee creators, they are by far the most likely source of fee waivers. Half of consumers who say they found a hidden fee on their credit-card bills told us they were able to call the company and get the fee waived; only 28 percent said such requests were outright rejected. The importance of this statistic can't be stressed enough. Credit-card firms clearly have made the business choice to throw every fee they can at the wall, and see what sticks. But they don't always put up much of a fight when consumers cry foul. They just count on consumers not speaking up. This means complaining about credit-card fees is time well spent.

3. Banks

Consumers rarely have nice things to say about their banks; three out of five of them singled out banks as a source of hidden fees. One-third of those said they were charged for services that were supposed to be free. That's no surprise. Free checking accounts are often expensive to maintain! Our research shows that the average consumer pays $83 each year in sneaky bank fees. And banks collect $12 billion each year.

The average monthly bank fee was $6.95, with 37 percent saying the fee ranged from $5 to $10 each month. Only 13 percent said the fee was between $10 and $20 and a tiny fraction said fees were more than $20. So there's that just-under-$10 sweet spot again. But banks apparently know how to pour on the charges. One-quarter of respondents said they found two or more such fees every month on their bills.

Refund outlook:

Now for the really bad news. Only 6 percent of consumers reported they managed to contact customer service and get bank fees removed. Compared to credit cards (51 percent) or even cell phones (19 percent), that refund rate is paltry. The data suggest customers don't even really try to get bank refunds, as only 12 percent indicated they tried but failed to talk their bank into giving back a sneaky fee it had collected. What about the other 82 percent who don't even try to contact the bank? Are consumers intimidated, and missing out thanks to bank-o-phobia? Or are they just wise, knowing there's not much point in banging their head against a bank vault? Our survey doesn't offer an answer to that question.

4. Airlines

The truth is, airline travel is remarkably inexpensive for what it is, and what it used to be. Airline travelers who plan ahead usually pay prices that are lower than travelers paid ten or twenty years ago. There are exceptions: smaller trips between places that have limited competition can still be pricey. But in general, airlines face rabid competition, and must always fear entry of the next JetBlue or Southwest Airlines to wreck their cost structure. Generally, this is great for consumers.

But it also means sneaky-fee watchers must be on high alert. Any time an industry faces this kind of deep price pressure, its only weapon to recover lost funds is hidden surcharges.

Most consumers know the drill pretty well. Outside of Southwest Airlines, JetBlue, and a few other rare exceptions, changing an airline ticket attracts a massive penalty, one that can be more than one-third the price of the ticket itself. Changing an international flight generally costs $200!

Airlines are constantly searching for other new fees you are certain to ignore while booking tickets. On Alaska Airlines, for example, food costs an extra $10 on a round-trip ticket. Extra-baggage fees are cropping up all over the industry, too. Don't be surprised when aisle-seat surcharges become common.

Alaska Airlines would probably debate the characterization of its $5 meals as a hidden fee. But it fits the bill: Consumers picking between two airlines on a travel site like Expedia are likely to pick the lowest fare, even if the difference is $5 or $10. After all, lower prices rank higher in Internet search lists. The price of a meal certainly could make the difference. By charging for meals on the plane, Alaska is gaming the system.

Perhaps this is why, in our survey, 85 percent of fliers said they were charged by airlines for services that were supposed to be free. *That's the highest-ranking fee-for-free-services rating in our survey.* About the same number of people said charges were made without their consent, and just shy of two-thirds said charges made were not clearly described in advance.

The consequences of not knowing the rules of the airline game are serious. Consumers feel airline penalties are the stiffest they face from among the industries in our study, coming in at an average of $33 per penalty. The average consumer pays $102 in extra airline fees every year.

These penalties are so common that people seem to believe hidden fees are an everyday part of flying. One-third said there was a hidden fee on "almost all airline tickets purchased," and another 37 percent said they were hit with such a fee on half the tickets purchased.

That same amount said fees made them switch airlines, but another one-third were fatalistic about airplane ticket fees and said they didn't bother switching. Thirty-five percent said their airline had the best price even with the fee included.

Refund outlook:

This fatalistic outlook by airline consumers makes them highly unlikely to contest hidden fees. Only 15 percent said they'd contacted customer service in an attempt to get a fee refund, and only 9 percent of all fliers said they'd been successful. Here's a hidden Ponemon Gotcha survey gem: Very few fliers try to get airline refunds, but many who try (60 percent) actually succeed.

5. Hotels

It's no mystery how consumers feel about hotel fees. A whopping 87 percent said charges for food, movies, drinks, and other incidentals were exorbitant. And more than half said they were charged fees without their consent. Average fees were high, about $25 dollars. And they were frequent. About half said such fees appeared on almost all their hotel bills.

But there's good news: The hotel business is awash in competition, and consumers seem to know it. Almost 60 percent said they'd switched hotels because of fees, *the largest "take-your-fees-and-shove-them" reaction in our survey.*

Refund outlook:

Consumers who complain about their bills see middle-of-the road results. For starters, consumers seem comfortable complaining about hotel fees. Fully 54 percent said they had contacted customer service to complain, among the highest rates (compare that to 15 percent who complained about airline and bank fees). Many of those complaints went unheeded, however: 34 percent said they'd failed to get a refund, but another 20 percent said they had, in fact, talked their way into getting some cash back. The other 46 percent just didn't bother complaining. The lesson: It's certainly worth calling or writing to complain, but hotels in recent years have begun to hold the line much more firmly, so don't always expect results.

6. Pay-TV

People don't hide their feelings about television-program providers, either. Cable and satellite consumers are the *most likely to contact customer service and complain*—we'll get to that in a moment.

TV fees aren't all that high—averaging $9.52 cents, once again in that sweet spot below $10. Of course, hidden, recurring subscription fees are far more insidious than one-time airline fees. Some 48 percent of consumers said these $10 extra charges appeared on every monthly bill, or even more frequently, raising the average annual pay-TV fee to $115 each year.

Three-quarters of consumers said extra TV fees were charged without their consent, and said that the fees were not clearly described on their monthly statements. And 35 percent said they were charged for services never received. Pay-TV consumers should pay heed to that number. Many consumers find themselves charged for premium channels they don't get or enhanced digital services they cannot receive.

Despite all this dissatisfaction, very few consumers—only 18 percent—acted on their anger and switched companies. That should be no surprise: 41 percent said their cable or satellite provider is the only one available in their location.

Refund outlook:

As for refunds, there's good news and bad news. Well, mostly bad news. Pay-TV customers are not shy about complaining. An incredible 85 percent said they had called to complain about hidden pay-TV fees. No wonder it's so hard to get through on the telephone! *Cable and dish customers are five times more likely to complain than bank or airline customers.* That's the good news. Here's the bad news: Complainers can't seem to get satisfaction. Cable and satellite firms are four times as likely to turn them down. Only 17 percent said they'd managed to squeeze a refund out of their TV provider while 67 percent said they were rejected.

7. Home Internet access

If there was a "winner" in our hidden-fee survey, it would be Internet service providers. Consumers reported average fees of only $3.71, and the total collected in average fees was only $700 million, an order of magnitude lower than banks, airlines, and hotels. Studying fees from Internet-access firms is tricky business, however, because broadband is increasingly bundled with cable-television service or phone service. Complaints about cable modems might show up more often as complaints about cabletelevision providers than complaints about Internet providers. That said, only 34 percent of all consumers named Internet access as a source of hidden fees, which ranked it near the bottom of our list.

Those who complained about fees said they were charged for services that were supposed to be free (71 percent) and the charges weren't clearly explained (61 percent). Consumers also indicate there is at least some choice for Internet providers: 36 percent said they had switched providers because of hidden fees, a sizable percentage.

Refund outlook:

That sense of choice apparently gives consumers a bit of power over their Internet providers. One third of consumers who complained to us about cable Internet fees said they'd contacted customer service looking for a refund, and half of those were successful.

8. Retirement

Hidden retirement-account fees generated the fewest number of complaints in our survey. There are two ways to interpret this: Consumers are either genuinely happy with the level of retirement-account fees, or genuinely being fooled by an incredible snow job. In Chapter 3, I explained that approximately $25 billion is taken from consumers' 401(k) accounts every year, an amount that never appears on any consumer's retirement statement, and that is almost impossible for any consumer to find or calculate. I suspect this incredible swindle may have skewed our survey results, and that those surveyed may have felt differently if such fees were itemized for them.

On to our results. Only 30 percent of those surveyed said they'd been hit by a hidden fee in their retirement accounts. The average fee was $9.83, and most people said the fee appeared either once each quarter or once each year—a relatively low rate. *Retirement savers were easily the least likely to switch to a new company out of fee frustration:* only 11 percent had done so. That makes sense, since consumers in 401(k) plans simply cannot switch providers (though they can often escape hidden fees by switching mutual-fund choices).

Refund outlook:

Predictably, fewer than one-quarter of retirement planners contacted customer service to complain about fees, and about half of them managed to squeeze a refund out of their providers.

9. Insurance

Insurance means a lot of things to a lot of people. There is, finally, a lot of competition in auto insurance, so consumers expectedly change providers when they become frustrated. There is some competition in homeowners insurance, though all providers share the same underlying risk and claim-history database, which somewhat limits real competition. Few consumers have choices among health-insurance providers, which like 401(k) plans, are often dictated by the place they work.

Still, insurance firms didn't fare badly in our survey. Hidden insurance fees only cost the average consumer $36 per year, buyers told us. The average fee was $13.50, and consumers only faced about three such fees each year. They also exercised their ability to switch providers when they could—48 percent of those who complained about fees said they had switched providers.

Of course, many consumers may find these results unbelievable, such as victims of Hurricane Katrina. But the results are not inconsistent. This survey did not ask about frustration with the insurance-claims process, only the presence of hidden fees when paying premiums. So it makes sense hidden-fee frustration would be low. The majority of Americans receive subsidized health insurance; home insurance is often a small sum tucked anonymously into a monthly mortgage payment, and auto insurance rates may be exorbitant, but they apparently are rarely a surprise. Despite the outrageous stories of claims frustration from hurricane victims and other insurance claimants, that pool of potential complainers remains a small percentage of the overall population, not likely to register high in a survey like ours.

Refund outlook:

People do complain to their insurance companies about hidden fees—some 39 percent told us they had. But only 11 percent managed to score a refund, ranking insurance complaints near the bottom of the potential success rating. Another 28 percent said their refund requests were rejected.

10. Groceries

Almost all of the fee frustration expressed by grocery-store shoppers centered around loyalty-card use. Nine out of 10 shoppers told us they'd paid excessive charges because they didn't have a loyalty card, *the highest rate of frustration for any question in the entire survey.* But in every other category, grocery stores were quite benign, consumers told us. Only 6 percent said they faced charges made without their consent, easily the lowest in our survey. And despite my complaints about the lack of price tags on items and rumbles of dissatisfaction with shelf price tags, only 11 percent complained that prices weren't clearly marked in stores.

Average hidden fees were tiny, coming in at just $2.47 per order. They were also rare, with 60 percent of people saying they were hit by sneaky fees less than 20 percent of the time they shopped, the lowest-frequency option we offered.

Consumers also have plenty of choices, thanks to hearty competition from grocery stores: 51 percent of complainers said they'd switched stores out of frustration.

And yet, despite all these positive results, consumers *lost more to grocery store fees than any other category, by far*—an average of $222 each year. Nothing reveals the power of repetitive fees more than grocery-store shopping. Consumers told us they shop for food an average of 7.5 times each month. Those $2.47 fees really add up.

Refund outlook:

Many consumers anecdotally report great success when challenging incorrect store pricing; particularly in states like Michigan and Massachusetts that have strict grocery-store pricing laws that provide "bonus" refunds to complainers. Unfortunately, very few consumers speak up at the store. Only 14 percent told us they complained about grocery-store fees. On the other hand, a majority of them received refunds, meaning it does pay to be a pain at the checkout line.

Ponemon Gotcha Study conclusion

Perhaps you already knew you were losing a lot of money to hidden fees. Certainly, you've felt it. But this study attempts to quantify just how much you are losing. Of course, some fees (like retirement fees) remain entirely out of view, making them almost impossible to quantify. The average $942.56 losses quantified in this study are a rough estimate, and almost certainly a lowball estimate. So is the total of $45 billion in regressive hidden-fee revenue we calculated is collected by ten important U.S. industries.

Still, the study offers valuable insights to consumers who want to fight back. The most valuable: Where to fire the few bullets you have when fighting hidden fees. Our research suggests that, while credit-card firms have a well-deserved, horrid reputation for being unfair, they are also the most likely to bend when consumers complain. It's possible this doesn't indicate largesse, but rather deft strategy: The banks may levy a truly outlandish spectrum of fees, see what they can get away with, then liberally give out refunds when caught. Such would be a profitable, if reprehensible, strategy. You don't care: You just want your money back. And you should know it is worth complaining to your credit-card company about sneaky fees.

On the other hand, it seems that much of the time you spend complaining to your cable company falls on deaf ears. Remember, this is an industry that had an employee change a customer's name to Bitch Dog—that's a tough neighborhood. Complaints to cell-phone firms are only a touch more successful. As we've seen, you'd be better off complaining about your food bill to your grocery store instead.

SUMMARY—COST PER INDIVIDUAL

Summary of Sneaky Fees	Fee	Fee Cycle	Annual Estimate
Cellular phone	$9.70	Per month	$116.36
Credit cards	$7.72	Per month	92.64
Banks including ATM fees	$6.95	Per month	83.46
Airline travel	$33.44	3.05 Tickets purchased per year	102.01
Hotels & lodging	$24.82	3.83 Stays per year	95.08
Cable/satellite services	$9.52	Per month	114.20
Home Internet access	$3.71	Per month	44.56
Retirement services	$9.83	3.65 Transactions per year	35.87
Insurance	$13.48	2.67 Transactions per year	36.00
Groceries	$2.47	7.5 Orders per month	222.40
Total		**Total Annual Cost Per Victim**	**$942.56**

COMPLAINTS AND SUCCESS RATE

Consumers don't always pick the wisest target

Type	Attempted	Successful	Success Rate
1. PAY TV	84%	17%	20.2%
2. CREDIT CARDS	79%	51%	64.6%
3. CELL PHONES	71%	19%	26.8%
4. HOTELS	54%	20%	37.0%
5. INSURANCE	38%	11%	28.9%
6. INTERNET	33%	17%	51.5%
7. RETIREMENT	23%	12%	52.2%
8. BANKS	18%	6%	33.3%
9. AIRLINES	15%	9%	60.0%
10. GROCERY	14%	8%	57.1%

Conclusion

The story of *Gotcha Capitalism* is really two stories. It's the story of last week's $30 cable TV fee you're still angry about, and it's the story of a fundamental shift in the foundation of America's economic system. In the age of the Internet, just-in-time manufacturing, and globalization, companies find themselves fighting to keep prices low like never before. Their response, almost universally, has been to compensate by lying about the true price of things. They've systematically dismantled other important market pressures, too, by tricking consumers into long-term contracts that virtually end real competition. They've invented tactics—like shrouding and reverse competition—that make it impossible to act like a rational consumer. They've abandoned old-fashioned ideas about customer loyalty and actually set out to drive away consumers their computers identify as less profitable. And they've created contracts with typography so small that they've had to make up a word—mouseprint—to describe it.

Add it all up, add up those ATM-denial fees, vehicle license-recovery fees, and handset-upgrade fees, and consumers say they lose $45 billion each year to small print. Other estimates place the figure at four times that amount. Whatever it is, you and I both know, deep down, that every day we're getting cheated by asterisks.

With no government agency acting as referee, our economy is operating as a free-for-all, and the result is widespread abuse. So much money is stealthily taken from consumers each year it artificially keeps the national inflation rate low.

The Internet was supposed to bring about the age of the consumer. With worldwide comparison shopping possible, and product information abundant, the World Wide Web was supposed to make us smarter and the resulting price transparency was supposed to force prices down toward a flat bottom. Instead, our technology age has been hijacked. We are outsmarted by computers that watch us constantly, calculating optimal ways to pick our pockets, to charge just a little more, to make it just a little harder to complain, to make us just a little more profitable.

Gotcha!

But now, you know better. You know the tricks they're using against you. You know where to look for hundreds of hidden fees in dozens of industries. You know how to complain, what buttons to push, and where to send those angry letters. You know the truth. They never really "Gotcha"—not as long as you have options. And you have many options—targeted complaint letters, small-claims-court lawsuits, summoning government regulators. You are not helpless, and you are not alone.

Of course, Gotchas are a moving target, so this journey does not stop here. Every week, more sneaky fees are unmasked at the *Red Tape Chronicles* blog I write. And now on the site there is a collection of tools you can download to help you fight and win these battles. The sample letters and telephone scripts in this book are just the beginning. Consumers from around the country are now sharing letters they wrote that got results on the *Red Tape Chronicles* Gotcha! site. They're transcribing customer-support calls that went their way, stressing the "magic words" that turned the tide—all so you can imitate their methods and enjoy their results. Databases have been turned against us for too long. Now, consumers have exactly the tools they need to tip the scales in our favor.

There is only one thing left for you to do: Have the courage to try.

Complaint phone calls are annoying and frustrating. They don't always end well. Sometimes they can ruin your afternoon. Complaint letters often feel like so many words thrown into a trash bin. And so, you often deliberate, procrastinate, hesitate, and then finally just plain skip it. You pay the fee, you avoid the battle, and you go on with your life.

That might seem the prudent thing to do, but by letting it go, you are letting go of our way of life. You are letting the Gotcha capitalists win—letting those who would cripple America's free market and America's love of fair competition have their way with you, and have their way with our economy.

Now, it's time for consumers to fight back against this systematic attack on fairness. Even if you don't always get optimal results, you must complain, complain, and complain to make sure the cheaters' victory isn't permanent.

To that end, here's the best plan of action:

1. Complain to state and federal legislators that you're tired of living in a lawless economy. You want truth-in-advertising laws enforced, you want fair-banking rules created, and you want companies to know there will be consequences for misbehaviors. Tell them regulation is not a dirty word; we all need rules before we play any game.

2. Stay a free agent. In every aspect of your life, avoid long-term contracts as much as possible. Always opt for the shortest contract when buying a cell phone or signing up for Internet access. Flexibility is key in a world where technology changes so quickly. Companies want to tie you up and then take advantage of you; don't let them. Similar to truth-in-lending requirements, long-term contracts should include provisions that indicate precisely how much the consumer will pay the company during the life of the contract.

3. Demand laws with expanded regret periods. For example: Cell-phone users should be able to return their phones at any time until they see their first monthly bill so they are sure they are paying a fair price.

4. Fees should be limited and commensurate with an actual expense incurred by a company—as in countries like the United Kingdom—rather than pulled from thin air. Such fee regulation is worth considering. So are European-style laws that require taxes and fees to be included in price tags, so there are no surprises.

5. Mouseprint shouldn't be legal. It's not impossible to specify minimum typeface requirements—workplace safety laws do. Some specify precisely what font size hazard-warning sign letters must be for the sign to be considered a fair warning. If the letters are too small, and workers can't read them, the company incurs additional liability. Consumers should not be bound by contracts that require a magnifying lens to read.

If this book were a cell-phone bill, or a credit-card contract, this final page would be jam-packed with Gotchas. And if there were fine print on this book, it would say this: "*Does not include information about every sneaky fee consumers might face. Some fees disappear, new ones are invented daily. *Gotcha Capitalism* can't protect you from every one."

That's where your imagination comes in. As we've seen, companies hire consultants and set up war rooms full of people who spend their entire day thinking of ways to trick you. Sneaky fees are a moving target. That's why only half this book was devoted to precise information about fees and refunds, and the other half is about the way these companies think. To really understand mouseprint, you have to think like a mouse. To really avoid sneaky fees, you've got to understand the sneaky mind. This book is stocked with lots of information, but much of it you won't remember, and some will be outdated shortly. Companies will keep dreaming up ways to screw you. That's where your imagination comes in.

The good news is this: Imagination is more powerful than information. (Thanks, Einstein.)

Armed with your imagination, you don't have to accept the rules of Gotcha Capitalism any longer. The world is full of people who close their eyes, hold their nose, and just pay their bills every month, while inside they know they've been cheated. They are the tourists in this new world. But not you. You know the rules. You're a local. You're a sophisticate. Your families don't have to be victims of cheating any longer. You are going to save a lot of money. Imagine what you'll do with it all!

Appendix

Gotcha Glossary

Aftercharge—Any amount you must pay over and above the amount listed on a price tag, an advertisement, or in a store window. These include surcharges, fees, taxes, and lots of other things companies dream up. Believe it or not, in some places on Earth (Europe), things actually cost the price listed on the price tag. Imagine that!

ARPU—Average Revenue Per User. The name cable companies use to describe you.

Asterisk—The twenty-seventh letter of the American alphabet. Avoid if possible. Usually leads to mouseprint.

Bottom-line shock—What consumers feel when they get their first cell-phone bill, cable TV bill, or otherwise learn the true price they are paying for something.

Contract of adhesion—A contract where one party has a drastically and unfairly superior bargaining position, and uses that position to offer a take-it-or-leave-it contract that's not open to negotiation over any of its terms. Many consumer contracts are contracts of adhesion. Unfair provisions in such contracts are not enforceable by law.

Expense ratio—Fees paid to mutual-fund managers. Also known as theft of 401(k) retirement funds by Wall Street money managers. These cut directly into investment returns. Fund managers give a portion to 401(k) administrators as revenue-sharing payments, an arrangement also called a kickback.

Freeloaders—Credit-card users who pay their bills in full every month. Credit-card companies hate them.

Fiduciary duty—A special legal relationship that requires a person or company to act in another person's best financial interest. Your 401(k) administrator should have a fiduciary duty to you. But she/he doesn't.

Gotcha Capitalism—An unfair, lawless playing field that's replaced America's former economic system, the market economy. Hidden fees are its most recognizable characteristic. The system rewards the sneakiest companies, rather than the most efficient companies with the best products.

Landing price—The teaser price that consumers are given for products when they arrive at a website. The real purchase price includes shipping and handling and other fees.

Loyalty card—Conspiracy by America's supermarkets to track all shoppers while tricking them into believing they are receiving discounts on items; an amusing euphemism.

Mouseprint—Small print so tiny only a rodent can read it. Usually written by rodents. Often on the other end of asterisks.

Myope—An economist's term for an unsophisticated consumer who's too busy to read every monthly twenty-eight-page disclaimer sent home by credit-card companies. Often seen carrying children instead of triple-checking for hidden fees in online hotel reservations or overcharged telephone calls. A.K.A., sucker.

Resort fee—Price of mini golf course at America's great hotels.

Revenue-sharing payments—Kickbacks accepted by 401(k)-plan administrators for giving you access to a few select, crappy, expensive mutual funds in your retirement plan.

Reverse competition—When someone bargaining on your behalf with another entity stands to benefit if your price for something goes up. Often paired with a trilateral dilemma, the economists' lover's triangle. Example: home purchase title insurance. Your Realtor or mortgage broker gets a kickback from the title company you pick, so both title company and your agent/broker benefit when you pay more. The price pressure is upward, not downward.

Revolvers—People who don't pay off their credit-card balances in full every month. Credit-card companies love them and bleed them dry.

Sophisticates—The coupon clippers of the electronic age. These are people who read mouseprint and avoid sneaky fees, thereby getting all the good deals. Myopes pay for the perks sophisticates get, like frequent-flier miles on credit cards.

Stealth inflation—Hidden fees are such a substantial part of the economy that they actually would impact the overall rate of inflation—if they counted. But the Bureau of Labor Statistics doesn't get accurate information on fees from companies, so the inflation rate doesn't reflect them, and as a result remains artificially low. But you feel it in your wallet.

Trilateral dilemma—See Reverse Competition.

VLRF—Vehicle license recovery fee. Snazzy name car rental companies give to one of their biggest fees, the extra charge you must pay to actually drive the car you rent off their parking lot. You could decline the fee, but then the car you get wouldn't be street legal.

Yield-spread premium—Kickback given to mortgage brokers who talk homebuyers into mortgages with higher-than-available interest rates. The brokers get one lump sum at closing; homeowners pay the bank back in tiny increments for 30 years.

Looking for Help?
Consumer Advocacy Groups

American Council on Consumer Interests (ACCI)
240 Stanley Hall
University of Missouri
Columbia, MO 65211 USA
Phone: (573) 882-3817
www.consumerinterests.org

Excellent starting point for finding area-specific experts and research. Search engine will link visitors to researchers and lawyers with expertise in elderly consumer law, health policy, consumer boycotts, and so on.

Better Business Bureaus, Inc.
4200 Wilson Blvd.
Arlington, VA 22203 USA
Phone: (703) 276-0100
www.bbb.org

Private organization run by 300,000 member businesses; it promotes self-regulation by corporate America. Consumers with complaints against any company should always register those complaints with the agency, which has about 150 local offices around the country. Not every complaint is resolved, however, as the agency has no legal authority. It can, however, revoke a company's membership, causing public embarrassment. That's its main enforcement tool.

Center for Responsible Lending
302 West Main Street
Durham, NC 27701 USA
Phone: (919) 313-8500
www.responsiblelending.org

Nonprofit research and policy organization devoted to protecting homeowner-ship and family wealth by working to stop abusive lending practices. CRL re-searchers write policy briefs, while CRL lawyers occasionally participate in litigation and file legal briefs on key predatory-lending issues.

Center for Justice and Democracy
90 Broad Street
Suite 401
New York, NY 10004 USA
www.centerjd.org

Nonprofit advocacy group that works to protect Americans' rights to equal ac-cess to the legal system. Specializes in medical-malpractice lawsuits and other health-related issues.

Consumer Action (CA)
717 Market Street,
Suite 310
San Francisco, CA 94103 USA
Phone: (415) 777-9635
www.consumer-action.org

Nonprofit advocacy group that provides free, nonlegal consumer assistance and referrals in English, Spanish, and Chinese. Also provides free educational mate-rials and supports pro-consumer litigation. Offers a popular "fee of the week" blog. Specializes in credit-card issues, other bank issues, and telephone com-plaints.

Consumer Federation of America
1620 I Street, NW
Suite 200
Washington, DC 20006 USA
Phone: (202) 387-6121
www.consumerfed.org

An umbrella group of 300 consumer-advocacy agencies from all around the country. It pools resources to take on large research projects and raise the pro-file of smaller advocacy organizations and their causes.

Consumeraffairs.com complaint agency database
(Find attorney general and other consumer-protection agencies by zip code)
www.consumeraffairs.com/db/consumerprotection.html

Consumeraffairs.com is a private website that pools consumer complaints and topic-specific stories related to all areas of consumer news. Its consumer-protection database is a quick tool consumers can use to find the right place to complain. Visitors simply enter their zip code and they receive a list of nearby agencies, including addresses and Web page links.

Consumers Union
101 Truman Avenue
Yonkers, NY 10703-1057 USA
Phone: (914) 378-2000
www.consumersunion.org

Consumers Union publishes *Consumer Reports,* the leading consumer-research magazine. In addition to testing all manner of consumer products at its three-hundred-acre facility in Yonkers, New York, Consumers Union also hires lawyers and other advocates to fight for consumer-friendly legislation around the country.

Federal Citizen Information Center
Pueblo, Colo. 81009 USA
Phone: 1-888-8 PUEBLO (1-888-878-3256)
www.pueblo.gsa.gov/complaintresources.htm

The Federal Citizen Information Center, in Pueblo, Colorado, is the federal government's consumer-information resource, run by the General Services Administration. The center publishes a family of websites, including usa.gov, kids.gov, and consumeraction.gov. At pueblo.gsa.gov, the site lists information on scams, product recalls, and newsletters that explain consumer rights. The complaint resource page lists government agencies that take complaints.

Foundation for Taxpayer and Consumer Rights
1750 Ocean Park Blvd.
Suite 200
Santa Monica, CA 90405 USA
Phone: (310) 392-0522
www.consumerwatchdog.org

California-based advocacy group focusing on issues like health care, homeowners insurance, taxation, and gasoline prices.

National Association of Consumer Advocates
1730 Rhode Island Avenue NW
Suite 710
Washington, DC 20036 USA
Phone: (202) 452-1989
www.naca.net

A nationwide association of consumer lawyers who defend consumers against abusive, fraudulent, and predatory practices by businesses. Its Web site includes a handy "Find a Lawyer" tool that lets visitors search by geographic area and legal topic—auto fraud, bankruptcy, debt-collection abuse, military consumer rights, and more. The group also advocates reform in several areas, including binding mandatory arbitration, credit cards, bank fees, and others.

National Consumer Law Center (NCLC)
18 Tremont Street
Boston, MA 02108 USA
Phone: (617) 523-8089
www.consumerlaw.org,

Advocacy group with consumer lawyers who initiate targeted litigation to advance consumer rights, with special focus on immigrants, vulnerable elders, homeowners, former welfare recipients, victims of domestic violence, and military personnel, among others. The center also offers advice and research to local consumer lawyers. It does not give advice to individual consumers.

National Consumers League (NCL)
1701 K Street, NW
Suite 1201
Washington, DC 20006 USA
Phone: (202) 835-3323
www.nclnet.org

A hundred-year-old consortium of state consumer-league groups, this nonprofit organization focuses on workplace safety and labor rights, along with food-safety issues and privacy. It also runs fraud.org, a site devoted to stopping Internet scams.

U.S. Public Interest Research Group
44 Winter Street, 4th Floor,
Boston, MA 02108 USA .
Phone: (617) 747-4370
www.uspirg.org

The U.S. Public Interest Research Group is a consortium of state advocacy Public Interest Research Groups (PIRGs) that tackle issues like problems with credit reports, conservation, free speech, toy safety, and education. About half of U.S. states have their own local PIRG, available from the group's main website. The agencies are chiefly concerned with policy issues, legislation, and attracting media attention to unfair practices.

Sample
TROUBLESHOOTING WORKSHEET

GENERAL SUBJECT OF DISPUTE: _____

COMPANY: _____

MAIN NUMBER: _____

CONTACT NUMBER: _____ DATE: _____

PERSON WHO ANSWERED: _____

OTHERS ON THE CALL: _____

NOTES: _____

_____

_____

_____

FOLLOW UP: _____

- -

CONTACT NUMBER: _____ DATE: _____

PERSON WHO ANSWERED: _____

OTHERS ON THE CALL: _____

NOTES: _____

_____

_____

_____

FOLLOW UP: _____

- -

CONTACT NUMBER: _____ DATE: _____

PERSON WHO ANSWERED: _____

OTHERS ON THE CALL: _____

NOTES: _____

_____

_____

_____

FOLLOW UP: _____

Sample
TROUBLESHOOTING WORKSHEET

GENERAL SUBJECT OF DISPUTE: _____

COMPANY: _____

MAIN NUMBER: _____

CONTACT NUMBER: _____ DATE: _____

PERSON WHO ANSWERED: _____

OTHERS ON THE CALL: _____

NOTES: _____

_____

_____

_____

FOLLOW UP: _____
- -

CONTACT NUMBER: _____ DATE: _____

PERSON WHO ANSWERED: _____

OTHERS ON THE CALL: _____

NOTES: _____

_____

_____

_____

FOLLOW UP: _____
- -

CONTACT NUMBER: _____ DATE: _____

PERSON WHO ANSWERED: _____

OTHERS ON THE CALL: _____

NOTES: _____

_____

_____

_____

FOLLOW UP: _____

Sample
TROUBLESHOOTING WORKSHEET

GENERAL SUBJECT OF DISPUTE: _____

COMPANY: _____

MAIN NUMBER: _____

CONTACT NUMBER: _____ DATE: _____

PERSON WHO ANSWERED: _____

OTHERS ON THE CALL: _____

NOTES: _____

_____

_____

_____

FOLLOW UP: _____

- -

CONTACT NUMBER: _____ DATE: _____

PERSON WHO ANSWERED: _____

OTHERS ON THE CALL: _____

NOTES: _____

_____

_____

_____

FOLLOW UP: _____

- -

CONTACT NUMBER: _____ DATE: _____

PERSON WHO ANSWERED: _____

OTHERS ON THE CALL: _____

NOTES: _____

_____

_____

_____

FOLLOW UP: _____

Sample
TROUBLESHOOTING WORKSHEET

GENERAL SUBJECT OF DISPUTE: _____

COMPANY: _____

MAIN NUMBER: _____

CONTACT NUMBER: _____ DATE: _____

PERSON WHO ANSWERED: _____

OTHERS ON THE CALL: _____

NOTES: _____

_____

_____

_____

FOLLOW UP: _____

- -

CONTACT NUMBER: _____ DATE: _____

PERSON WHO ANSWERED: _____

OTHERS ON THE CALL: _____

NOTES: _____

_____

_____

_____

FOLLOW UP: _____

- -

CONTACT NUMBER: _____ DATE: _____

PERSON WHO ANSWERED: _____

OTHERS ON THE CALL: _____

NOTES: _____

_____

_____

_____

FOLLOW UP: _____

Sample
TROUBLESHOOTING WORKSHEET

GENERAL SUBJECT OF DISPUTE: _____

COMPANY: _____

MAIN NUMBER: _____

CONTACT NUMBER: _____ DATE: _____

PERSON WHO ANSWERED: _____

OTHERS ON THE CALL: _____

NOTES: _____

_____

_____

_____

FOLLOW UP: _____

CONTACT NUMBER: _____ DATE: _____

PERSON WHO ANSWERED: _____

OTHERS ON THE CALL: _____

NOTES: _____

_____

_____

_____

FOLLOW UP: _____

CONTACT NUMBER: _____ DATE: _____

PERSON WHO ANSWERED: _____

OTHERS ON THE CALL: _____

NOTES: _____

_____

_____

_____

FOLLOW UP: _____

Notes

"Connecticut Attorney General Says Even Reputable Telecom Companies Cheat Consumers, On *60 Minutes*," press release issued by CBS Television Network describing *60 Minutes* episode, December 13, 2001. Broadcast occurred December 16, 2001.

Section 1
Chapter 1

"Some will rob"—lyrics from Woody Guthrie's song "The Ballad of Pretty Boy Floyd," 1939.

"fastest-growing crime in the country"—Identity Theft Survey Report, Federal Trade Commission, September 2003.

"million-dollar diamond heists"—an allusion to James Jackson, perhaps the world's most accomplished identity thief, and the subject of my first book, *Your Evil Twin: Behind the Identity Theft Epidemic.*

"two-hundred-million cell phones"—CTIA, the wireless industry trade association group (formerly the Cellular Telephone Industry Association), estimated in April 2007 that there were 235 million U.S. cell-phone users.

"around $216 billion annually"—*Consumer Reports,* "Don't Get Taken by Hidden Fees," May 2004, pp. 34–38.

"inflation rate is held artificially low"—Emily Thornton, "Fees! Fees! Fees!" *BusinessWeek,* September 29, 2003. Cover story.

"can constitute a binding contract"—refers to Carnival Cruise Lines Inc.

V. Shute, 499 U.S. 585 (1991). A more thorough discussion appears in Chapter 3 of the Toolkit section.

"This tale of deception"—The AT&T narrative is constructed from U.S. District Court Northern District of California ruling, Darcy Ting et al. vs. AT&T. January 15, 2002. Legal citation Ting v. AT&T, 182 F. Supp. 2d 902 (N.D. Cal. 2002). The ruling was affirmed by a federal appeals court in 2003.

"I hit the brakes hard"—Billboard viewed by the author in Lake Forest Park, Washington, during February 2006.

"save 3 cents per gallon"—Jeff Leonard, "Common Cents," NACS Magazine, published by the Association for Convenience & Petroleum Retailing, April 2007. Draft provided by author.

"Gabaix and Laibson boiled"—Xavier Gabaix and David Laibson, "Shrouded Attributes, Consumer Myopia, and Information Suppression in Competitive Markets," The Quarterly Journal of Economics, May 2006.

"Economists sometimes call this"—an excellent discussion of the trilateral dilemma can be found in "Kickbacks or Compensation: The Case of Yield Spread Premiums," by Howell E. Jackson and Jeremy Berry, a paper published by Harvard Law School on January 2, 2002.

"Some 30 percent of its budget"—Hal Taylor, "FTC Chairman Doubts More Cuts to Agency," Daily News Record, November 1984. Archived online at http://findarticles.com/p/articles/mi_hb4298/is_198411/ai_n14959514

"the FTC budget fell"—Peter G. Germanis and Thomas M. Humbert, "Budget Cuts: The Key to Economic Recovery," paper published by the Heritage Foundation, September 18, 1981. Archived online at http://www.heritage.org/Research/Budget/bg151.cfm

"A review of FTC actions"—Peter G. Germanis and Thomas M. Humbert, "Budget Cuts: The Key to Economic Recovery," paper published by the Heritage Foundation September 18, 1981. Archived online at http://www.heritage.org/Research/Budget/bg151.cfm

"In 1979, there were 1,746 employees"—"FTC Full-Time Equivalent History," http://www.ftc.gov/ftc/oed/fmo/fte2.shtm

"forced to refund," "Marketer of Free Credit Reports Settles FTC Charges," press release issued by the Federal Trade Commission, August 16, 2005.

"Even companies that are directly"—For a discussion of the battle between the Federal Trade Commission and the nation's credit bureaus, see Bob Sullivan, Your Evil Twin: Behind the Identity Theft Epidemic, Chapter 4.

"which traces its roots"—For a thorough discussion of Karl Rove's role in the tort-reform movement, see the excellent PBS *Frontline* special "Karl Rove: The Architect," which originally aired in April 2005. It can be accessed online at http://www.pbs.org/wgbh/pages/frontline/shows/architect/texas/tort.html

"While it is true"—*New American Bible.* Luke 18:4–5.

Section 2
Chapter 1: Credit cards

"Owning a credit-card"—"New GAO Credit-Card Study Highlights Anti-Consumer Practices in the Credit Card Industry," press release issued by The U.S. Public Interest Research Group, October 11, 2006.

"Wesley Wannemacher was the perfect"—reconstructed from Wesley Wannemacher, testimony before U.S. Senate Permanent Subcommittee on Investigations, March 7, 2007.

"Merchants pay banks a hefty fee"—"Vermont 'Mom and Pop' Store Owner Tells Leahy Panel of Struggles Confronting Small Businesses in the Face of Escalating Credit Card Fees," press release issued by U.S. Senator Patrick Leahy, July 19, 2006.

"eight billion preapproved credit-card applications"—Elizabeth Warren, "You Are Pre-Approved—8 Billion Times," TPMCafe.com, February 26, 2007, http://warrenreports.tpmcafe.com/blog/warrenreports/2007/feb/26/you_are_pre_approved_8_billion_times

"about half of American consumers don't"—Liz Pulliam Weston, "The Truth About Credit Card Debt," column on MSN's *Money,* http://moneycentral.msn.com/content/Banking/creditcardsmarts/P74808.asp, accessed April 14, 2007.

"eighth-grade reading level"—"Increased Complexity in Rates and Fees Heightens Need for More Effective Disclosures to Consumers," report to Congress by the U.S. Government General Accountability Office, September 2006.

"twenty-seventh-grade level"—Ibid., p. 38.

"*If you pay late*"—Ibid., p.47.

"It has no right to pass a law"—For an intriguing discussion of the birth of South Dakota as a financial hub, see the PBS *Frontline* special, "Secret History of the Credit Card," which first aired in November 2004. The segment "The Ascendancy of the Credit Card Industry," by Robin Stein, can be accessed at http://www.pbs.org/wgbh/pages/frontline/shows/credit/more/rise.html

"That decision declared credit card penalty fees"—Supreme Court ruling: Smiley v. Citibank (S.D.), N. A., 517 U.S. 735 (1996).

"one in every three cardholders were issued a penalty"—"Increased Complexity in Rates and Fees," GAO report, p. 5.

"a 160 percent increase"—Ibid, p. 18.

"a whopping 15 percent increase"—Kathy Chu, "Credit Card Fees Can Suck You In," *USA Today,* December 15, 2006, accessed http://www.usatoday.com/money/perfi/credit/2006-12-15-card-fees-usat_x.htm

"you'll owe $35 in interest on that $20 balance"—Example adapted from Senator Carl Levin, opening statement, "Hearing on Credit Card Practices: Fees, Interest and Grace Periods," Permanent Subcommittee on Investigations, March 7, 2007.

"one-third of credit card firms used double-cycle billing"—"Increased Complexity in Rates and Fees," GAO report, p. 27.

"trick you into a fee"—Ibid.

"Pay to Pay"—Senator Carl Levin, opening statement, "Hearing on Credit Card Practices: Fees, Interest and Grace Periods," Permanent Subcommittee on Investigations, March 7, 2007.

"Banks pay off the cheapest part of the loan first"—"Choosing a Credit Card," online brochure published by The Federal Reserve Board, accessed April 14, 2007, http://www.federalreserve.gov/Pubs/shop/

"their credit limit was lowered below"—Michael Donavan, testimony before the Senate Committee on Banking, Housing, and Urban Affairs, January 25, 2007.

"The effective limit is a dynamic amount"—Diane E. Thompson, council for Land of Lincoln Legal Assistance Foundation Inc., public letter to the Board of Governors of the Federal Reserve, in advance of Truth-in-Lending rulemaking, March 27, 2005.

"Fourteen of the twenty-two most popular credit cards took the lowest road"—"Increased Complexity in Rates and Fees," GAO report, p. 22.

"so did Steve Monteith"—Monteith described his episode in interviews with the author in February 2006.

Chapter 2: Banks

"Miss Piggy"—Jim Hightower, blog post on Alternet.org, April 26, 2000. Accessed April 15, 2007. http://www.alternet.org/columnists/story/8956/

"they'll talk dirty to you"—As quoted in Timothy L. Keiningham et al., *Loy-*

alty Myths, John Wiley & Sons, September 2005, p. 34. The book's first chapter retells the pay-to-talk teller experiment in lively detail.

"Profits jumped 28 percent"—Ibid., p. 36.

"$32 billion bite," "Banks: Protection Racket?" *BusinessWeek Online,* May 2, 2005. http://www.businessweek.com/magazine/content/05_18/ b3931085_mz020.htm

"fee income has soared 44 percent," Richard Burnett, "Few Complain As Rising Fees Boost Profits of Banks," *Baltimore Sun,* May 28, 2006, p. 3C.

"about half of bank income," Liz Pulliam Weston, "Don't be duped by bounced-check 'protection,'" *MSN Money,* accessed April 15, 2007. http://articles.moneycentral.msn.com/Banking/BetterBanking/DontBe DupedByBouncedCheckProtection.aspx?page=all

"can cost you $100 or more a year," "Foolish Checking." The Motley Fool. http://www.fool.com/money/banking/services/checking.htm, accessed April 11, 2007.

"fifty-five pages long"—"Banks: Protection Racket?" *BusinessWeek Online,* May 2, 2005.

"most banks don't disclose fees"—Jean Ann Fox and Patrick Woodall, "Overdrawn: Consumers Face Hidden Overdraft Charges from Nation's Largest Banks," Consumer Federation of America report, June 9, 2005, p. 9.

"Service Fee. Quantity: 1," Andy Gallagher told his story to the author during a series of interviews in January 2007.

"These folks stay up all night"—E-mail to the author, January 12, 2007.

"They are quite aware of the money that they are making"—Comment left on the author's blog, *Red Tape Chronicles,* on January 12, 2007. http:// redtape.msnbc.com/2007/01/the_quest_for_m.html

"Chasing away undesirable customers"—Keiningham, p. 36.

"*BusinessWeek* tells the story of"—"Banks: Protection Racket."

"but have so far stopped short"—"Joint Guidance on Overdraft Protection Programs," issued February 16, 2005 by these federal banking regulators: Office of the Comptroller of the Currency, Treasury (OCC); Board of Governors of the Federal Reserve System; Federal Deposit Insurance Corporation (FDIC); and National Credit Union Administration (NCUA).

"The Banks don't care. It's not their money"—Bob Sullivan, "A quest for more info on bank fees," comment left on blog, January 12, 2007, http:// redtape.msnbc.com/2007/01/the_quest_for_m.html

"We've heard from customers"—"Banks: Protection Racket."

"fees, which total about $17.5 billion," "Out of Balance: Consumers Pay $17.5 Billion Per Year in Fees for Abusive Overdraft Loans," Eric Halpern and Peter Smith," paper published by the Center for Responsible Lending, July 11, 2007.

"more electronic payments than paper check transactions"—"Federal Reserve Studies Confirm Electronic Payments Exceed Check Payments for the First Time," press release issued by the Federal Reserve, December 6, 2004.

"check writing has been on the decline since 1995"—Josh Funk, "Check Writing Going Way of Clerks, Quills," *Chicago Tribune*, February 7, 2007, p. 5.

"Blacks and Latinos are twice as likely"—Jean Ann Fox, Director of Consumer Protection, Consumer Federation of America, letter to the Federal Deposit Insurance Corporation, in response to a request for comment on agency overdraft study, October 16, 2006.

"No bank is going to advertise"—Kathy Chu, "Rising Bank Fees Hit Consumers," *USA Today*, October 4, 2005, p. B1.

"Banks cash your checks and clear your other transactions"—Kathy Chu, "Banks' Check-Clearing Policies Could Leave You with Overdrafts," *USA Today*, November 20, 2006, p. B1.

"Banks rake in about $4 billion a year"—Greg McBride, "Bankrate's Fall '06 Checking Study: Fees Rise Again," released October 30, 2006, http://www.bankrate.com/brm/news/chk/chkstudy/2006_fall_checking_study_main.asp

"America's customer service champ"—"Customer Service Champs," *BusinessWeek*, March 5, 2007.

"ATM Denial: $1.50"—This story is told in more detail on the author's *Red Tape Chronicles* blog, "In Denial: ATM Fee for Getting Nothing," published October 28, 2005.

"according to an HSBC study in 2005"—"Are You Financially Fit in the Event of a Hit," Bob Sullivan, *Red Tape Chronicles*, November 11, 2005.

Chapter 3: Retirement/401(k)s

"If we had to disclose fees"—David Nicklaus, "Hidden Fees Could Drain Many 401(k)s," *St. Louis Post-Dispatch*, March 18, 2007, p. E1.

"Changes Needed to Provide 401(k) Plan Participants and the Department of Labor Better Information on Fees," Government Accountability Office report GAO 07-21, November 2006.

"A Look at 401(k) Plan F Fees," report issued by the U.S. Department of Labor Employee Benefits Security Administration, undated.

This hard-to-believe result of sixty-five years of investing is elegantly explained in the PBS *Frontline* special: "Can You Afford to Retire?" which initially aired in May 2006. The 80–20 split claim was made by John C. Bogle, founder of Vanguard, and defended by a benefits expert who provided a year-by-year table of earnings to PBS. The table is available online at http://www.pbs.org/wgbh/pages/frontline/retirement/interviews/bogle.html#2

Jeff Robertson, "The Opportunity Cost and Fiduciary Implications of Retirement Plan Fees," guest article, 401K Help Center, undated. Robertson does not supply his underlying math in the article, but here's a typical scenario, computed using the excellent calculator at Bloomberg.com at http://www.bloomberg.com/invest/calculators/401k.html A single 35-year-old with a $50,000 account who earns $100,000 each year and aggressively saves 12 percent of his salary, along with the maximum 3 percent employer match, will put away $15,500 yearly, the annual maximum limit in 2007. Assuming all those factors remain constant until age 65 (including no salary increase), our saver will have $2,334,221 million in his 401(k) account. If expense fees were 1 percent higher, dropping returns to 7 percent, our saver's balance would be $1,899,700 million, a startling loss of $434,521! The real effect would be even worse than that, as the annual maximum contribution will certainly rise during the next 30 years. http://www.401khelpcenter.com/401k/robertson_opportunity_cost.html

Nicole Bullock, "10 Things Your 401(k) Provider Won't Tell You," *SmartMoney*, Nov. 14, 2006.

Lisa Shidler, "Balances in Active 401(k) Plans on the Rise; Stock Market, Higher Contributions Spark Growth," *Investment News*, August 28, 2006, p. 18.

Lynn O'Shaughnessy, "A 401(k) Picks a Mutual Fund. Who Gets a Perk?" *New York Times*, February 15, 2004.

"Insurance Giant Agrees to Sweeping Reforms: ING to Compensate Upstate Teachers After Probe Reveals Hidden Influence over Union," press release issued by New York State Attorney General's Office, October 10, 2006.

For a priceless discussion of the flaws in many annuities, see Liz Weston's
    MSN Money column, "High fees, more risk? Here's why you should be
    skeptical of an insurance salesman's pressures to buy a variable annuity,"
    undated, http://articles.moneycentral.msn.com/Insurance/AvoidRipoffs/
    BewareOfTheAnnuitySalesmansScareTactics.aspx

For more information, the Federal Trade Commission has initiated a Re-
    verse Mortgage Education Project, in conjunction with the AARP. More
    information is available at http://www.ftc.gov/bcp/conline/pubs/homes/
    rms.shtm

Chapter 4: Mortgages and Rentals

"something of a tragedy . . ."Stephen Gandel, Closing Cost Scams, CNN
    Money.com, October 10, 2006, http://money.cnn.com/2006/02/13/real
    _estate/closingcosts_money_0603/index.htm

"Nikole and Josh Didier," Ibid.

"We thought we had paid"—Ibid.

"Consumers pay $110 billion buying and selling homes," Elisabeth Leamy,
    "Save Thousands on Closing Costs," ABCNews.com, http://abcnews
    .go.com/GMA/Business/story?id=1704406&page=1

"It could not do this"—Jack Guttentag, "Legal Thievery at the Closing
    Table," Yahoo Finance, posted December 26, 2006, http://finance.yahoo
    .com/expert/article/mortgage/18781

"as little as $110 elsewhere"—J. Robert Hunter, testimony before the
    House Committee on Financial Services, Subcommittee on Housing
    and Community Opportunity, April 26, 2006.

"as little as 1 or 2 percent"—Ibid., pp. 3–10.

"Five companies ultimately own more than 90 percent"—Joseph B.
    Treaster, "Iowa Cuts Added Costs in Title Insurance Policies," *New York
    Times,* July 6, 2005, p. 3.

"a flat cost of $110"—Hunter, p. 13.

"70 percent of mortgages,"—Jamie Smith Hopkins, "Raising Broker Loan
    Fee Decried: Senate to Take Up Bill That Foes Say May Cost Borrowers
    Thousands," *Baltimore Sun,* March 30, 2007.

"American families spend $2.9 billion more"—"Yield Spread Premiums: A
    Powerful Incentive for Equity Theft," Center for Responsible Lending
    report, June 18, 2004.

"The total compensation to [the broker]"—"Broker Compensation," blank
    form on The Mortgage Professor website, http://www.mtgprofessor.com/

A%20-%20Upfront%20Mortgage%20Brokers/dealing_with_an_upfront
_mortgage_broker.htm

"sleazy lenders would brag to her at lunch"—Carolyn Warren, *Mortgage Rip-Offs and Money Savers,* John Wiley & Sons, 2007.

"take an interest rate that's 0.5 percent higher"—"Bloated Mortgage Costs," ConsumerReports.org, May 2004, http://www.consumerreports.org/cro/ personal-finance/financial-services-hidden-fees-504/mortgage-costs/ index.htm

Chapter 5: Cell Phones

"Consumer Groups Urge California Regulators to Adopt New Consumer Protections for Cell Phone Users," press release issued by Consumers Union, August 26, 2003.

"I'm currently in the middle"—"Locked in a Cell: How Cell Phone Early Termination Fees Hurt Consumers," California Public Interest Research Group report, published August 2005.

"Fully 36 percent said fees"—Ibid.

"crystal clear, uninterrupted"—Brian Williams, "Dead Sea Diarist," *The Daily Nightly,* dailynightly.msnbc.com/2006/11/dead_sea_diaris.html

"The exodus eventually brought the company to its knees"—For a comprehensive look at AT&T Wireless collapse, see "The Fall of AT&T Wireless," by Dan Richman, a set of stories that appeared on the front page of September 21, 2004 editions of the *Seattle Post Intelligencer.*

"the industry took in more than $1 billion"—Kyle Stock, "Consumer Advocates Worry that Recovery Fees Mask Cell Company Rate Increases," Knight Ridder/*Tribune Business News,* May 17, 2004.

"announced it would begin pro-rating"—The Verizon Wireless early-termination fee isn't, strictly speaking, pro-rated. Instead, the $175 fee drops by $5 each month, making it much cheaper to get out of your contract as time passes. Of course, the fee is still hefty—$110 if you try to leave a two-year contract after one year. Still, it's something. Unfortunately, other wireless providers did not immediately follow suit.

"Cell-phone firms fought back, but often relented"—website Consumerist .com offers frequent updates on cell phone cancellation tactics at http:// consumerist.com/consumer/early-termination-fees/

"Only a few carriers require copies of death certificates"—See "Getting Out of a Two-Year Cellphone Contract Alive," Damon Darlin, *New York Times,* March 10, 2007.

"Courts had also ruled in favor of generic garage door"—Jennifer Granick, "Cell Phones Freed! Poor Suffer?" commentary on Wired.com, published December 6, 2006, http://www.wired.com/politics/law/commentary/circuitcourt/2006/12/72241

"Jessica and her husband Colin"—Jessica Persson described her experience during a series of interviews with the author in January 2007.

"In Nebraska, fully 22 percent is added"—Dennis Cauchon, "City, State Cell Phone Taxes on the Rise," *USA Today,* May 8, 2005, http://www.usatoday.com/news/nation/2005-05-08-cellphone-taxes_x.htm

"Nebraska proposed a 4 percent cell-phone tax"—Jeffrey Silva, "Nebraska Town Uses 4% Cell-Phone Tax to Offset Declining Landline Revenues," RCR Wireless News, October 16, 2006.

Richard Roesler, "Cell companies fighting taxes," *Spokane Spokesman-Review,* May 31, 2005, p. A1.

"In recent years, policy-makers have viewed wireless"—Ben Charney, "Clash Over Cell Phone Fees," News.com, March 17, 2005, http://news.com.com/Clash+over+cell+phone+fees/2100-1039_3-5623824.html

"taxes on wireless skyrocketed at nine times the rate"—Scott Wooley, "How to Duck Cell Phone Taxes," Forbes.com, June 6, 2005, http://www.forbes.com/technology/2005/06/06/cz_sw_0606cellphone.html

"His taxes shrunk to $1.15 a month"—Ibid.

"My letter was very brief and to the point"—Jill Kurz described this incident to the author during a series of interviews conducted in January 2007.

"your second call should be to your local state legislator"—Cell Phone User Bill of Rights laws and regulations have been proposed in many states around the country, including Massachusetts and New York. In a setback for consumer rights, California's Public Utilities Commission passed a Bill of Rights in 2004, then promptly rescinded it at the urging of the telecommunications industry. The bills offer varying protections, but they all target misleading marketing campaigns and robust "regret" clauses that allow consumers longer spans of time to return phones after purchases when reception is poor or monthly bills are unexpectedly high. One version of the rules is available at the Massachusetts Public Interest Research Group website at http://masspirg.org/MA.asp?id2=16134&id3=MA

Chapter 6: Home Phones

"she paid $3.45 as insurance"—Telephone activist Bruce Kushnick argues his case at his website NewNetworks.com. His detailed phone bill comparison, matching Aunt Ehtel's 1980 bill to her 2006 bill, is available at: http://www.newnetworks.com/NYClocal%20charges19802006.htm

"do nothing more than soak consumers"—National Association of State Utility Consumer Advocates' Petition for Declaratory Ruling, petition filed with the Federal Communications Commission, March 30, 2004.

Patricia Horn, "Dialing Up for Answers; Cost of Local Phone Service Is Debated," *Sun-Sentinel Ft. Lauderdale*, August 26, 1998, p. 1D.

"literally zero percent of the consumers"—New Networks Institute survey, described on agency's website, http://www.newnetworks.com/phonebillinto.html

"taxes and surcharges on the average bill were 112 percent"—Ibid.

"dinged customers more than $27 a month"—Beatrice E. Garcia, "A Call to Phone Companies: Stop Charging Odd Fees," *Miami Herald*, September 19, 2004, p. 1E.

"charges provided by small Ohio-based Toledotel"—The chart on Toledotel's website was subsequently removed.

"About $13,700 per home"—Hao Sean, "Firms Reap Telcom Bonanza," *Honolulu Advertiser*, June 19, 2005, p. 1.

"We acknowledge that carriers in the past"—"Report and Order," Federal Communications Commission, FCC 02-329, released December 13, 2002.

"new line items with generic names"—"Nation's Consumer Advocates Call for Stronger Telephone Billing Rules, More Customer Protections," press release issued by the National Association of State Utility Consumer Advocates, June 27, 2005.

"they argued the fees were 'political speech' "—"Nation's Consumer Advocates Fight Telephone Industry's Misleading Surcharges," press release issued by the National Association of State Utility Consumer Advocates, August 13, 2004.

"95 percent of those errors"—Norm Alster, "Taking Charges," CFO IT, January 12, 2005.

"two years worth of refunds"—"Verizon New Jersey Settles Class Action on Overbilling for Circuits, Law Firm Says," Dow Jones News Service, August 1, 2006.

"was billed $3.63 for one minute"—Roark vs. GTE California Incorporated, Case No. 01035862, Third Amended Complaint, filed in California Superior Court, Santa Barbara County, May 4, 2001. Available online at http://www.foleybezek.com/verizon2/Final-GTE.pdf

"agreed to refund about $14 million"—Jim Finkle, "A $14 Million Wrong

Number: Error on O.C. Woman's Phone Bill Rings Up Compensation for Thousands of Californians," *Orange County Register,* October 15, 2003, p. 1.

"then we're to re-rate it"—Nick Welsh, "Wake-Up Call," *Santa Barbara Independent,* April 24, 2003 edition. Article reprinted on plantiff's attorney website at http://www.foleybezek.com/verizon2/article.pdf.

Chapter 7: Pay TV

"Unfortunately, the FCC"—"Cable Mergers, Monopoly Power, and Price increases," Mark Cooper, paper published by Consumers Union, January 2003.

"I have a Comcast service plan"—Internet complaint filed with consumeraffairs.com, November 13, 2006.

"soared from around $22 a decade ago to $60"—Mark Cooper, Consumer Federation of America, testimony before the U.S. Senate Judiciary Committee, February 11, 2004. Average revenue per user, 2006, from Robert Serrano, analyst at JupiterKagan, interview with the author, December 28, 2006.

"Comcast, and its predecessor"—"Comcast to Pay $1 Million, Improve Advertising and Customer Service Practices," press release issued by the Office of the Massachusetts Attorney General, March 16, 2006.

"Time Warner offered three-month teaser rates"—"Time Warner Cable Agrees to Alter Promotional Practices," press release issued by the Office of the New York Attorney General, May 18, 2005.

"Cable's unceremonious invention is often credited"—Ed Parson's role in the invention of cable television is told in great detail by George Mannes in "The Birth of Cable TV," published by *Invention & Technology Magazine,* Fall 1996. It can be accessed online at americanheritage.com at http://www.americanheritage.com/articles/magazine/it/1996/2/1996_2_42.shtml

"People would drive"—Ibid.

"resolving 18,000 complaints"—"FCC Role in Cable Rate Regulation Ends," consumer alert issued by the Federal Communications Commission, March 1999.

"cable prices exploded"—"The Telecommunications Act: Consumers Still Waiting for Better Phone & Cable Services," press release issued by Consumers Union, February 6, 2002.

"now rank among the worst rated businesses"—Constance Mitchell Ford and Patrick Barta, "A Silver Lining for Airlines: Fliers Are More Satisfied, Survey Finds," *Wall Street Journal,* May 20, 2002.

"I don't know why people don't"—Jeffrey Strain, "50% Off Cable TV Bill," PFAdvice.com, June 15, 2006. http://www.pfadvice.com/2006/06/15/50 -off-cable-tv-bill/

"the 20-most-popular channels"—David Lazarus, "Cable Strangles Choice," *San Francisco Chronicle,* May 16, 2004, p. J1.

"systems must make available"—"Cable Television Fact Sheet: Where to File Complaints Regarding Cable Service," Federal Communications Commission, July 2000. Available online at http://www.fcc.gov/mb/ facts/complain.html

"Cablevision obtained control of seven of the nine"—"The Failure of Cable Deregulation," U.S. Public Interest Research Group, August 2003, p. 3.

"about 30 percent of the U.S. population"—Ibid., p. 4.

"cable prices are about 17 percent lower"—Ibid., p. 1.

"Tell them if these phone lines"—DIRECTTV Techs: Policy Makes Lying Part of Job," television report aired May 1, 2006 by Local 6, accessed online at http://www.local6.com/problemsolvers/9142100/detail.html

"Contract terms were spelled out in unreadable fine print"—"Madigan, 21 Other Attorneys General Announce $5 Million Settlement Agreement with DIRECTV to Refund Consumers Misled by Advertisements," press release issued by the Illinois Attorney General's Office, December 12, 2005.

"repeatedly ignored consumers' wishes"—"DIRECTV to Pay $5.3 Million Penalty for Do Not Call Violations," press release issued by the Federal Trade Commission, December 13, 2005.

" 'free-to-pay' fee"—"Attorney General Salazar Announces Settlement of 13-State Consumer Protection Investigation of Echostar over Dish Network Sales," press release issued by Oregon attorney general's office, May 22, 2003.

"Under duress, I subscribed"—"DIRECTV Install Techs Claim They Were Forced to Lie to Customers," Techdirt.com, comment left on story, May 3, 2006.

Chapter 8: Internet Access

"Damned if you do," "The Fake Broadband War," anonymous comment, TechDirt.Com, http://www.techdirt.com/articles/20060711/122200.shtml, posted July 11, 2006, accessed August 18, 2007.

"in its place would appear a new line item"—The Verizon "supplier surcharge" incident was covered extensively by newspapers around the country.

"On balance your total bill"—Letter sent by Verizon to DSL customers in August 2006. The letter was posted online in various outlets. Here's one: http://www.isp-planet.com/marketing/2006/fee_editorial.html

"Its euphemism was perhaps"—Marguerite Reardon, "No Price Cuts for Verizon, BellSouth DSL Customers," CNet News.com, August 22, 2006. http://news.com.com/2100-1034_3-6108471.html?tag=nefd.top

"Old: Federal regulatory"—Alex Goldman, "Editorial: Verizon's Fee Error Is an ISP Opportunity," ISP-Planet.com, August 23, 2006, http://www.isp-planet.com/marketing/2006/fee_editorial.html

"What $14.95 price?"—Author's personal experience, December 2006.

"Let's examine one such offer"—Offer listed at Comcastoffers.com, accessed January 2007.

"Starbucks T-Mobile Wi-Fi service"—Terms and conditions listed on T-Mobile's website, accessed April 17, 2006. http://hotspot.t-mobile.com/services_plans.htm

"an oddly-long 15 months"—DirecWay terms and conditions, accessed April 18, 2007 at http://direcway.cc/terms.htm

Chapter 9: Travel

"Hilton surprises guests"—Conor Dougherty "Lawsuit Says Hilton Charged Resort Fees Under Guise of a Tax," *Los Angeles Business Journal,* Sept. 16, 2002, accessed at http://findarticles.com/p/articles/mi_m5072/is_37_24/ai_92138376

"Kyle Leung thought"—Linda Burbank, "Resort Fees Add Up to a Pain," *Traveler's Aide* column, *USA Today,* September 5, 2006, p. D7.

"Hotel fee revenue tripled"—Christopher Elliot, "How Much? Many Answers," *New York Times,* September 16, 2006. Available online at http://travel.nytimes.com/2006/09/19/business/19hotels.html

"reached a $2.3 million settlement"—Christopher Boyd, "LXR Resorts Settles with State, Drops Undisclosed Hotel Fees," *Orlando Sentinel,* August 2, 2006, p. B1.

"In Miles City, Montana"—Author's personal travel experience.

"the four-star Fairmont hotel"—Author's personal travel experience.

"at the Wynn Las Vegas hotel"—Author's personal travel experience.

"hotel phone revenue peaked in 2000"—"PricewaterhouseCoopers Finds

US Hotel Telephone Revenues Declined 16 Percent Since 2000," press release issued by PricewaterhouseCoopers, October 16, 2006.

"we found that abandonment rates were higher"—"How Much? Many Answers." Op. Cit.

"Many airports impose a fee on revenue"—"Taxes, Surcharges and Fees," Alamo rental policies from Alamo.com, accessed April 25, 2007, http://www.alamo.com/alamoctx/itemDetails.do?HelpItemID=TAX

"a flat $4.50-per-rental fee"—Donna Hogan, "Fee-for-all," EastValley Tribune.com, April 10, 2005, http://www.eastvalleytribune.com/index.php?sty=39353

"turn a $194 rental car into a $281 rental car"—Toni Salama, "Study Shows Rental Cars Can Be Taxing at Airports," *Houston Chronicle,* March 11, 2007, p. 5.

"the fee can vary by a full 2 percent"—Rates can change frequently, so check with your bank a few weeks before you take your trip. To find rate information now, type "currency conversion rates" and Bankrate.com into your favorite search engine.

"car rental agencies to put a 'hold' on credit or debit transactions"—Ellen Cannon, "Don't Use Debit Card for Car Rental," bankrate.com, undated, http://www.bankrate.com/brm/news/cc/20061122_debit_card_car_rental_a1.asp

Chapter 10: Groceries

"called 'padding' by retailers"—Donna Montaldo, "The Truth Behind Grocery Store Discount Cards," http://couponing.about.com/od/groceryzone/a/disccards.htm

"one in thirty items scanned incorrectly"—"Price Check II Shows Scanner Accuracy Has Improved Since 1996," press release issued by the Federal Trade Commission, December 16, 1998.

"It's the most basic thing"—Interview with the author.

"Cost to price every item in a typical store"—Brian Mohl, "For BJ's, Ignoring Item Pricing Is a Bargain," *Boston Globe,* May 14, 2006.

"three out of four scanners failed"—"Retailers Flunk Scanner Test: Shoppers Stuck without Price Stickers," press release issued August 4, 2004, Consumer World. Dworsky operates Consumer World and ConsumerWorld.com.

"10 percent of self-service scanners weren't working"—"Consumer Affairs Gauges Retailer Pricing Accuracy: Strong Compliance at Checkout, But

In-Aisle Scanner Concerns Mount," press release issued by Commonwealth of Massachusetts Office of Consumer Affairs and Business Regulation, December 20, 2005.

"81 percent of store purchases"—Barbara Salsbury, *Beating the High Cost of Eating: The Essential Guide to Supermarket Survival,* Horizon Publishers & Distributors: May 2005, p. 4.

"Hellman's shrank its standard quart-sized jar"—"Hellmann's Mayo: Introduces the 30 oz. Quart*" mouseprint.org, published August 28, 2006. http://www.mouseprint.org/?p=122

"jars of paint are now 124 ounces"—"House Paint: Introducing the 116 oz. Gallon*," mouseprint.org, published October 9, 2006. http://www.mouseprint.org/?p=136

"a homeowner was charged with arson"—Brandon Sprague, "Fireman attempted to set fire to house, charges say," *Seattle Times,* October 6, 2004, p. B3. All charges against the suspect were dropped.

"standard for stores that implement such programs to raise prices"—An excellent discussion of pricing tricks and privacy problems created by supermarkets that initiate loyalty card programs can be found at the Consumers Against Supermarket Privacy Invasion and Numbering website, NoCards.org. For specific examples of upward price adjustments when the programs start, see John Vanderlippe, "Supermarket Cards: An Overview of the Pricing Issues," at http://www.nocards.org/overview/index.shtml

Chapter 11: Gift Cards

"bank cards carry fees that become scary"—"Gift Cards 2005: Many Good Retail Cards. Any Good Bank Cards?" report issued by Office of Consumer Protection, December 1, 2005.

"investigating Red Lobster"—"National Restaurant Company Settles FTC Charges for Deceptive Gift Card Sales," Federal Trade Commission press release, April 3, 2007. Red Lobster's parent company, Darden Restaurants Inc., admitted no wrongdoing but agreed to refund customers and beef up its disclosure notices.

"I recently had a humiliating experience"—Bob Sullivan, "Red Lobster Pinched Over Gift Card Fees," comment left on *Red Tape Chronicles,* December 8, 2006.

"only two of the forty gifts cards"—"Gift Cards 2006: Retail Cards Continue to Improve (with Prodding); Bank Cards Still Have Problems," report published by the Montgomery County Division of Consumer Affairs, November 20, 2006.

"each withdrawal incurs a $2 fee"—Ibid.

"up to 10 percent of all gift card money"—Stephen J. Dubner and Steven D. Levitt, "The Gift Card Economy," *New York Times Magazine,* January 7, 2007.

"$43 million in unused gift cards"—Lisa R. Schoolcraft, "Unused Gift Cards Deliver $43 Million to Home Depot," *Atlanta Business Chronicle,* June 10, 2005.

Chapter 12: Rebates

"All it took was 29 e-mails"—Sid Kirchheimer, "Scam Alert: Rebate Runaround," *AARP Bulletin,* June 2007. http://www.aarp.org/bulletin/consumer/rebate_runaround.html

"Vento thought she had spotted a cell-phone deal"—Marie Vento told her story to the author during a series of interviews in January 2006.

"In some low-margin businesses"—Interview with the author, January 2006.

"InPhonic's BBB membership was revoked"—Ed Johnson, CEO, Washington-area Better Business Bureau, interview with the author, January 2006.

"attorney general's office sued InPhonic"—Annys Shin, "D.C. Sues InPhonic Over Rebate Restrictions," *Washington Post,* June 9, 2006, p. D4.

"then later settled the lawsuit"—Annys Shin, "InPhonic Settles Lawsuit Over Rebates," *Washington Post,* November 7, 2006; p. D5.

"the FTC argued that the retailer"—"The Rebate Debate: Why Were They Late? FTC Settles Charges Against CompUSA," press release issued by the Federal Trade Commission, March 11, 2005. Additional details on the case, including a copy of the FTC's civil complaint, are available at the agency's website, http://www.ftc.gov/opa/2005/03/compusa.shtm

"retailers now know they can be held responsible"—Ibid.

"Here's a compilation of other rebate recovery tricks"—A similar version of this list originally appeared on MSNBC.com on January 27, 2006 at http://redtape.msnbc.com/2006/01/free_the_ad_scr_1.html

Chapter 13: Student Loans

"students get served up like turkeys"—"Sallie Mae's Success Too Costly?" *60 Minutes,* May 7, 2006.

"close to $13,000 per year"—"The Cost of College Continues to Increase While Average Pell Grant Decreases," press release, Democratic Policy Committee, October 25, 2006, http://democrats.senate.gov/dpc/dpc-new .cfm?doc_name=fs-109-2-151

"about $880 billion during that time"—Total student debt figure courtesy of Mark Kantrowitz of finaid.org. Credit card debt figure provided by the Federal Reserve June 7, 2007, press release: "Consumer Credit."

"$35,000 or more"—"Student Loans," finaid.org. http://www.finaid.org/ loans/

"$400-a-month payment"—finaid.org calculator, http://www.finaid.org/ calculators/loanpayments.phtml

"a starting salary of $30,000"—Jeanne Sahadi, "Lucrative Degrees for College Grads," CNNMoney.com, April 19, 2005, http://money.cnn.com/ 2005/04/15/pf/college/starting_salaries/

"to 20 percent in 2006"—Kathy Chu and Sandra Block, "Reforms? Not for rates on private student loans," USAToday, May 30, 2007 http://www .usatoday.com/money/perfi/college/2007-05-29-student-loans-usat_N .htm

"an $85 billion market annually"—Kevin Drawbaugh, "Senator to seek private student loan crackdown," Reuters news service, June 8, 2007, http://www.boston.com/news/nation/articles/2007/06/08/lawmakers _bill_targets_private_student_loans/

"Rates as high as 28 percent"—Bethany Mclean, "When Sallie Met Wall Street," Fortune Magazine, December 26, 2005.

"4 to 10 percent of the outstanding payment," This information was not generally available on Sallie Mae's site, but provided to current loan after they log in to their website accounts. Here is the language on the site: "Sallie Mae will charge a late fee if you fail to make your monthly payment when it is due. . . . the fee is charged 15–21 days after your payment due date and is 4%–6% of the installment amount of your loan(s). In some cases a maximum of $5 applies. For SLM Financial loans, late fees will be assessed after 10–15 days at rates of 4%–10% according to the loan type."

"50 percent of the monthly payment"—"The Importance of Ontime Payments," http://blog.wellsfargo.com/StudentLoanDown/2007/04/the _importance_of_ontime_payme.html

"$10,000 at 6.8 percent has a monthly payment"—Adopted from "Student Loan Consolidation," http://www.finaid.org/loans/consolidation.phtml

"students can theoretically use private consolidation loans"—Student loan consolidation brings with it many caveats. There is a case where a Stafford Loan and a PLUS loan can be consolidated together—when both loans are owed by the same person. That is, when a parent is still paying their own Stafford Loan, and then takes out a PLUS loan for their child.

"more than triple the price of the loan"—Calculations courtesy of FinAid, www.finaid.org/loans/preferredlenderlists.phtml

"only one in ten former students make it"—"A Hot Knife Through Butter," http://www.newamerica.net/blogs/2007/01/a_hot_knife_through_butter

"one-third of all college students leave school with $10,000 or more in credit-card debt"—"Sallie Mae launches new 'Be Debt Smart' campaign," http://www.salliemae.com/about/news_info/newsreleases/021407 _bedebtsmart.htm

"managed to collect $5 billion in loan debt"—Liz Weston, "3 Ways to Avoid the Student-Loan Trap," http://articles.moneycentral.msn.com/ SavingandDebt/ManageDebt/3waysToAvoidTheStudentLoanTrap.aspx

"the student loan–home equity loan swap can be smart"—"Q&A with Liz," http://www.asklizweston.com/home-equity-to-pay-student-loan.htm

Chapter 14: Sneaky Fees Everywhere

"America used to be the land of the free"—Emily Thorton, "Fees! Fees! Fees!," *BusinessWeek* magazine, September 29, 2003.

"one in four consumers paid marked-up interest rates"—"The Hidden Markup of Auto Loans: Consumer Costs of Dealer Kickbacks and Inflated Finance Charges," report issed by the Consumer Federation of America, January 26, 2004.

"Hispanics paid an average rate of 8.52 percent"—Ibid.

"Only when the loan crosses $33,000 does trading the rebate"—Calculators can vary slightly. I used the nifty one at Valley Federal Credit Union, https://www.valleyfcu.com/calculators/auto-rebate.htm. Bankrate.com offers another good one at http://www.bankrate.com/brm/calc/rebate .asp

"unless the savings is truly substantial"—Ibid.

"consumers are penalized as much as 50 percent on auto insurance"—In a set of interviews with the author, April 2007.

"it's fair to use credit scores in premium formulas"—In a set of interviews with the author, April 2007.

"shopping around is your only defense"—The insurance/credit score dilemma looks to be with us for a while. In June 2007, the U.S. Supreme Court ruled insurance firms generally don't have to send home notices of adverse action—one justice, in the opinion, noted that consumers might be irritated by such notices and would treat them as "junk mail."

"part cautionary tale"—Based on an e-mail exchange with the author, June 29, 2006.

"The survey studied clubs from eight different chains"—"Beware of the Fine Print: Council Investigation Finds Unfit NYC Health Club Policies," press release issued by the Council of the City of New York, July 2, 2003.

"In a settlement, Bally said it had done nothing wrong"—"Consumer Complaints Lead to Health Club Sales Reforms: Spitzer's Office Obtains Settlement with Bally Total Fitness," press release issued by the Office of the New York State Attorney General, February 16, 2004.

"Note that 'rush order' doesn't mean faster shipping"—For an excellent description of 'rush orders,' landing prices, and the like, see "Shipping Charges Tested," *Marketing Experiments Journal,* January 19 2004, accessed online at http://www.marketingexperiments.com/improving-website-conversion/shipping-charges.html

"The average customer is not so gullible"—Ibid.

Section 3
Chapter 1: Customer-Service Calls

"25 percent had one incident that took at least nine hours"—Scott Broetzmann described his survey results in an interview with the author, January 2007.

"Lands' End, Dillard's"—A comprehensive list of companies that really answer phone calls can be found at GetHuman.com.

"Have a Copernican Revolution." "The Zen of Placing Customer Service Calls," Mother Tongue Annoyances, online blob, http://www.mtannoyances.com/?p=216, accessed April 19, 2007.

"i'm a CSR and i must say one thing"—blog comment to *Red Tape Chronicles* post "Cell Phone Complaints That Get Your Money Back," August 30, 2006.

"Bitch Dog"—Don Oldenburg, "Demonizing the Customer; Some Company Help Staffs Disdain the People They Serve," *Washington Post,* November 13, 2005, p. F5. For a very funny interview with Govan, who works in customer service, see Keith Olbermann's *Countdown* interview with her, available online at http://www.msnbc.msn.com/id/9040808/

"CSRs enter copious notes about calls"—Broetzmann interview.

"The strongest tool a customer has is call length," Blog comment to *Red Tape Chronicles* post "Win Customer Service Battles," January 16, 2007.

"That's gonna be kinda hard"—Comment left on customerssuck.com, topic name "Is This Illegal?" Dec. 27, 2006, http://www.customerssuck.com/board/archive/index.php/t-6218.html

"My all time favorite is 'Sir' or 'Ma'am,' "—Ibid.

"Customerssuck.com top-ten list"—provided in an e-mail to the author, January 2007.

Chapter 3: The Legal Options

"When he was granted a judgment of $3,500"—André-Tascha Lammé told his story to the author during a series of interviews in February and March 2007.

"Small-claims courts can hear any kind of case"—The best way to find out about the particular small-claims court requirements in your jurisdiction is to do an Internet search for your county and small-claims court. One compilation of small-claims court rules can be found at http://law.free advice.com/resources/smallclaimscourts.htm

"Binding mandatory arbitration agreements are part of"—The best source for information on Binding Mandatory Arbitration cases is GiveMeBack-MyRights.com.

"It is agreed by and between the passenger"—Carnival Cruise Lines, Inc. V. Shute, 499 U.S. 585 (1991)

"If I'm a retired lawyer turning out"—Richard Neely, "Arbitration and The Godless Bloodsuckers," The West Virginia Lawyer, September–October 2006, pp. 12–13.

"success rate was still well over 99 percent"—Caroline E. Mayer, "Win Some, Lose Rarely?; Arbitration Forum's Rulings Called One-Sided," *Washington Post*, March 1, 2000, p. E1.

"79-year-old Stella Liebeck"—Douglas McCollam, "Demon in the Court-room: Stephanie Mencimer's New Book Details How Republicans and Their Corporate Allies Have Tried for Decades to Defang the American Trial Lawyer," *The American Lawyer*, February 1, 2007, Volume Vol. 29, No. 279. For those who are counting, Liebeck did not receive millions of dollars for her troubles. A judge reduced her award to $640,000, and the parties settled for an undisclosed sum before legal appeals could run their course.

"He ultimately got his $249"—Steve Taplits described his experience in several e-mails to the author, August 30, 2006.

"victims sued Cingular after the firm purchased AT&T Wireless"— Anne Broache, "Cingular accused of duping ex-AT&T subscribers," CNET News.com, July 7, 2006, http://news.zdnet.com/2100-1035_22 -6091853.html

"lawsuits filed around the country"—for a compilation of the the latest legal action, see givemebackmyrights.com

"operated principally by Experian, Equifax, and TransUnion"—There are other credit reporting agencies, too—the largest being ChoicePoint, better known as an exployment backgrounding company, and Innovis, which few have heard of.

"Their addresses are in the notes section for this chapter"—As of this writing, Experian, Equifax, and TransUnion can be reached at: Equifax: 1-800-525-6285; www.equifax.com; P.O. Box 740241, Atlanta, GA 30374-0241; Experian: 1-888-EXPERIAN (397-3742); www.experian .com; P.O. Box 9532, Allen, TX 75013; TransUnion: 1-800-680-7289; www.transunion.com; Fraud Victim Assistance Division, P.O. Box 6790, Fullerton, CA 92834-6790. Updated information may be available from the Federal Trade Commission at http://www.ftc.gov/bcp/edu/ microsites/idtheft/consumers/defend.html.

"Other things debt collectors can't do"—"Facts for Consumers: Fair Debt Collection," Federal Trade Commission publication, March 1999.

Ibid.

"A sample "get off my back" letter"—A thorough discussion of consumer rights, with additional sample letters, is available from the ExpertLaw library at http://www.expertlaw.com/library/consumer/fair_debt_collection .html

Chapter 4: Sneaky-Fee Survey

"which you can read about in this book's endnotes"—This Internet-based survey was conducted in November 2006 by the Ponemon Institute. A volunteer panel of 2,068 consumers, selected to mirror demographic and geographic characteristics of U.S. adults, participated. Each was compensated for their participation with a coupon for an online retailer.

The total margin of error for the study is plus or minus 3 percent. Financial results and cost estimates are based on extrapolation of generally available demographic information and additional data provided by industry sources. Some of those sources provided the data under the condition that their company name would not be published. The annual period described in the survey represents December 2005 to November 2006. In general, participants were asked what percentage of the prior month's bill was the result of a sneaky fee, and given ranges to pick from. In the bank and retirement categories, participants provided an exact dollar figure. Total U.S. adult population assumed to be 241 million. Other assumptions as follows:

Cell phones: Average invoice value determined by data provided by two national wireless telecom providers. Total number of bill-paying cellphone users: 96 million.

Credit cards: Average monthly bill provided by one international creditcard provider. Total number of bill-paying credit-card holders: 120 million, who hold an average of 1.93 credit cards.

Banks: Total number of bank account holders: 168.7 million, who maintain an average of 1.44 bank accounts.

Airlines: Average ticket price provided by one international airline. Number of Americans who fly at least once each year: 120 million, averaging three ticket purchases per year.

Hotels: Average hotel-stay bill provided by one international hotel chain. Total number of Americans who stayed in a hotel last year: 120 million, who averaged 3.83 hotel stays.

Cable and Satellite TV: Average invoice value provided by one national cable provider. Total number of Americans who pay a cable or satellite bill each month: 96.4 million, who average 1.04 accounts.

Internet access: Average invoice value provided by one national Internet service provider. Total number of Americans who pay a cable or satellite bill each month: 96.4 million, who average 1.06 accounts.

Retirement: Total number of Americans who pay for retirement services: 84.35 million, who average 1.28 accounts.

Insurance: Average invoice value provided by one national cable provider. Total number of Americans who pay for insurance: 120.5 million, who average 1.63 insurance payments monthly.

Groceries: Average shopping bill provided by one national supermarket chain. Total number of Americans who pay for grocery trips each month: 120.5 million, who average 7.5 trips to the store each month.

"the top ten issuers controlled 90 percent"—Robert Manning. Testimony before the Senate Committee on Banking, Housing, and Urban Affairs, January 25, 2007.

"$25 billion is taken from consumers' 401(k) accounts every year"—This is explained in greater detail in Chapter 10 of Section II, but in 2005, the Investment Company Institute estimated that 47 million Americans have $2.4 trillion parked in company 401(k) accounts, much of it in mutual funds. Assuming a rough average of 1 percent "expense ratios"—fees—on each fund, Wall Street makes $25 billion for babysitting all this retirement money. The actual amount is probably higher—many estimates say the average 401(k) fee is 1.3 percent, which would make Wall Street's take closer to $32 billion.

Acknowledgments

I'm sorry I had to write this book. It was a pain to write. I don't really like reading small print. It's more of a compulsion. And I really don't like confrontation much, either. I'm actually kind of shy. When I'm nervous, I even stutter. I'm not the kind of person who whips out witty comebacks with ease, or who has an immediately intimidating presence or commanding voice. That means, when faced with an unfair situation, I have only one tool at my disposal: the law. And after a good part of my adult life, I've come to realize that's become a pretty blunt tool.

I love our country, and our way of life. I even love capitalism, though after reading this book you may question that. But let me make my case for that this way: Gandhi once said he might become a Christian if he ever met one; I would support a free market if I ever saw one.

Instead, our economy is laced with unchecked unfairness. Why? As my CNBC colleague Jim Cramer likes to say, we have a government that is of the corporations, for the corporations, and by the corporations.

So I'd like to thank everyone who has ever tried—successfully or not—to fight for fairness. In particular, I thank all readers of the *Red Tape Chronicles*, especially those tens of thousands of readers who've taken the time to leave comments on my blog. These voluntary comments are often much more than complaints or criticisms. Many writers share incredibly clever solutions to typical consumer dilemmas, or thoughtful insights into maddening situations. You'll see many of their comments in this book, and I owe them thanks for their contributions. I hope those who haven't yet seen the blog (redtape.msnbc.com) will take the time to look it up, and to browse through the notes consumers leave on it.

There has been much talk lately about the usefulness of bloggers and blog commenters. Will self-made Internet journalists and the Wisdom of Crowds completely overtake traditional media? Or is the coming Cult of the Amateur the death of society and culture as we know it? This being my second go-round in a hype cycle of Internet Revolution, I'm pretty sure I know how this one will play out. Bloggers will not slay professional media nor civilization. The phenomenon will simply continue to open up doors for talented people who might otherwise have been overlooked (some bloggers will even be hired by the *New York Times*!), while others will serve the incredibly important function of keeping journalists honest. There will still be experts and professional reporters for a long, long time. Millions of people can play a little piano, but they don't all get to play Carnegie Hall. Still, blogging will push the world forward, just a little bit, and a very important little bit. So, dear reader, don't let anyone pin the label of amateur on you. Everything you have to say is important.

In addition to the thousands of readers I want to thank for helping me with research for this book, I feel like I have thousands of friends and colleagues to thank. First and foremost, MSNBC.com editor in chief Jennifer Sizemore. Most new columns and projects at big media companies take months or even years to conceive, design, and implement. The *Red Tape Chronicles* went from idea to publication in about four days. The idea arose in the wake of Hurricane Katrina, when I heard from thousands of victims who'd been denied assistance from the federal government because of various maddening computer-related glitches. Computers were denying aid to unrelated roommates, for example, because they'd been programmed to adopt a "one aid check per address" rule. Next came a story about Katrina victims being in danger of ruined credit reports, and word that the nation's credit bureaus refused a request to grant victims temporary credit-score amnesty. Clearly, Red Tape was—and is—the second storm surge that hit Gulf Coast residents. But here's what I didn't expect: An endless cascade of "me too" stories from all walks of life, from all corners of the country. These were twenty-first-century headaches, many of them owing to various stupid computer tricks. I told Jennifer I wanted to start a blog and encourage people to complain about this Red Tape openly, that we'd get an endless string of leads about stories that really mattered to people. She was in the middle of her own Red Tape battle with her cable television company, so I didn't even need to finish my project pitch. Despite the frenetic pace of news in the wake of Hurricane Katrina, she allowed me to steal time from MSNBC.com's fine graphics art team and programmer Jim Ray, and we had the new venture up and running in just a few days. Thousands of comments poured in. Barely a year passed before we had 50,000 comments, and counting. No one's looked back since.

I'd also like to thank my direct editors at the time, Gary Seidman and Lori Smith, who both put up with me as I stumbled around for the right formula for Red Tape stories in the early days, and technology section editors Michael Wann and Kristin Kalning for their constant encouragement.

Next on the list is Michael Brunker, himself an extraordinary reporter, who has been my editor for the bulk of the *Red Tape Chronicles*. His gentle encouragement and support is a style rarely found in today's newsrooms. And he's the one who had to put up with my unusual schedule while I wrote this book. In fact, I am grateful for the support and patience of everyone at MSNBC.com—particularly the patience of CEO Charlie Tillinghast, who has unflinchingly supported my ability to speak my mind without censure, even though there have been times when I've made advertisers and lawyers a bit uncomfortable. That's something else you'll have trouble finding today. I am fully aware that without the great success and enormous audience of MSNBC.com, which gives me the chance to speak to nearly 30 million readers every month, there would be no *Red Tape Chronicles,* and I am grateful for that.

The next debt of gratitude I owe to my friend Lisa Napoli, one of the best reporters of the Internet age, now a correspondent at American Public Radio's Marketplace program. It was Lisa's interview with me that brought me and my project to the attention of the good folks at Random House.

At Random House, it was Jane von Mehren who heard the program and jumped on the idea. Her enthusiasm overcame my immediate reluctance to take on the task of turning a blog into a book. Thanks also to Ben Loehnen, the acquiring editor, who convinced me that I was better off writing a book people wanted to read, rather than the everything-is-unfair diatribe I initially approached him with. He wanted a book full of solutions, not complaints, and he was right.

Many, many other people at Random House shared their enthusiasm and wisdom with me along the way; working with them was refreshingly easy and helpful in a world where authors are increasingly treated like a commodity. You won't find a more enthusiastic and dedicated bunch than Jane, Sanyu Dillon, Brian McLendon, Lisa Barnes, Tom Nevins, and Lydah Piles, who worked so hard to make sure this project caught your eye, and Becca Shapiro, who all helped make sure it arrived on time and in all the right places. But the biggest helping of thanks belongs to Jill Schwartzman, my level-headed editor and fellow outrage-ee. Jill put her heart and her checkbook into this project. From day one, she "got it," and believed in it, but she did much more than that. *Gotcha Capitalism* is full of stories, puns, paragraphs, and at least one entire chapter that she deserves co-author's credit on. Editors rarely get that kind of credit, but Jill should.

A host of other people helped make sure I didn't run off the rails on this project. Leading experts in each subject area read sections of the book for me and offered helpful suggestions and improvements. I owe each of them much professional gratitude. They are:

Edgar Dworsky, founder of ConsumerWorld.com
Jack Guttentag, The Mortgage Professor
Robert Manning, author of *Credit Card Nation*
Esther Shapiro, Detroit Office of Consumer Protection, retired
Gail Hillebrand, lawyer for Consumers Union
David Szwak, consumer advocate
Liz Pulliam Weston, personal finance columnist and author of
    Your Credit Score
Evan Johnson, Montgomery County (Maryland) Department of
    Consumer Protection
Bruce Kushnick, founder of Teletruth
Rob Douglas, PrivacyToday.com
Chris Hoofnagle, senior fellow, Berkeley Center for Law and
    Technology
Elizabeth Warren, Harvard Law professor and author of *The Two-
    Income Trap*
Lorna Rankin, of GetHuman.com
Mark Kantrowitz, publisher of FinAid

And finally, I owe a tremendous debt to Larry Ponemon, of The Ponemon Institute, who spent endless hours (and real money) helping me study the Gotcha phenomenon and quantify the pain it causes consumers every day.

I'm sorry there are companies and employees who think it's okay to confuse and mislead people. I hope this book will convince you that cheating is not "just good business," and in fact, it's bad business and bad for our country. Most of all, I hope this book will save you some money and restore your faith that you do have rights. Then, when you succeed, I hope you will come see me at the *Red Tape Chronicles* and share your success story.

PHOTO: © CHRISTINE GACHARNA

BOB SULLIVAN has been a reporter for nearly two decades. For the past ten years, he has covered computer crime and consumer affairs for MSNBC.com. Today, his work appears on MSNBC.com's "Red Tape Chronicles" blog. He also appears regularly on MSNBC television, NBC Nightly News, the *Today* show, and various local NBC affiliates. He is the winner of the prestigious 2002 Society of Professional Journalists Public Service Award for a series of articles on online fraud. His first book, *Your Evil Twin: Behind the Identity Theft Epidemic*, investigated the root causes of credit card fraud and other identity-related crimes. He lives in Maltby, Washington, with his golden retriever, Lucky.